Punters

How Paddy Power Bet Billions
and Changed Gambling Forever

Aaron Rogan

HarperCollins*Ireland*

HarperCollins*Ireland*
The Watermarque Building
Ringsend Road
Dublin DO4 K7N3
Ireland

a division of
HarperCollinsPublishers
1 London Bridge Street
London SE1 9GF
UK

www.harpercollins.co.uk

This edition published by HarperCollins*Ireland* in 2022

1 3 5 7 9 10 8 6 4 2

A catalogue record of this book
is available from the British Library

PB ISBN 978-0-00-846391-5

Typeset in Sabon LT Std by
Palimpsest Book Production Ltd, Falkirk, Stirlingshire

Printed and bound in the UK using 100% renewable electricity
at CPI Group (UK) Ltd

MIX
Paper from
responsible sources
FSC™ C007454

This book is produced from independently certified FSC™ paper
to ensure responsible forest management.

For more information visit: www.harpercollins.co.uk/green

Punters

AARON ROGAN is currently News Correspondent at the *Business Post* and was previously Senior Reporter at *The Times* Ireland. Rogan's journalism has focused on investigatory work into the online gambling industry and general reporting on the business of Flutter, the parent group of Paddy Power Betfair.

For Ash and Rose

Table of Contents

Introduction   1

 1: Origin Story   15
 2: Tax Wars   34
 3: Political Punt   55
 4: Cat and Mouse   72
 5: Online from the Bunker   94
 6: Let's Make Things More Interesting   115
 7: Quants   131
 8: The Kennedy Era   156
 9: We Hear You   168
10: Future Expected Margin   190
11: The First Europeans   196
12: Tony10   222
13: Vanguard   240
14: Spot the Stallions from the Mares   251

15: Vatican City to Pyongyang, via Tallaght   262
16: Nobel Prize, or an Oscar?   283
17: Betty Power   304
18: Rise of the FOBTs   326
19: Green Street   336
20: Addiction by Design   354

Epilogue   385
Acknowledgements   403

Introduction

Stewart Kenny says he walked away from Paddy Power because his conscience wouldn't let him stay.

There was a time, however, when the personas of Kenny and the gambling company he co-founded in 1988 were inseparable. So much so that English journalists even believed his name was actually Paddy Power, long before the man who actually had that name became the face of the company.

In August 2016 Kenny had just helped orchestrate a €12 billion merger with the rival Betfair – a deal that increased his own personal wealth by many millions and created more than 200 millionaires. He was about to turn sixty-five so it seemed like a natural enough time to retire for good.

Kenny had actually retired once before, over a decade earlier, when he fulfilled a promise to himself to leave the company by the age of fifty. He stood down as chief executive, pursued his interest in Buddhism, shaved his head, visited temples in Tibet and began studying psychiatry with a view to becoming a counsellor. The rest of his time he planned to fill with his other new hobby, long-distance cycling.

But the bookmaker-turned-Buddhist didn't separate himself completely from Paddy Power and stayed on as a director, mentoring younger executives and revelling in the controversy sparked by the marketing gimmicks he continued to be in.

For three decades Kenny had been one of the best marketing men in Irish business, on a par with Michael O'Leary at Ryanair in ensuring his brand was talked about as part of the national conversation, hiding a ruthless business intelligence by playing the part of the hapless bookie. 'People like to see a bookie caught with his nappy down,' he said in 1995 after overseeing a media campaign presenting a calculated loss as an accidental error.

But as the business model was supercharged by the advent of the Internet and high-powered data-harvesting tools to nudge gamblers to bet on products designed to trigger psychological urges that caused concern they were leading people into addiction, a group in Paddy Power tried to temper the damage the gambling industry was causing.

I didn't know any of this about Kenny when I got a call out of the blue in the summer of 2018. I was in the Dublin newsroom of the London *Times*, where I had been covering the business model of Paddy Power Betfair for a couple of years, exposing technological advancements that made it more difficult for gamblers to win, and much easier for addicts to lose everything.

A number I didn't recognize flashed up on my iPhone screen and when I answered, the posh Dublin accent on the other end introduced itself.

'Hi there, is that Aaron Rogan? This is Stewart Kenny.'

I must have sounded confused, not because I didn't recognize the name, but because I didn't know what was coming next. 'I used to work for Paddy Power . . .' he offered before I interrupted and explained I knew who he was. He vaguely complimented my reporting on his old company, and asked to meet for a coffee the next day.

I half expected to get a bollocking for a couple of embarrassing inaccuracies that I had reported in my stories, or maybe he would tell me to back off from scrutinizing the company.

I braced myself with responses to the expected accusations of having a biased agenda to do down betting as an immoral pastime and planned to explain that I was not some flag-waving, anti-gambling crusader, I was a typical Paddy Power customer. Since I was in college in the mid-2000s I had spent a good chunk of my hung-over Saturday mornings putting together football accumulators that might pay for the next night out but rarely did, and backed almost every horse-racing tip I got, even if the horses were running in the same race.

When I met Kenny I was disarmed when he said he thought I had got to the crux of the problem with the gambling industry: that they couldn't claim they didn't want to take advantage of gambling addicts if they were not willing to make their products less addictive and take the hit on profits that came with cutting off the high-staking losers who are not in control of their behaviour.

This would not be an unconscionable interference in its customer base, as Paddy Power and all other bookmakers already restrict some customers from betting: those who win too much.

The €10 punters who make up the vast majority of Paddy Power's customers are mostly unaware that a certain subset are unable to get a bet on: they have shown an insight that means that in the long run they can beat the bookie and take a profit – rather than the other way round.

Since gambling began, bookies have always courted losers and baulked at customers who displayed more knowledge than them, but the new model of Internet gambling had taken this to a whole new level. Gambling companies these days identify the type of gamblers they are up against within a few bets, using a computer monitoring system that determines how profitable each new account will be to the firm. Most customers are given incentives to gamble more, with the company knowing that they will lose in the long run. A tiny minority are effectively banned from placing bets because they display intelligence that suggests they might win. Those who display the strongest disregard for winning are offered incentives to gamble on casino games that guarantee returns for Paddy Power with no risk to the company's profits. And a small percentage of these show such a great aptitude for losing money that Paddy Power filters them into a system of management where they are referred to as 'VIPs'.

It might sound obvious but you don't ever want to be considered a 'very important person' by a gambling company. What is very important to them is not likely to be what is good for your bank balance in the long run.

In High Nelly's, a café on Haddington Street around the corner from one of Paddy Power's most profitable shops, I explained my reasoning to Kenny while he nodded and scoffed greasy rashers folded into slices of buttered toast. He was going for a cycle later that day, he offered by way of explanation for the fat and carb intake, and then told me that the reason he had left Paddy Power Betfair in 2016 was not because he was exceptionally rich and about to reach retirement age, but because he could no longer stomach the company's complacency in taking action on the social costs of the massive profits it was generating.

This was big. Here was the founder of a stock-market-listed giant on the Irish and British corporate landscape, telling me that he had a moral distaste for the company's business model.

My reporting had already drawn out sources within the company and people who had recently left because they were unhappy with how certain issues were handled by the company, but this was not just a trader, data analyst or risk manager who had found it hard to stomach the social cost of the betting industry's billions in profits. This was the founder and face of Paddy Power.

I began to ask around about Kenny and got a sense that he really had pushed for changes in the way Paddy Power operated while at the company, and learned that he was not alone in this, but he was not particularly influential either. By the time he left, he was a non-executive director and the direction of the company was on the same course as other gambling firms in pursuing fast profits from any avenue where they became available, even when it seemed clear that the gamblers were in the throes of addiction.

An internal analysis in 2013 – known as Project Vanguard – found that using the same type of data analysis Paddy Power employed to get the most money from customers to root out people falling into addiction could cost between 15 per cent and 20 per cent of profits, but as Paddy Power merged into Paddy Power Betfair, the project was sidelined.

This and other efforts to lower the level of harm caused by gambling were designed not out of altruism but because public opinion, political scrutiny and regulatory oversight were growing increasingly harsh on the corporate giants sucking up profits from punters.

'Self-regulation won't work and hasn't worked. There are bonuses for profits, not for social responsibility,' Kenny told me in 2019 for an article in the *Business Post*. 'As someone with experience on the board, I can tell you boards look to governments for regulation.'

That regulation has been piecemeal and the subject of intense lobbying by the industry, but the tide is turning in many countries where online gambling is already regulated. The gambling corporations have realized this and are making last-ditch attempts to reduce addiction among their client base, without risking too much profit.

As Kenny sees it: 'This is the way the industry want

to play it – to act as a fire brigade putting out fires rather than changing the design and materials used in the building of the house to prevent any fires breaking out.' He believes that the solution is relatively simple: make the products less addictive, or gambling 'will get a stench like cigarettes'.

When the news of the reasons behind Kenny's 2016 departure broke, it confirmed his position as a gadfly on the ever-fattening rump of the industry where he made his millions. But rivals and cynics question whether his crusade against gambling corporations' excesses is the work of a fox-hole convert trying to clear his own conscience.

Kenny's reputation in the gambling industry as a ruthless businessman was honed over his three decades as a senior executive in one of Ireland's most successful and controversial businesses, which is now worth €30 billion and rising. In a similar way to Ryanair, Paddy Power used the Internet and Irish entrepreneurship to create an international success that upended the very industry it is part of. Aggressive expansion, ballsy marketing and a healthy disregard for the competition led both companies to heights which would have been implausible when they were founded as parochial outfits in the 1980s.

Under Kenny's stewardship, Paddy Power courted

controversy with advertising campaigns skewering Catholic sensibilities and gimmicks such as offering bets on murder trials. This was all good fun for Kenny, but by the time he made the decision to walk away, his company's reputation was being torn to shreds in a way it could no longer control.

The reports of young and middle-aged suicides, broken homes and defaulted mortgages caused by gambling addiction among customers were piling up in newspapers across Ireland, Britain and Australia, clashing with the firm's tongue-in-cheek adverts showing how much fun gambling is:

'VIOLENCE, DEBT AND DEVASTATION
BROUGHT BY THE SPIN OF A WHEEL'
The Times

'Gambling addiction becoming
"public health issue of a generation"'
Irish Examiner

'MESMERISING HORROR OF WATCHING
A MIDDLE-CLASS ACCOUNTANT LOSE
£3,000 IN AN HOUR ON CRACK-COCAINE
GAMBLING MACHINES'
The Mail on Sunday

'Mum's crusade against "crack cocaine of gambling"
machines which drove her son to suicide'
The Mirror

'PADDY POWER "ENCOURAGED GAMBLER"
UNTIL HE LOST HIS HOME, JOBS AND FAMILY'
The Guardian

'A teenager drowned himself after racking up
£5,000 in online gambling debts, an inquest heard.'
The Sun

These stories are all from the year before Kenny decided to walk.

Over the last two decades gambling has gone through an existential change. Smartphone and technological innovations have made it more fun, more accessible and more dangerous.

The stories of men, and it is usually men, slowly boiling themselves alive financially by chasing losses on every type of product offered by Paddy Power and its rivals should have caused a reckoning. Instead the firms added heat to the problem through supercharging their use of customer data, reckless incentive schemes and aggressive cross-selling of customers into more addictive forms of gambling.

More than anyone else in modern Irish bookmaking,

Kenny succeeded in making the average person believe that losing money by gambling is entertainment they can't afford to miss out on. He burst the bubble that the industry had inflated about punters being able to get rich from gambling and shifted the focus onto entertainment and fun, not money. Paddy Power's brand guidelines wanted punters to think of gambling in the same way that they think about slipping out of the office at half four for a sly pint – sure, it's not going to make you a better person but it will add a bit of divilment to the day. Irish people have the third biggest gambling losses in the world annually, behind only Australia and Singapore, so understanding the psyche of the Irish punter is a valuable piece of analysis.

Since property tycoon and bookmaker John Corcoran approached Kenny and Richard Power about combining their chains of shops in 1988, the company has grown from a high-street operation into a technology-powered multinational conglomerate, merging with rival firms to rev up the use of data and psychological techniques to make people bet more money, more often.

Kenny knows that lots of people turn their nose up at gambling but he knows too that for most people life is enhanced with a bit of risk. These are the people he has succeeded in turning into Paddy Power customers. From betting on who shot Mr Burns in *The Simpsons* to the outcome of the Oscar Pistorius murder trial, there was little that Paddy Power didn't think was worth letting people have a punt on. But as the technological power of Paddy Power kicked into gear, Kenny began to see that too many people were being chewed up by the machine. These guys weren't having a cheeky beer in the early evening – they were twisting the cap on the vodka bottle by mid-morning.

When he went public about the reasons for leaving Paddy Power, business rivals and industry cynics scoffed. Kenny had a reputation as someone who never took his foot off the throat of a smaller competitor too soon and his company's courting of controversy made it seem like they didn't take anything seriously.

But Kenny was actually alive to the dangers of his industry long before he walked away and he had made some efforts to redirect Paddy Power's course. He had developed strategies with other executives that tried to root out addicts before they ran into danger. When still a non-executive director at Paddy Power he lobbied the Irish government, warning them against changing the law to allow fixed-odds betting terminals, known as FOBTs, which had been a goldmine in the UK. Discreet dispatches to departmental officials are nothing strange in the world where politics meets corporate interests, but Kenny's 2009 intervention was startling. Here was the founder of a stock-market-listed company telling the government not only that their products were addictive, but likening them to street drugs. Kenny warned that FOBTs were 'the crack cocaine of gambling' and 'particularly enticing to younger gamblers in disadvantaged areas'.

Kenny is an unusual personality even in the world of rascals and rogues who make up parts of the gambling industry. He entered middle age proclaiming himself to be a 'two-bit hustler' unsuited to corporate life and exited it as an '*à la carte* Buddhist' who had spent almost thirty years on the board of Paddy Power. During his tenure he used every trick in the book to fight for his company, taking on vested interests in the politically connected horse-racing industry, going to war with fellow bookmakers and using government contacts to ensure favourable tax arrangements to see Paddy Power's profits soar. This makes his conversion into a critic of the company he built all the more cutting.

Some people I spoke to while writing this book believe Kenny's attempts to rid gambling of FOBTs and other addictive products were born out of pragmatism – he could sense the political campaigns forming and wanted to get out in front of them. Others agreed with the views of Paddy Power's rivals, that Kenny was only interested in limiting FOBTs because it would damage Paddy Power's competition more than his company, which was already making fortunes from its online operations and did not need increased high street turnover as much as smaller independents.

But Kenny has continued crusading, talking behind the scenes with the most vociferous and uncompromising anti-gambling campaigners and politicians to limit the damage caused by the industry. He admits himself that he should have done more when he was in a position of power but it is too late for that now and, whatever his motives, he is having an effect.

As one person who first got to know him when he was a bookie with a pitch at Harold's Cross greyhound track in early 1980s said: 'I like Stewart Kenny, I just preferred him when he didn't let his conscience get in the way.'

I

Origin Story

'There's no need to hedge your bets on this one.'

Stewart Kenny was typically cocksure as he made the announcement that he was merging his chain of bookmakers with a group of rival firms.

'It's a dead cert that we will be successful, both here and in Britain,' he said, adding that the nascent group would move to float on the stock exchange even though they hadn't yet taken a bet. Then Kenny played to the crowd.

'If the English companies can come in here, there is no reason why we can't go over there. I find the English companies a little clinical in their approach. We are going to introduce a degree of razzmatazz and flair, which they can't match.'

This sort of ballsy jingoism was rare among Irish businessmen in 1988, but Kenny wanted to make a splash. He has something about him of the barker outside the circus tent: 'Roll up! Roll up! Enter and behold the sights and sounds of the most amazing Irish bookmaker . . .'

The announcement of the well-known and well-liked Kenny O'Reilly chain's merger into a new Irish super-group was front-page stuff. Not just because it was a decent business story, but because Kenny has a knack for framing stories in a way that is irresistible to editors. The headline of the *Irish News*' page-one coverage on 12 February 1988: 'Bookie wages war on British.'

Kenny declared that the new outfit would have a network of fifty 'bright green offices around the country, with ultra-modern facilities' within a month and would attract 10 per cent of the £200 million spent by Irish gamblers that year. It was a clear statement of intent in an uncertain time. Dublin in 1988 was the capital of an economic wasteland in a celebratory mood. It was a hungry and dirty city. About one in five Irish people were unemployed, 70,000 (mostly young) people were about to emigrate and interest rates were in double figures as decades of faulty policies and economic mismanagement had the country on the precipice of catastrophe.

"Dublin's Great in '88" the branding on milk bottles said, almost sarcastically, above a depiction of the city's emblem of three castles, coloured in a garish blue, yellow and red design to commemorate 1,000 years of the city. As part of this so-called millennium, a 70ft-long fibreglass, aluminium and plywood body of Gulliver had been commissioned by Dublin Corporation and sat partially submerged in the water off Dollymount Strand.

In a satirical flourish illustrating the carelessness of Irish officialdom that Jonathan Swift himself would have been proud of, this celebratory Gulliver was made by thirty-five young men on an unemployment scheme for a millennium party that was held in the wrong year. The founding of the city by the Gaelic King Máel Sechnaill II's conquest of the Viking city Dubh Linn had actually occurred in 989 and medieval scholars complained that the conquest itself was of little histor-ical consequence as the area had long been home to a settlement. Central Dublin was dilapidated and needed a lift, but even the year-long festivities of the phoney millennium could not hide the fact that for many in the capital at the time, life was a grim slog.

A special report by *The Economist* magazine in January 1988 was illustrated on the front cover with a photograph of a beggar woman sitting on the street, a child sleeping in her arms while a man in an overcoat strolls by ignoring them. 'Poorest of the rich' the stark headline said. The article's introduction was equally damning of Ireland's prospects as the 1990s approached:

Take a tiny, open, ex-peasant economy. Place it next door to a much larger one, from which it broke away with great bitterness barely a lifetime ago. Infuse it with a passionate desire to enjoy the same lifestyle as its former masters, but without the same industrial heritage of natural resources. Inevitable result: extravagance, frustration, debt.

The report – illustrating a poverty-stricken nation tied up in knots of bureaucracy – provoked anger in the governing Fianna Fáil party who accused *The Economist* of damaging Ireland's reputation, but it was in fact a fair encapsulation of an international view that Ireland's economy was headed for catastrophe and its best and brightest citizens would always be emigrants. As the joke went at the time, last one out please turn off the lights.

But what *The Economist* didn't capture were the early stirrings of an entrepreneurial and innovative spirit in a new generation no longer happy to live in the shadow of the economic giant on the neighbouring island. The government's Industrial Development Authority was seeking occupants for the International Financial Services Centre (IFSC), which was set to begin construction. This building marked the start of a corporate tax honeypot in one of the most deprived areas of Dublin, and with it a long-standing commitment to the capitalist spirit that would define the Celtic Tiger of the late 1990s and new millennium – the real one, that is.

By 1988 small seeds were being planted that would bear fruit to achieve those goals in the next decade. The .ie domain registry was started, giving Ireland its own address on what was to become the World Wide Web. In a more established field of connectivity, Tony Ryan had built Guinness Peat Aviation from scratch to become the world leader in aircraft leasing, outstripping all expectations. In 1988 Ryan had just appointed a mouthy accountant named Michael O'Leary – who had left KPMG to start a newsagent's business – as chief financial officer of Ryanair, which won approval to run routes between Ireland and England despite the government's efforts to protect Aer Lingus. Denis O'Brien, another entrepreneur who would go on to become a billionaire tycoon and who also worked under Ryan in his early years, was about to take advantage of the loosening of the state's grip on the airwaves by launching Communicorp, a commercial radio network.

And on a freezing winter's day in the year of Dublin's phoney millennium, John Corcoran bumped into Stewart Kenny outside the Department of Industry and Commerce on Kildare Street. Corcoran, an imposing figure known to some as 'the Colonel', had an ambitious vision. He wanted Kenny to do a deal merging their betting businesses.

Corcoran said they would need to think big and long-term and when he called Kenny and two other Irish bookmakers, David Power and Liam Cashman, to a meeting in the offices of Green Property on Earlsfort Terrace, he outlined a strategy in which a new Irish chain could beat the British firms into retreat. Kenny was excited and Power was agreeable as they both saw the influx of British firms muscling in, but Cashman's involvement was short-lived as his demands for family members to be involved frustrated Corcoran, who was clear in his own vision for the new company.

The multimillionaire property tycoon had retained his father's interest in the P. Corcoran bookmaking business alongside founding Green Property, a trans-formative developer that would help to facilitate the growth of Dublin in the 1990s. When announcing a one million square-foot retail development in Blanchardstown in 1986, he bluntly told reporters: 'It's not a shopping centre, it's a town centre.' Always forward-minded, Corcoran had been sitting on the suburban tract of land since the 1970s when he bought it from farmers. He was ready to realize his vision to coincide with the new ring road now diverting more traffic towards Blanchardstown. 'The town is going to be here in 200 years' time, so we'd better get it right,' Corcoran observed at the time.

The Enniscorthy, Co. Wexford man had a similarly optimistic and determined plan for merging the betting businesses. What about the prospect of taking on the British firms starting to crowd out the traditional Irish bookies and beating them at their own game – in both Ireland and England?

There had been a gold rush west across the Irish Sea since 1986. The old colony was viewed as another part of the British gambling market and independents were under pressure. When betting tax was reduced from a punitive 20 per cent to a slightly less punitive 10 per cent in 1985 there was an almost immediate 44 per cent increase in turnover in bookmakers, as punters were happy to bet more rather than giving it straight to the taxman. It will come as no surprise that the Irish bookmaking industry's diligence in collecting the tax from punters was less than thorough. The increase in turnover had actually been facilitated mainly by a focus from Revenue Commissioners' special investigation unit working under-cover and legitimate bookmakers ratting out their less honest rivals. Whatever the reasons behind the higher turnover, it attracted the attention of the British giants Ladbrokes, Coral and Mecca, who were well-established operations and had the coffers to run large chains of shops undercutting independent retail operations.

Kenny had himself just struck it rich in that gold rush when in August 1986 he sold the chain of ten betting shops he had built up with business partner Vincent O'Reilly, a wealthy publican. But it was not a particularly popular deal. The £3 million sale to Coral needed High Court clearance after rival Irish bookies in Dublin objected and got politicians to lobby the Garda Commissioner asking him to block the granting of new betting licences, which would allow the British outfit to take over the shops. The attempt to block the sale failed after Kenny and O'Reilly lodged a case in the High Court against the Garda superintendents who were refusing to grant new licences for some shops. Newspaper coverage of the court hearing claimed that the deal would revolutionize betting in Ireland and more pressingly – in the minds of many out-of-work Dubliners – lead to Coral spending £1 million on decorating and renovation work.

Ladbrokes and Coral had together spent £10 million buying up sixty of Dublin's premier shops by the time of the Kenny O'Reilly deal, valuing them at fifteen times their weekly turnover as they planned to blitz out the Irish competition by offering costly satellite racing feeds from tracks all across Britain, which many Irish outfits could not afford. The *Evening Herald* headlined the details of Coral's take-over of the Kenny O'Reilly chain as 'UK bookies in Dublin coup.'

It was becoming increasingly clear that Irish shops would not be able to compete with the might of Ladbrokes, Coral and Mecca but Kenny didn't view the windfall as enough reason to leave the mischief of bookmaking behind. On the same day as Coral officially took over the ten outlets, Kenny and O'Reilly opened up a new set of four shops, much to the British firm's disgust – it would not have paid such an inflated price for the original chain had it known how few obstacles there were to opening competing shops in Ireland. As Coral did not see the value in buying the brand name Kenny O'Reilly, the business was free to restart as long as it did not open within half a mile of a Coral shop.

Coral initially hoped to attract punters by pushing up its payout limits to £250,000, eight times the £30,000 maximum win available in only the most generous of Irish bookies. Without missing a trick, Kenny used the windfall from the Coral deal to push the Kenny O'Reilly payout up to £100,000 and alerted journalists to this detail so it would be included in their coverage of Coral's announcement.

Kenny, the son of a Supreme Court judge, stood out from the urban rogues and rural gentry who generally had deep family lineages in the Irish betting industry, either through horses or greyhounds. Kenny had only been drawn to horse-racing as a young child when his father, Mr Justice John Kenny, who had no interest in sport beyond cricket, was advised by colleagues in the Law Library to take his wheezy son to Leopardstown races for a day of fresh air to help with the boy's eczema and asthma. He was hooked, and began taking bets as a bold boarder while a fourteen-year-old attending the Benedictine school Glenstal Abbey. After Glenstal he sacked off his commerce degree in University College Dublin – having needed to repeat exams to pass his first year in 1970 – and moved to London where he got a job working in a Ladbrokes shop. In a line he has repeated like a good joke throughout his career, Kenny said that when he told his Supreme Court justice father and Methodist mother that he wanted to be a bookie, he may as well have told them he'd 'got the neighbour's daughter up the pole'.

The anti-establishment bent in Kenny attracted him to the rascality of gambling but he was regarded as a strange fish by the plain punters at Harold's Cross dog track when he set up his pitch there. They soon warmed to the newcomer, however, as in desperation to attract business he offered higher odds than the bookies beside him, starting a career-defining trait. After his first day at the south Dublin track, a more experienced bookie pulled Kenny aside and gave him some advice. 'Any fool can fill a satchel – it's filling it at the right price that counts.' However, it was not just his upper-class upbringing that made Kenny an outsider in the bookmaking fraternity – unlike the other outfits, he always approached bookmaking from a punter's point of view.

He soon decided that he wanted to follow in the footsteps of Terry Rogers, a flamboyant character who redefined Irish betting in the 1960s. Rogers was a giant in Irish betting. He was the man who brought Texas hold 'em poker to Europe by starting the Irish Poker Open in 1980 and founded Dublin's Eccentric Club above his betting shop on Hanlon's Corner, Phibsborough. This card club drew in punters, politicians, professional snooker players, bookies and other hardy souls who wanted to gamble with the country's best.

At horse-racing tracks, punters flocked to the cabaret-style flamboyance of Rogers' pitch to hear his banter and wager on the unique bets he offered – including on the outcome of elections, which at the time was a rarity. Kenny regards Rogers, who died in 1999, as the father of modern Irish bookmaking and believes Paddy Power's take on the industry is a continuation of Rogers' mantra that betting is about fun and customers should be treated with respect.

In 1972, armed with a £6,000 overdraft from Bank of Ireland guaranteed by his father, Kenny opened two shops, one on Wexford Street in Dublin and another in Athy, Co. Kildare. From this point on Kenny started to inject a bit of fun in the stuffy world of off-course betting by appealing to a wider audience. He and Alan

Tuthill, another independent bookmaker, are credited with ushering in a new era of gambling in Ireland by offering odds on all sorts of events from the Eurovision Song Contest to whether it would snow on Christmas Day.

They may have been innovators in Ireland but they were mainly using the gimmicks of Graham Sharpe, a local newspaper hack who became William Hill's head of public relations in 1972, pioneering wide-ranging political markets and causing stirs in the tabloids by offering bets on weather events and TV programmes. Sharpe wanted to make betting more customer-friendly and felt that offering odds on, for example, how many seats Labour would win in a general election would allow punters to back something they couldn't accuse the bookies of rigging.

When Sharpe caused a sensation by opening a book in 1980 on who shot JR in the television phenomenon *Dallas*, Kenny immediately followed suit with his own bookmaker's and earned himself invitations onto RTÉ radio and full pages of press coverage to talk about the potential shooters in a programme he had rarely even watched. It was the start of a long-running career of media manipulation that would serve Kenny's book-making brand well.

It was also a breath of fresh air in the gambling industry in Ireland. Throughout the 1970s and 80s, off-course bookmakers were dingy places with bare walls except for the tacked-up racing pages from newspapers, bolshie staff and, in several premises, buckets on the floor collecting rainwater from leaking roofs. Gambling was allowed but not acceptable in Catholic conservative Ireland. The archaic law governing the pastime placed a holy host of unworkable conditions on where bookmakers could work from: they could not be situated close to a place of worship, a religious institution, a school, an employment exchange, a factory, any place near where large numbers of people congregated, or in a residential area. The 1931 Betting Act also banned bookmakers from being 'in close proximity to premises known to be resorted to habitually by evilly-disposed persons', which would have been particularly bad for business had it ever been enforced.

As a rule, bookmaker shops had to be drab as the Betting Act made it illegal to offer anything considered an 'attraction'. This might incite loitering and – depending on the temperament of the local Garda superintendent – could be interpreted to mean that no seating was allowed. It was only in 1979 that an enterprising bookie in Dublin challenged a fine he received for having a television set in his premises and the district court ruled that TVs were necessary for the business of bookmaking. The newer bookmakers such as Kenny and Tuthill made their shops colourful and offered bets on all sorts of markets, which other firms didn't believe were worth pricing up. Kenny wanted to make betting a form of entertainment and set himself up as the punter's pal.

An opportunity to show his mettle came in June 1975 when Barney Curley landed his first major betting coup. The now infamous gambler's plot involving his horse Yellow Sam exposed a flaw in the off-course book-makers' armoury by taking advantage of poor telephone facilities at the Bellewstown track. Curley had a number of acquaintances and hired accomplices wait in shops around the country with sealed envelopes containing cash and instructions to be opened upon a call from Curley, who was at the track. The trainer called a small number of friends at 2.50, ten minutes before the 20–1 Yellow Sam was to run. They in turn called others and dozens of wagers totalling £15,000 were placed on the horse. But because another of Curley's friends was blocking the only available phone line at Bellewstown (the private line belonging to the Extel company which supplied racing data to betting shops had been myste-riously cut), pretending to have a conversation with his dying aunt, the unusually high level of bets could not be communicated. Normally the starting price would have been slashed to much lower odds, but Curley had successfully jammed the network at the track, which he had selected especially for its poor communication lines.

Yellow Sam won by two and half lengths, landing Curley £300,000 (around €2 million adjusted for inflation) and sending the off-course bookmakers apoplectic. Curley had literally hidden in the long grass, watching the race from gorse so as not to arouse suspicion from the bookies on-course who were already aware of his reputation as a dangerous gambler. Rogers and dozens of other bookmakers refused to pay the winnings at first but when they realized there was no illegal activity they conceded – and quickly concocted a new 'anti-coup' rule to block anything similar from happening in future. From then on any bet more than £20 placed less than half an hour before a race would be limited to odds of 2/1. This would apply to any Irish racetrack with a telephone set-up deemed inadequate, which would have meant all but the main courses.

The daring nature of the coup and the enraged bookies' reactions led to widespread media coverage, with Rogers claiming that the industry wanted the 'genuine punter' but would do well enough without the '£100 man and coup merchant'. But the genuine punters Rogers wanted to take bets from were already bound by all sorts of rules limiting pay-outs and they delighted in seeing so many of the bookies caught with their pants around their ankles. The rule was a PR disaster for the bookies who signed up to it. In response, Kenny took out adverts in national newspapers reassuring his customers that no such restrictions would be applied in his shops. The slogan on the advert stated: 'You do the betting – we do the fretting.'

The young bookie's reputation was growing and over the next decade Kenny would join with Vincent O'Reilly to build up a chain of ten well-known shops in Dublin. Having retained the brand following the sale to Coral, he was again in a position to define the new era of Irish bookmaking.

After the impromptu meeting on Kildare Street, Corcoran laid out the plan he had been mulling over. He wanted to merge his twenty-one shops with Kenny's nine and a small group of others to fight back against the British invasion. Corcoran was clear in his vision. He told Kenny that it would have to be a long-term strategy, similar to how he had sat on the Blanchardstown farmland. It would value market share above other metrics, leaving the short-term profits to the outsiders, and they absolutely would not sell up.

While they didn't have a lot in common from the outside, one thing Corcoran and Kenny understood was that Irish gamblers had different tastes to British ones. They would play on the nationalism of the time by wrapping the new brand in Kelly-green shopfronts. Coral, Ladbrokes and Mecca had bought up about 20 per cent of the Irish market by the late 1980s, so any pushback from an indigenous group had to be from a running start.

On the same day Kenny's declaration of war on the British bookies appeared on the news-stands, the insurrection began. One of his offices in Rathfarnham had been put under pressure when Ladbrokes opened up beside it and began offering the extremely attractive proposition of 'tax-free' betting to customers. This was a show of strength by Ladbrokes as it would badly cut into the shop's profits but its intention was to push Kenny's shop out of business as smaller operations could not operate on such tight margins. On 12 February the new Irish venture hit back by renting an office beside the Ladbrokes in Ballymun and doing the same.

With Corcoran they had the money to push the boat out on these punter-friendly but profit-draining ideas and with Kenny they had the marketing. For this high-turnover, low-profit model to work, the new chain needed to start with a bulky high-street presence. Added to Corcoran's twenty-one shops and Kenny's nine were four independent outlets and twelve previously operated under the Richard Power banner.

David Power was a third-generation on-course bookie who also oversaw his family's chain of shops around Ireland and who had built a private-client business to give high-profile punters some much-needed confidentiality. His partnership would give the firm the standing among serious horse-racing punters that it may have otherwise lacked. A pipe-smoking turf accountant of the old school, Power was an equally shrewd businessman and could see the potential of the proposition.

Power's pedigree as a bookmaker was second to none. His grandfather Richard Power is said to have begun running bets from the drapery store where he was employed in 1896 to a local illegal bookmaker and soon realized he was rarely required to go back for any winnings. Instead of making the trip to the local bookie, he began keeping the money and paying back from his growing bankroll when the rare bet was a winner. Soon after he started working on-course at the Tramore races, shouting his odds from a tea chest.

This origin story of a poor boy taking bets from his elders and realizing they were rarely sending him to collect any winnings is shared by many bookies but other aspects of the Power's story gave him a unique standing in the trade. Richard Power stood in the same betting rings as William Hill at British courses. The name had an eight-decade-long association with horse-racing and a long list of wealthy private clients when David inherited his grandfather's business at the age of sixteen when his father Paddy died. By the time David took over the running of the family business in 1970 on finishing his accountancy studies, the firm also held a chain of off-course shops. With the addition of John O'Reilly as financial controller and Jimmy Mangan as head of operations, the principals were now in place to give the new business a fighting chance against their better-funded rivals.

As part of the opening, the in-your-face British icon of Channel 4's betting coverage, John McCririck, was flown in to launch the new brand. The famous side-burns, deerstalker hat and tweed suit arrived from Wexford racecourse in an open-top convertible at Corcoran's Northside Shopping Centre on a Thursday afternoon in April 1988 to open the chain's flagship outlet.

In total, forty-six bookmaker shops spread across eleven counties were kitted out in the new brand's patriotic green livery and the shop signs installed, revealing the name and a cheeky two-fingered salute to the British betting giants: Paddy Power.

2

Tax Wars

Paddy Power might have been started in opposition to the British giants moving into Ireland but the first to feel the strength of this new green-jerseyed outfit were its compatriots.

In June 1988 an upstart firm named Celtic Bookmakers sought to cash in on the new model of bookmaking, offering comfort and fun to punters as it took their cold hard cash. Celtic's first two offices were right in the firing line of Paddy Power, one opposite a rebranded R. Power office in Tramore, Co. Wexford. Celtic opened its second outlet in Wicklow town and began offering 'best odds guaranteed', which meant that if you backed a horse that drifted out to higher odds at the starting price set at the course you would get paid out at that higher price. It was an attractive proposition for punters and won Celtic some customers in the busy market town.

But it was not as attractive as Paddy Power's retaliatory offer. As Kenny had been treated by Ladbrokes in Rathfarnham so too would Paddy Power treat Celtic. The bookmaker offered to pick up the 10 per cent betting tax for customers in Wicklow town. This forced Celtic to do the same, and a local independent bookmaker named Brian Carthy also had to follow suit. It soon emerged that Celtic was owned by Ivan Yates, the outspoken Fine Gael TD from Wexford, and his wife Deirdre, details of the dispute between local retailers somehow made it to the national press.

Kenny would tell the story years later that Yates rang him early on in the row and told him he had three ambitions in life: to be a successful farmer, a successful politician and a successful bookmaker. But before he could make his point, his rival cut him off. 'Listen Ivan, it's as simple as this: two out of three ain't bad,' he said as he hung up the phone.

Powers would not relent and Celtic could afford to see them off for a period so long as the sporting results were in their favour, but like all small operators Carthy operated off a tighter profit margin and complained that he was being sent to the wall. Carthy was buried within months and Paddy Power dropped the tax-free offer, leaving just it and the Yates' Celtic Bookmakers in the town. Yates rang him again and said that it was such a great tactic they should try it again in some other town. Indeed, it would not be the last time Kenny crossed paths with the TD.

The tax wars continued in towns and villages around the country with Paddy Power joining Ladbrokes and Coral in trying to win customers from local independents by using their own financial muscle to absorb the squeeze on profits caused by paying customers' taxes along with all the other overheads. Tax-free offers had been used sporadically by larger firms in Ireland but what was happening now was widespread. The smaller firms were bruised but were not going to give up.

Terry Rogers pulled together 200 small independents to form the Irish Independent Betting Offices Association (IBOA) to lobby the government to ban the practice of offering tax-free betting. Rogers warned that local shops could be wiped out along with their jobs if they were not protected.

By 1989 the British firms had around 80 per cent of business in Limerick City and just under half of the market in Dublin and Cork, according to the IBOA. The industry group's members did not complain about Power or other Irish firms engaged in offering tax-free betting but accused the multinationals Ladbrokes, Coral and Mecca of operating a predatory practice.

The British firms hit back that they were offering value to customers, which had been absent until they arrived in Ireland. In order to bolster their argument, an economic analysis commissioned by the lobby group of small bookmakers showed that hundreds of jobs could be lost in the industry and would ultimately damage Irish horse and greyhound racing. It was enough to persuade the Minister for Finance Albert Reynolds to outlaw the practice in the Finance Act 1989, making it a criminal offence to offer tax-free betting and imposing a fine of £1,000 for offenders.

But the practice was too lucrative and too leaky to make any difference and the tax wars continued, occasionally at the behest of Paddy Power looking to squeeze out competition in areas they deemed to have too many shops. By the mid-1990s Paddy Power had developed a reputation among Irish bookies as a ruthless outfit no different in its tactics from the British beasts it had set out to stop taking over Irish bookmaking. It was buying out independents and crushing the competition.

John Corcoran's firm belief was that if the firm went for market share then it could absorb bad days much more easily than the competitors and gain more than them on the good days. If Paddy Power was miserable, then the smaller bookies must have been suicidal. If they were delighted, then Paddy Power was ecstatic.

The firepower of this new Irish mega-chain was putting the frighteners on local independents – who had no idea how much of a drain it was on Paddy Power. John Corcoran was parsimonious in his business dealings so arranged for Paddy Power's head office to be located in an unused room on the site of his son Andrew's APC Scaffolding firm on the Greenhills Road in Dublin. The four full-time principals – Kenny, John O'Reilly, Jimmy Mangan and Corcoran's daughter Roseanne – crowded around one table with two phones between them. Roseanne Corcoran shared her father's aversion to waste and made sure costs were kept low in her role of fitting out the shops. She would later boast that in the first thirty orders of Paddy Power-branded betting dockets, each order was cheaper than the last.

Soon after the company moved to a new office above the Paddy Power shop on the Clonard Road in Crumlin, John Corcoran arrived to see a pile of twenty *Racing Posts* on the floor. Why would four people need that many copies of the paper, he asked Kenny. How much would have to be taken in over the counter to pay for the *Racing Posts* that were thrown out? Kenny added up the cost of sixteen papers, but Corcoran re-asked the question more specifically. How much net? The firm was operating on 3 per cent margin so the real cost of those papers was getting around £400 over the counter, giving Kenny an early lesson in cost saving.

The principals of the young company were initially disillusioned at the effort needed to compete with the British firms and Irish rivals, but two signs of weaknesses from the foreign invaders soon changed that. In 1991, when Paddy Power was still in its infancy, Corcoran arranged a meeting with Bob Green, the chief executive of Mecca Bookmakers, which was owned by Grand Metropolitan, the leisure conglomerate that would later merge with Guinness plc to form Diageo in 1997.

The meeting was held under the premise of Paddy Power purchasing some of Mecca's Irish shops, but Corcoran and Kenny hoped to make a pitch to convince the British firm that the Irish chain could be purchased for around £3 million. After the second meeting it became clear that Mecca was trying to sell as well, and Green and Corcoran burst out laughing. 'We'll have to run these businesses then, I suppose,' Corcoran said as he left the meeting with Kenny.

The incident that really gave belief that the new firm could be a success was when Joe Jennings, an Essex bookie who had come west in the gold rush, wanted to sell a shop on Moore Street. Kenny was obsessed with placing Paddy Power shops in positions of prominence on shopping thoroughfares as a way of guaranteeing footfall and building the brand. Jennings had tried to implement the same style of shop that had worked in the south of England and lost the customers who had frequented the shop once owned by Donnacha O'Dea, a teenage Olympic swimmer who had gone on to great success in poker and opened bookies around Dublin.

Just as Tesco had departed Ireland in 1986 (only to return again in 1997) because Irish shoppers didn't take to buying products with Union Jacks on the packaging, British bookies were finding that Irish punters were different from their English counterparts.

Ladbrokes declined to take Jennings' offer of £30,000 to take the lease off his hands, but Kenny and Mangan arranged a deal for £33,000 to cover the cost of refitting the shop – knowing its location would be perfect for Paddy Power. In its first year in trading the Moore Street shop made more than £100,000, mostly from its Lucky Numbers game, which was beginning to attract women into betting shops to place bets on three numbers in the National Lottery draw.

This sort of turnaround in fortunes was becoming common for Paddy Power shops, with profits often covering financial outlay within months of take-overs. The company was also finding it increasingly easy to do deals with Irish bookmakers who felt they were being screwed over by Ladbrokes. The British firm employed a tactic of negotiating with two bookmakers in the same town and agreeing terms with both, only to play them off each other to lower the price. This caused ill will among the independents and word travelled fast.

Kenny delighted in getting up the nose of Ladbrokes. Ireland's richest handicap race was sponsored by the British giant, and the corporate boxes at Leopardstown were filled with visiting clients and associates of the bookmaker for the Ladbroke Hurdle after it announced a massive sponsorship deal in 1987. As the attrition between the British firm and Irish operators ratcheted up, Paddy Power tried to spoil the party by buying up billboard space all the way from Dublin city centre to Leopardstown, making its own offer to pay out on the first six places – more than the race's own sponsor was offering. When Ladbrokes responded by matching Paddy Power's offer, Kenny would call John McCririck of Channel 4 racing and alert him to how Irish customers of a British brand were getting a better deal than the Brits themselves.

Kenny was focused to the point of paranoia on Ladbrokes' market share in Ireland and he made it his mission to hunt down their best-performing shops and open nearby, but Paddy Power was no friend to independents either.

On Ashe Street in Tralee, Co. Kerry, the summer of 1994 should have been a busy one for Colm McLoughlin with Jack Charlton's boys in green's appearance in the USA World Cup being the highlight of the packed sporting calendar. McLoughlin was going back into business as an independent after selling his last shop to Paddy Power, which was by now following the Starbucks model of aggressive expansion. Instead, McLoughlin was squeezed by Paddy Power from the start of June when it offered to cover the 10 per cent tax for customers in its Tralee shop. McLoughlin was enraged and complained that they were trying to force him and the other independents in the town out of business. 'They don't want the independents getting on. It's as simple as that,' he told *The Kerryman* in a front-page article. But punters didn't care as it offered them fair value and Stewart Kenny was resolute that it was not in breach of the law. Rather than offering tax-free betting, Paddy Power was merely offering a 10 per cent discount on the punter's stake as a promotion and all taxes were paid by the bookmaker. 'We are making no apologies to anyone for this,' Kenny told the newspaper.

This was the new world of ultra-competitive book-making and illustrated the often confrontational attitude Paddy Power had towards the rest of the industry. Their mega-chain model was based on keeping the customer happy, not their rivals, so why should they care if the others couldn't keep up? Kenny in particular would develop a reputation in the bookmaking fraternity as being a man who had little interest beyond his own firm. Yates himself remembers the Paddy Power approach as being to engage in any industry-wide efforts 'timidly and at arm's length'.

But it had not always been this way. Before the establishment of the Paddy Power brand Kenny had been a leading figure in the retail committee of the Irish National Bookmakers Association (INBA) throughout the 1980s, along with its chairman Brian Fogarty and another forward-looking young bookie, Dan Daly. The INBA was primarily focused on the interests of on-course bookmakers at the time but under the new young businessmen it began to focus on making book-making a more respectable trade and one that could get its voice heard in the corridors of power.

The group cunningly linked a call for a reduction in the original 20 per cent betting tax to a drive for a clampdown on illegal bookmakers. These pleas made front-page news but initially there was little sympathy for the trade among the public. Generations of young Irishmen had been warned by their mothers as they left the house on Saturday mornings that 'you never meet a poor bookie', so the idea that this trade was struggling seemed laughable to many. But Fogarty, Kenny and Daly found a more sympathetic ear from the TDs whose constituencies depended on the horse-racing and blood-stock industries.

In January 1983 Kenny and Daly met with Revenue officials and explained a widespread tax-dodging fiddle used by bookies to save themselves the cost of the betting tax. Rogue bookies would accept, for example, a £5 bet but not stamp that docket and instead issue a stamped receipt for a 5p bet. The customer would be able to collect on the full price of the bet in the unlikely event they won, but in any case would have saved themselves £1 on placing the bet. The 'penny in the pound' tax scam was widespread at the time and was particularly lucrative. Kenny told reporters at a meeting of bookmakers in the Gresham Hotel that he could have creamed £200 a day by doing it in one of his shops at the time. Daly claimed he could have taken in up to £250,000 a year in his outlets. Despite many bookmakers availing of the fiddle, a widespread militant action was taken and the INBA organized its members into withholding the tax they collected until Revenue took action on the rogue and pirate bookmakers.

The decision by an industry group of ostensibly wealthy men to withhold more than £1 million of tax in the middle of a crippling recession drew little comment from the main political parties and came with little risk. The protest was cleverly deferred until January when most members had renewed their licences, which required a tax certificate to be granted. After a meeting with Alan Dukes, the Fine Gael finance minister at the time, the tax protest ended and it became compulsory for bookies to issue carbon copies of bets to customers. The group failed to convince Dukes of the merits of cutting the betting rate to 10 per cent but there was a separate, surprising political intervention that would play in the bookies' favour.

In an April 1984 segment on the RTÉ programme *Public Account* about the prevalence of illegal gambling in Ireland, two TDs unashamedly said they did not pay the levy when they placed bets and one even claimed the tax was 'immoral'. Charlie McCreevy, a Fianna Fáil TD who was also a horse owner and punter, and Brendan McGahon, a Fine Gael TD, were subsequently interviewed by Revenue inspectors in Leinster House but refused to give any details of where they placed the bets. McCreevy told reporters afterwards that Revenue's interview was an invasion of his privacy because his relationship with his bookmaker 'was the same as with my bank manager'. McGahon's reason for keeping schtum about where he placed illegal bets was 'because getting information about that is their job to find out'. McCreevy said they had not broken the law because it was the bookmakers' duty to pay the tax and accused the politicians criticizing them of 'sanctimonious hypocrisy'. 'It gives me a pain in a place where I can't be quoted,' he told *The Irish News*.

The controversy fizzled out quickly with no official rebuke from the Fianna Fáil or Fine Gael leadership and perhaps surprisingly – given their warnings about the peril their industry was in because of such tax evasion – there was no criticism from INBA. The scrutiny of the sector, however, led to the Revenue Commissioners launching a sting operation during the Galway Races that summer. Undercover inspectors mingled among the crowd at Ballybrit Racecourse finding some on-course bookmakers not collecting tax and during the festival caught out some busy off-course outlets with the same tactic. Rather than offering praise for the new efforts of the taxman in rooting out rogue operators, Kenny complained of a 'revenge vendetta' for the previous year's tax protest.

The campaign may not have been happy with the actions of Revenue but their complaints about the high rate of betting tax compared to Britain and prevalence of illegal activity was now firmly on the agenda. After Kenny, Daly and Fogarty held another meeting with Dukes in 1984, the rate was cut to 10 per cent in the following year's budget. For its part of the bargain, the INBA launched a 'squeal on a bookie' campaign, encouraging punters to contact Revenue if they knew of rogue operators, and the association vowed to oppose the licences of anyone they knew not to be collecting tax. The plan worked and the lower tax rate was kept in place to facilitate a more respectable betting industry and with the empowerment of the INBA. The groundworks for invasion of the British giants and the formation of Paddy Power were set by the new level playing field. Ten years later, when Kenny was defending the firm's own tax-free betting, it was a very different landscape.

In 1994 Paddy Power had eighty-two shops, including seven that had been bought back from Coral in a clear sign that the domestic chain's strategy was working. It was already Ireland's biggest bookmaker, with 18 per cent of the market, and was moving towards 100 shops. The expansion was driven without big debt as Corcoran's property power allowed the firm to finance new outlets by selling the freehold on other shops. Jimmy Mangan was the head of operations and he ensured everything ran as smoothly as possible and made sure that the shop staff were happy and engaged. He was so hands-on that it was joked he wouldn't be back in the office until Christmas after the Galway Races in July because he made a habit of stopping into every shop on the way home to check in. The humanity of Mangan got buy-in from the shop staff in how he dealt with changes to the workings of the shops – he even declined to prosecute thieves so long as they were not violent because he believed they must be down on their luck if they were stealing.

With a dominant business, 1994 marked Kenny's first foray into the brand building that would set the tone for Paddy Power's trademark trolling of politically correct sensibilities.

*

On a drizzly Sunday February morning, mass-goers in Dublin were greeted by a picture of the Holy Father blessing them from bus stops around the city. 'Glasgow Rangers' next signing,' read the block white letters imposed on the picture, referring to the staunchly Protestant Scottish team. Below that was the logo of Paddy Power along with odds of 100,000–1 and the tagline: 'Bet you anything you like.' It was a fortnight before the Cheltenham Festival and Kenny wanted to maximize his brand's exposure to the casual punter ahead of the busiest betting week of the year. The Pope to Rangers idea had actually been drawn up in secret by an Irish advertising agency who worked for Paddy Power, because they did not want to jeopardize a large contract with the National Lottery by associating with a controversial bookmaker.

Kenny wanted to change public perception that the betting industry was only about taking bets on horse and dog races, which had a limited appeal to most people. At the time only about 12 per cent of Irish people ever gambled in bookmakers but Kenny knew that others were interested in betting if it could be made accessible to them. If the average person saw betting as a bit of fun rather than something that required specialist knowledge it would open up the industry to a whole new market.

Fintan Drury, a PR guru who went on to become the

chairman of the Paddy Power board, created the character of Kenny as Mr Bookmaking. Drury wanted the Paddy Power chief to be the face of the high-street sector and reframe gambling as a respectable pastime for an added bit of entertainment in life. As part of this effort, Kenny had hoped to cause a stir.

The first comments on the posters were from Bishop Tom Flynn, a conservative cleric who served as spokesman during some of the Catholic Church's worst scandals in Ireland. He laughed it off. 'I'm not sure if the Pope himself would take much offence,' he said. Jim Cantwell, the Catholic press director who had been in charge for the Pope's visit in 1979, also saw the funny side. 'I imagine the Pope would laugh, if he knew the context,' he told the *Irish Press*.

The plan was to cause enough controversy so that the ads could be adorned with a yellow ribbon stating 'Bless me Father for I have sinned' covering the reference to Rangers, thus generating a second round of chatter about Paddy Power. It appeared to be a bit of a damp squib, however, as no one was taking offence. Celtic supporters in Ireland started asking in Paddy Power offices if they could get copies of the adverts for their bedroom walls. Even Rangers supporters got in on the joke, with the Lagan Village Rangers Supporters Club in Belfast saying they would welcome the chief pastor of the worldwide Catholic Church so long as he could help them win. Only two punters took Paddy Power up on the bet and they were refunded in April when the Pope broke his leg after slipping while getting out of the shower, apparently scuppering his chances of moving to the Scottish champions.

But as the posters stayed up, those which were strategically placed close to churches led to complaints from parishioners. The Advertising Standards Authority of Ireland wrote to Kenny and described the posters as being 'in extremely bad taste, offensive and involving undertones of bigotry'. This was more like it. The advertising watchdog did not order the removal of the posters, but Kenny decided to pull the campaign and live to fight another day.

The Pope to Rangers posters are considered a foundational text in the Paddy Power brand guidelines, but Kenny knew that it would take more than splashy ads to change the general public's perception of bookmakers. John Martin's Punters Platform column in the *Evening Herald* was the de facto arbitration system for disputes between bettors and bookmakers. Issues around lost dockets, illegible handwriting and other grounds for complaint were adjudicated by Martin with bookies generally falling in line with his view. As Paddy Power's retail network expanded throughout the 1990s, it began to feature regularly in Martin's column.

And Kenny always endeavoured to make sure the

firm appeared friendly to its punters. He often offered partial pay-outs where a customer felt hard done by but was not entitled to anything and even used the column in 1992 to track down a customer who had placed a £200 bet on Albert Reynolds to replace Charles Haughey as leader of Fianna Fáil in the mid-1980s.

This was all part of Kenny's work to position Paddy Power as an entertainment brand in contrast to the way the turf accountants of old operated. In his position as managing director he won newspaper coverage for his take on the political issues of the day and used his journalistic contacts to ensure the Paddy Power brand was included in all manner of stories. A front-page story in the *Irish Independent* in 1994 revealed that the Taoiseach had won £60 by betting on Ireland to win the Eurovision. Paddy Power and the British chains had spruced up the industry's image – with bookmakers' offices no longer merely social clubs for out-of-work men and bored pensioners, betting was becoming an increasingly respectable and desirable way to spend cash.

Market research commissioned by Paddy Power in 1992 drove the expansionary strategy. It found that rather than being a working-class pursuit, middle- and upper-class people were as likely to have a flutter in bookmakers: 45 per cent of adults in the country bet but only 14 per cent went to racetracks. This legitimized

Kenny's pursuit of non-racing people in Paddy Power's marketing. Less than five years after its formation, when the market researchers asked people to name a betting chain, 21 per cent said Paddy Power. It should have come as no surprise that the company's branding was working – turnover increased from £29 million in 1990, to £44 million in 1991, to £53 million in 1992 and to £60 million in 1993.

The Paddy Power main players were on a single-minded mission to squeeze out competition, challenge perceptions on betting and unseat vested interests. The year after its foundation the company managed to convince Leopardstown racecourse to allow them to operate a bookmakers' office at the track on race days where they could take bets on meetings in other venues. The presence of a Paddy Power shop on-course was an affront to the track's bookmakers but Kenny, Corcoran and Power had convinced the Irish Racing Authority that it would attract more people to the meetings.

Michael Smurfit, the chairman of the Racing Board, was trying to push the government to give it a chunk of the money collected through taxes in off-course bookmakers, a move firmly resisted by the bookies. Opening a shop within a racecourse would show that the money from betting was only possible because of the Board's activities and strengthen the argument for more cash from the tax.

There was immediate resistance from the on-course bookies who lobbied to ensure that Paddy Power could not take single bets on races at Leopardstown and had to charge the full 10 per cent tax, rather than the 5 per cent rate for on-course bets. The Tote operated by the Racing Board had a minimum bet of £1, which was too steep for many families attending the races, so the Paddy Power shop was immediately attractive. Ultimately it was doomed by its own success and forced to close when the on-course bookies found out that it was taking some bets on Leopardstown races. As was his wont, Kenny turned the dispute into publicity and offered to return the £3,000 taken from punters on losing horses in a gesture of goodwill. The in-fighting between Paddy Power and the on-course bookmakers reached a head in 1993 and a note was posted on the door of the shop reading 'Closed by order of the Racing Board' with no further details.

With the traditional lobbying power of the horse-racing industry and the new might of Paddy Power, the issue around the Leopardstown shop became political. Joe Walsh, the agriculture minister, announced an over-haul of the structures governing the horse-racing industry. The sweeping reforms would create a new authority to oversee the various interests of racecourse operators, horse breeders, owners, trainers and book-makers.

By the end of 1993 Paddy Power was already exceeding £1 million in annual profits after costs and tax, despite its modus operandi of aggressive expansion into new areas and generous offers to win over customers from the British mega-chains and domestic independents. As John Corcoran had envisaged, the company was in it for the long haul. And while its retail network expanded Paddy Power was also developing political savvy, further securing its dominance of the Irish market.

3

Political Punt

When bookmakers were granted a pre-budget meeting with Charlie McCreevy in 1998, the Department of Finance offices turned into a betting ring. The minister – from the horse-racing heartland of Sallins, Co. Kildare – was steeped in the sport and in gambling. So when the bookies turned up to outline their case for reducing tax and gaining state support, McCreevy could not resist going from seat to seat trying to get the best odds on his fancies at Cheltenham.

McCreevy was a minister who prided himself in making political decisions against the advice of his departmental advisers. While in office, he cut betting tax and resisted efforts to end tax exemption for stud fees. As a backbencher he had been close to the industry – it was remarked among bookies that during a heave against Charles Haughey in October 1982 McCreevy wouldn't take calls from journalists, but did so from his bookmakers so that they could get some insight into the prospects.

Political betting had become a feature of many Irish bookmakers since Stewart Kenny gained notoriety and front-page stories when, on opening his first shop in 1974, he offered odds of 4–1 on the resignation of US president Richard Nixon.

He got rinsed when Tricky Dickie fell on his sword over the Watergate scandal but Kenny believed that the publicity was worth it. A political junkie, Kenny fostered close relations with politicians and political journalists. His parents were friends with Fine Gael Taoiseach Garret FitzGerald and Kenny chummed around in a circle that included people with ties to Labour and Fianna Fáil.

Kenny knew the benefit of having politicians on the side of the industry as it expanded; his operating procedure was to develop relationships with friendly TDs while they were backbenchers and use them to sow the seeds of industry campaigns. When McCreevy became finance minister in 1997, the corridors of power had been well trodden by Kenny as he had led campaigns over the past two decades seeking tax cuts, and Paddy Power's day at the Christmas racing festival in Leopardstown was marked in the diary of politicians and advisers of every political party. Many politicians of the time were punters, frequenting Harry Barry's bookies on Baggot Street where anyone looking for the ear of a TD could find them in a more relaxed environment.

When British bookmakers began to move their telephone operations to the Isle of Man, which had cut its rate of betting tax to 0.3 per cent, in 1998, a theatrical campaign of codology began to push McCreevy into cutting the Irish rate in half. Kenny complained that three of Paddy Power's biggest customers, worth more than £1 million, had left its client base to take advantage of the minimal rate of tax being offered by Victor Chandler and William Hill. The managing director of Ireland's biggest bookmakers and employer of 700 people across the country said that if the rate did not reduce here, he would move its increasingly popular Dial-a-Bet operation, having secured a Manx licence.

A picture of Kenny boarding a Ryanair flight with his bookie's satchel in his hand was published in the *Evening Herald*, apparently illustrating the departure of a proud Irish company to the piddling British Crown dependency. In fact, there was no flight that day – the picture had been concocted with the *Herald* photographer and Kenny had not even secured a licence with the Isle of Man, a fact he later claimed was irrelevant.

Putting on the poor mouth wasn't a good look for the bookies and Paddy Power had just passed a milestone of more than £100 million in turnover, an average of £1 million per shop. The firm grew by 18 per cent over 1996. It controlled 25 per cent of the market, more than 10 per cent above its nearest rival Ladbrokes, and was making just under £3 million in profit. But cutting the tax was in the common man's interest, the bookies claimed, and punters were asked to sign petitions in support of the tax cut and hand them over the counter with their dockets. A flat-bed truck pulled up outside the Department of Finance and 20,000 petitions signed by customers were moved by winch onto the steps of McCreevy's office.

On Budget Day 1998 Stewart Kenny sat in the invitation-only public gallery of the Dáil wearing a bright orange tie watching over proceedings on the parliament floor below him. McCreevy announced a cut to the betting tax, from 10 per cent down to 5 per cent, as the opposition benches heckled and hooted their disapproval.

McCreevy announced that he was halving the tax in order to disincentivize people being attracted to offshore bookmakers, 'I have received strong representations,' he said. 'I bet the minister did,' Nora Owen, the Fine Gael opposition TD, knowingly interjected.

As McCreevy was wrapping up his budget speech he attempted a soliloquy urging prudence from the people who benefited from changes in the budget. 'If they do not have a care in the world they will shop and shop and shop. However, if they have cares and worries and owe money, things would be different. Perhaps they would be wise to hold on to that extra few pounds and put it towards reducing the size of their debt,' McCreevy said.

Michael Finucane, a Fine Gael TD, offered his own sage advice from the other side of the house: 'They should not put it on a horse.'

McCreevy was on the bookies' side even before the public campaign and seemed to have almost free rein over fiscal policy, cutting tax and ramping up spending as the Celtic Tiger began to mature. In this party time of politics, Paddy Power was a perfect court jester. By the time of the Leopardstown Christmas meeting on 27 December 1998, every race bar one was sponsored by the bookmaker and the corporate boxes were filled with people there at the expense of Paddy Power. It was a well-fed and well-watered crowd long before the winter sun set in south Dublin. And while the marketing was politically incorrect, the annual blowout was evidence of Paddy Power's political connections.

Paddy Power did not always play nice with politicians, however, and when TDs got in their way Kenny was quick to turn the pressure on them. When Ruari Quinn, the Labour finance minister, threatened to outlaw bookies taking bets on the National Lottery in

1995, he was met with the full force of the bookmaker's political savvy and campaigning power.

Like many innovations at Paddy Power, the success of the shops was down to cleverly taking a competitor's idea and making it simpler. By the late 1980s Coral's had started taking bets on the National Lottery. Ladbrokes followed suit with Rou-lotto, a comically convoluted coupon, which allowed customers to pick numbers from the televised draw and use them in a new game. Jimmy Mangan brought Rou-lotto into Paddy Power shops but after a few weeks it had made little impact. Even Kenny struggled to make sense of the Rou-lotto docket and realized if it was to work in its aim – of attracting women gamblers who had little knowledge of bookmakers' shops and weren't necessarily au fait with roulette – it would have to be made simple.

Paddy Power launched Lucky Numbers, where customers were able to pick three Lotto numbers and bet on them coming up. At the time the National Lottery only paid out for combinations of four and above. This simple concept was foundational for Paddy Power. It was based on Kenny's understanding of the gambler's psyche: the excitement of nearly winning. He would later alter his money-back special, which gave losing gamblers their stakes back if they came close to winning on a certain event, based on the same understanding of trying to elongate the feeling of excitement and joy in the gambler's mind. The first iteration of money-back specials gave the stake back to customers who, for example, bet on Manchester United to win if Eric Cantona scored first. But Kenny realized that if Cantona didn't score first then the excitement of the bet was dampened, so he switched to money-back specials based on the last goal-scorer, keeping the punter on the edge of their seat into the dying seconds of a match.

Most bets lose, leaving the punter feeling like a fool and resenting the bookie. But if Paddy Power could keep the buzz of engagement with the outcome of the match going for the full ninety minutes, then that feeling of losing would be a tiny fraction of the gambler's emotion.

Lucky Numbers was launched on 14 February 1990, which of course was Valentine's Day – but more impor-tant, it fell on a Wednesday that year; the day of the weekly Lotto draw. Paddy Power made it clear that Lucky Numbers had no affiliation with the National Lottery. That would have been illegal. Queues formed outside Paddy Power shops as mothers and grand-mothers in town to do the Lotto hedged their chances of a fortune in the millions by picking numbers to come up – the odds were 5/1 for one number, 40/1 for two, 450/1 for three and 4,000/1 for four. The gimmick was immediately successful and generated repeat business due to the twice-weekly draws.

Instead of smoking men in wool coats moaning about fallen favourites at Goodwood, women in town to do their shopping were being assisted in filling out their Lucky Numbers. This change in clientele did not go unnoticed by the usual patrons and Kenny and Mangan became increasingly aware that if Paddy Power were to retain the new, female customers it would have to change the layout of its shops.

Initially bookies were designed to draw the customer as far into the dingy office as possible, with the odds boards on the far side of the room to the entrance. But with the success of Lucky Numbers, which was generating profits of 40 per cent on the turnover on the bets, it was decided that the counters should be closer to the door to save the women from the eyes of the men inside.

Of course with any market offered, the bookies did not always come up smelling of perfume and when, in a Wednesday draw in September 1997 the numbers 4,7 and 11 came up, John O'Reilly had a face like thunder. Kenny didn't grasp the significance, being entirely unaware of an eau de cologne named 4711, which was being heavily promoted with a catchy jingle in radio ads at the time. Those three numbers cost the firm more than £500,000 – the equivalent of millions today.

Never one to waste a good day for the punters, Kenny alerted the press, which garnered a front-page story in the Thursday *Evening Herald* as shop staff around the country bought small bottles of the perfume to give away to the lucky customers who came in to collect their winnings. The profits from the Lotto were so big by the mid-1990s that Paddy Power's market share of almost 100 shops allowed them to run the rest of the business as a loss leader. The era of generous specials on horse-racing and other more traditional bets began in earnest, putting the pressure on smaller operators to follow suit or get left behind.

Lotto betting was a nice add-on for most bookmakers, but it was core to Paddy Power's profits. Coupled with the tax-free tactics being employed as well, the new mega-chain was really putting its rivals under the cosh.

A rep for Stanley Leisure – the Belfast bookmaker and casino group which had fifty shops in Ireland and ten times as many in Britain – threatened to collapse the Lotto betting, which was being probed by the Department of Finance at the time for potential breaches of the National Lottery Act, by advertising it. This would bring it under greater scrutiny and force the government's hand in dealing with the issue. But Kenny offered a better option, by explaining that there was enough money in it for everyone if they all followed the Paddy Power Lucky Numbers model.

The crisis was averted until Shane Ross, the *Sunday Independent* columnist and later minister for sport, rang Kenny and asked for comment about the upcoming legislation that was going to ban Lotto betting. This was the first Kenny had heard of the plans, but thanks to his media and political contacts he was now up to speed and could begin the fight back. Ray Bates, the director of the National Lottery, was claiming that the bookies were taking £30 million a year from the state Lotto and the worthy charities and local sporting organizations it funded were the ones losing out at the expense of bookmaker's profits. That line of argument could have been persuasive had it been allowed to take hold, but the bookies went on the attack.

Fintan Drury chaired a meeting of representatives from all the bookmakers that weekend who agreed that Kenny should be the spokesman for the campaign. The Paddy Power managing director duly appeared on *Morning Ireland* on Monday and tore into Ruari Quinn. How could a Labour minister put through legislation that would cost hundreds of jobs? This set the agenda for the campaign: half-page ads were bought in newspapers talking about unemployment figures, under the Lotto's own slogan, 'It could be you.' The bookmakers began to lobby back-bench TDs and constituency rivals of ministers, but after Kenny's appearance on *Morning Ireland* a grass-roots campaign was formed that made any effort to ban Lotto betting politically unpopular. When Joe Kemmy, the brother of Jim, a Labour TD in Limerick, went into his local Paddy Power on William Street, he was met with a barrage of complaints from the punters queueing up to do their Lucky Numbers. The ban was quietly dropped.

While political campaigns were chugging along in the background, Kenny was more upfront in his efforts to present Paddy Power as the punter's pal. The internal notes were that staff should represent the company as 'fun, fair and friendly' and this was bolstered by Kenny's media efforts to make the bookmaker seem almost hapless.

In 1995, when the world was gripped with anticipation over who had shot Mr Burns in *The Simpsons*, Paddy Power opened a market on who was the perpetrator. A group of students stung the bookie for £9,000 when the market was left open, after the episode revealing that baby Maggie Simpson had pulled the trigger had aired in the United States. 'I think people love seeing a bookie being caught with his nappy down,' Kenny said, announcing the cartoon coup.

A bigger bet that same weekend was when a Finglas punter landed a £286,000 double with Paddy Power – the biggest payout in Irish history. The £4,000 bet was on Cap Juluca at 12/1 to win in Newmarket and

Lammtarra at 9/2 to win the Prix de l'Arc de Triomphe in Paris.

Kenny revealed the winnings at a press conference announcing Paddy Power's sponsorship of a race at Leopardstown. To gain maximum publicity out of the sponsorship he played up his schtick and held up an oversized cheque and copy of the docket.

'This man is quite clearly very lucky or a genius,' Kenny said, but the real smarts were not revealed.

Paddy Power's racing room in Tallaght had caught the potential exposure to the bet early and traders had laid off £130,000 by placing their own bets with rival firms, but took the publicity for the full amount.

By the late 1990s Kenny and Drury had beaten back campaigns from the National Lottery, off-course book-makers and the horse-racing industry, but the real fight came in 1998 when the cocky Kenny was invited to give a speech at the Irish Turf Club's annual Moyglare Dinner during the festive party circuit in December. Other speakers over the years have included the Aga Khan and Queen Elizabeth's racing manager, the Duke of Devonshire, but Kenny was not interested in offering up niceties to the great and the good of the horse-racing fraternity.

He was the first and last bookmaker to be invited to speak at the event. He used the pulpit to attack the

Irish Horseracing Authority's plans to offer its own Tote betting (which offers winner a portion of a pool determined by the total amount of stakes, rather than guaranteeing returns based on pre-agreed odds) in pubs and accused Noel Ryan, the chief executive of the Irish Horseracing Authority and the rest of the decision-makers, of imperialism, being socially irresponsible and lacking cop-on:

> It is wholly inappropriate to take a sizable percentage of the gambling industry and put it into an environment where people are not in full control of their senses. I have no interest in growing my profits by helping create an environment that loosens the punter's faculties. We have enough problems in our society without creating the potentially lethal cocktail of booze and betting in the cosy environment that is everybody's local,

Kenny thundered as McCreevy watched on. 'Those who want deregulation of the pub market should cop on. It will fail economically, damage the National Lottery and, at the same time, break fundamental principles of good social management.'

Paddy Power had fought hard and invested a million pounds in a deal to get Irish horse-racing streamed into its network of shops. The brand wanted to serve every demand its customers might have and negotiated a £1 million deal with Pierce Moloney of the Irish Association of Racecourses to ensure all Irish races were shown in its stores. Up to now Irish racing was only shown if the Satellite Information Service (SIS), which charged bookmakers to show its broadcasts from meetings in their shops, deemed it to be of interest to British bettors, which enraged Paddy Power. Efforts to use the Irish industry lobby to force SIS to run the pictures were stalled so Kenny went direct to the courses. Offering Irish racing would also keep punters in-store to watch races rather than the time-honoured practice of flitting from the bookies to the pub between flutters. The arrival of betting into pubs as mooted by the Turf Club's Tote would swing this trend the other way.

Kenny wanted the off-course Tote operation to be housed in bookies' shops, where Paddy Power and the rest could cream off 10 per cent commission. Ryan and the Irish Horseracing Authority were wary of the power of bookmakers already and didn't relish the prospect of housing their operations in-store, but Kenny knew he had the upper hand because it was already investing in the systems to bring bookmaking into the new millennium.

Like a Young Turk staring down the mob bosses whose turf he had moved in on, Kenny laid out the new reality of who held the power now:

Before the IHA picks a fight, they should think about how bloody a nose they might get. If anyone tries to stop us from selling Tote products, we may be less inclined to promote Irish racing. This would mean the loss of over £200,000 in sponsorship from Paddy Power alone, and a £1 million investment in live pictures. If we were to freeze out Irish racing, newspapers would not cover it to the same extent. Shop customers could not bet on it and fewer people would go racing as the interest in Irish racing waned further. Wise up, fellas.

By now Kenny and Paddy Power were part of the political conversation in Ireland. The bookmaker was regularly quoted by political correspondents, offering his insight into the chances of Haughey resigning, or Dick Spring becoming the next Labour leader, or the number of seats Fine Gael would win in the next election. The bookmaker even became a political pundit on RTÉ when he reached an agreement with the producers of the influential *Today with Seán O'Rourke* programme to give them exclusive access to Paddy Power's polls with Kenny invited on to talk about the state of the parties.

Kenny's apparent savviness on these matters was part-borrowed from an enigmatic Fine Gael insider named Jim Nolan. The legend in Paddy Power was that

Nolan had taken Kenny for thousands on bets on the outcome of elections a few too many times in the early eighties when he was given the ultimatum: 'Work with me or you're barred.' Nolan became a consultant sooth-sayer on all matters political for Paddy Power from then on. When canvassing for Fine Gael he preferred to do it alone so he could get the best sense of what the real issues for people were, rather than being interrupted by another volunteer trying to steer the conversation.

It was said that Nolan could grasp the mood of the nation by knocking on a dozen front doors. This was first evident in 1989 when Paddy Power was offering its first market on a snap general election. Charles Haughey had hoped to catch the opposition parties unawares by dissolving the Dáil while Fianna Fáil was buoyant in the opinion polls and an overall majority was in sight for the minority government party. Paddy Power's odds were based on opinion polling but were quickly revised after a night of canvassing by Nolan revealed that Fianna Fáil's belief that people wanted a stable government more than anything else was not reflective of the real mood, where people were focused on the issue of health and employment. In the end Haughey lost seats and the party needed the Progressive Democrats to form a government.

While Haughey's grasp on power was slipping as the 1990s progressed, Paddy Power's closeness to the political system intensified. Paddy Power's influence was self-perpetuating as politicians wanted to be close to the company that could guarantee press coverage and make the elite TD look like a man of the people. Kenny fostered relationships with backbenchers including McCreevy, Enda Kenny (the future Taoiseach) and dozens of others about to advance in their political careers.

Such was their hold on politicians by 2002 that Bertie Ahern spent his very last pound in the Paddy Power shop on Baggot Street. The Taoiseach – who famously didn't have a bank account while finance minister and claimed at a tribunal into corruption that the £15,000 lodged into his building society accounts in question was money he had won on horses – marked the introduction of the euro in Ireland by putting his final punt on a bet in Paddy Power. In the same way as visiting dignitaries are taken to traditional pubs to pose with a pint of Guinness, politicians placing a bet on themselves in Paddy Power became an enduring part of the democratic pageantry. It became so commonplace that it seemed to be part of the process of dissolving the Dáil and calling a general election.

The 1990s allowed Paddy Power to reach new heights as the Irish economy roared into life and politician connections led to favourable conditions for the bookies. But the country's biggest bookmaker was not just a favourite haunt of high society.

4

Cat and Mouse

John Gilligan whispered in the ear of one of his barris-
ters, who took a quick note on the legal pad in front
of him. As he walked to the witness box, Stewart Kenny
noticed just how short and squat the five-foot five-inch
Gilligan was. The most notorious crime boss in Ireland
at the time, Gilligan's hulking shoulders and biceps
stretched the fabric of his designer shirt to the point
where the creases were flattened. Though he was the
same age and ever so slightly taller, Kenny's slender
frame and impish demeanour made him appear a fraction of Gilligan physically. In about every other way
they were opposites too.

Gilligan had grown up the eldest of nine children in
the hardscrabble of 1950s Ballyfermot, a working-class
suburb in west Dublin. Kenny was born in 1951, a
year earlier than the crime boss, and raised in the leaf-

iest of suburbs, Donnybrook, just ten kilometres east of Ballyfermot but a world away. Gilligan left school with a larceny charge at the age of fourteen while Kenny was playing bookmaker to his boarding-school chums in Glenstal Abbey with its idyllic lakes, forests and terrace garden.

Both boys carried their schoolboy hobbies – theft for Gilligan, bookmaking for Kenny – into their adolescence and made successful careers of them. Gilligan began hijacking delivery drivers and raiding warehouses in the 1970s and 80s before becoming the head honcho of the Factory Gang, stealing freight containers filled with goods on their way to shops and factories. The gang tied up and terrorized warehouse staff and took off with vanloads of vacuum cleaners, sweets and whatever else they could move on quickly in the black market.

After a few short stints in prison Gilligan soon realized that the drug trade was a lot more lucrative and having established a connection in the Netherlands, he soon became the biggest hash dealer in Ireland, importing tens of thousands of kilograms of cannabis every couple of years for sale on Irish streets, which in total was worth £37 million, according to the Gardaí. He travelled to Amsterdam so often that he was given a frequent flyer's gold card by Aer Lingus and amassed so much cash that he lived a life of luxury similar to the wealthiest stud farmers and horse trainers. His prized asset was the £2 million Jessbrook Equestrian Centre in Meath, a dedication to his love of horses.

Of course, since Gilligan had come up as a petty criminal and had served time for serious robberies, his newfound wealth did not go unnoticed by An Garda Síochána. The problem was they could do very little about it as he became richer and more powerful with each kilo of cannabis transported into the country. It was an affront to the country that such a criminal could continue about his trade untouched. Crime reporters such as Veronica Guerin of the *Irish Independent* risked their lives by tracking Gilligan's exploits and earnings. It seemed no one could stop him.

When a tax official in the Revenue Commissioners posted Gilligan a tax form to account for his earnings, he replied with a short self-assessment of his affairs: 'I've no fucking money for you. Fuck off.'

Everyone knew Gilligan was a drug-dealing gangster, so how could he get away with such ostentatious displays of wealth? Like many mobsters before him, gambling laundered his money. Gilligan could hide in plain sight because he was posing as a businessman who was bulking up his personal wealth as a professional gambler in the casinos of Amsterdam and, of course, the bookmaker shops of Dublin. Unless the detectives tracking him like bloodhounds could prove his earnings were from illegal means, Gilligan could continue to live his high life, shielded by stacks of casino chips and betting-shop slips. It was not just the Garda detectives and crime correspondents keeping abreast of Gilligan's affairs, however. In Paddy Power's head office was a book containing betting slips faxed by staff every evening from shops around the city and traders' columns detailing wins and losses on horse-racing from customers who were monitored.

This was not just out of any interest in Gilligan's criminality – it was also because Paddy Power was concerned that he might win. Just as checks were put in place to alert the racing room in the Tallaght office (which monitored wagers across the company) to unusual betting patterns that might indicate a Barney Curley-style coup in the offing, all big bettors were monitored so that their transactions could be laid off with rivals or curtailed by restricting how much they could get on a particular race.

This was done discreetly, with staff in shops across the country noting the amounts placed by high-staking customers and alerting senior management, who would then make decisions on what to do. To get around this, many gamblers with an edge (which meant they knew more about a race than the bookies or had a history of finding winning horses with big odds) would send a team of paid runners around the shops to get bets on so that they couldn't be tallied together by Paddy Power until it was too late. Gilligan's team included Derek Baker, an on-course bookmaker who travelled as part of a group with the mobster to Amsterdam casinos alongside Brian Meehan, a member of the drug dealer's gang. Baker's bets in Paddy Power shops were recorded in the account of Gilligan, along with those placed by the mobster's children and anyone else who was believed to be acting in concert with him.

In the early 1990s Gilligan was a frequent visitor to Paddy Power shops around Dublin. The short, seemingly friendly, grey-haired man would place stacks of notes on the counter as he wrote out his bets, sometimes leaving the stack in place while he trotted up to the clerk to place his bet. Why not? Who was going to touch it? These shops would not have been frequented by high-rolling gamblers and Gilligan's manner of stuffing wads of cash under the clerk's window to cover £20,000 to £40,000 wagers led to the not unreasonable suspicion among staff that he was involved in crime.

There was no obligation on bookmakers to know the identity of the person betting with them or where they had sourced the money, but the staff running the Paddy Power shops knew he was unlikely to be betting with money earned from washing windows. And so he was nicknamed 'the General's brother', referring to Martin 'the General' Cahill, Ireland's most notorious criminal in the early 1990s.

More often than not the bets would be so big that shop staff would inform him that they needed to get clearance from head office to process them. Gilligan would stand patiently in front of the clerk while Paddy Power management cleared his bets.

Kenny and the management team were aware of this customer and cleared the bets when the shop staff phoned them in, opening the conversation with, 'Hello Mr Kenny, "the brother" is back in.' 'Fine, give him whatever he wants,' was the usual reply. Gilligan was just another losing customer and Paddy Power wanted his business.

Derek Baker was in effect his racing manager and knew what he was doing, so while Gilligan was losing overall he was collecting on enough bets to make Paddy Power take heed that he could turn a profit with a good run. His stakes began increasing in the Summerhill and Parnell Street shops, reaching tens of thousands every day, and Gardaí began to monitor his activity more closely. One detective informed Kenny that his best customer in these shops was in fact one of Europe's biggest hash dealers, importing hundreds of thousands of kilos into Ireland. And the gang was using Paddy Power and other bookmakers to launder their money. It was a blunt mechanism, which led to the gang backing every horse in a race in bookies across the city on some occasions, but it worked for Gilligan. Between 1994 and 1996 he won back £4.8 million from £5 million bet mainly on Irish horse-racing. No accountant in the world would have been able to clear that amount of cash in such a cheap fashion and with no need to involve the Revenue Commissioners. The method was crude but the results were exemplary for the criminal.

As managing director Kenny kept a close eye on what was going on in the growing chain of shops and when he was alerted by the Garda he knew he had a duty to take it to the board. John Corcoran assured Kenny he was confident that, as managing director, he would be able to get the company out of this scrape like he had with other issues – such as opposition to tax-free betting and the political pushback against Lucky Numbers – in the past. There's a slight difference this time, Kenny told him, he had two kneecaps and two children to worry about. But an opportunity to get Gilligan off the books and save his patellae was about to present itself.

Gilligan, his unmistakable frame as wide as it was tall, strolled up to the counter in the Parnell Street Paddy Power on Saturday, 29 April 1995 and passed the docket over the counter. He wanted £18,000 on Sharatan, the John Oxx-trained 5/2 favourite in the 3.30, and a £10,000 double linking that bet with a shorter-priced favourite in a later race. The cash was stuffed under the counter and head office was called before it could be counted out to £30,800 including the 10 per cent tax needed to cover the bet. As with all of Gilligan's bets it was approved and there was a shout in the shop when Sharatan raced home a length ahead of Jim Bolger's Celladonia. But unfortunately for Gilligan there was a steward's inquiry: Sharatan was relegated to third. Gilligan walked out in disgust.

Half an hour after the race, there was another call to Paddy Power's office from Parnell Street. The wads of cash had been counted. 'He's after leaving us £19,000 short,' the clerk said through floods of tears, fearing the likelihood of signing on to the dole first thing on Monday morning. Kenny was in the office and grabbed the phone, told her not to worry and assured her that there was no threat to her job. Not only had Gilligan lost his bet, Kenny now had the perfect excuse for refusing to do business with the man he had reason to believe was a drug dealer.

The following Monday, Maria, the receptionist at head office, took a call for the managing director: 'There's a Mr Gilligan on the line for you.' The man known as Factory John for his spate of burglaries on industrial units said that he had left the company a few quid short at the weekend but assured them that he would pay it off by continuing to bet. He would allow Paddy Power to keep his winnings until the debt was settled. Paddy Power had a policy of never allowing anyone to bet on credit and Gilligan was told he would be treated no differently.

That appeared to be the matter settled as Gilligan was not seen in the shops for the next three weeks. Then another call came into head office. He said that he had £10,000 and would bet against the rest of the £19,000 until the debt was settled. Kenny again outlined that there would be no bets taken while there was a debt outstanding and that the board was being notified of the losses caused by the underpayment. Another three weeks passed with Gilligan being rebuffed every time he attempted to place a bet in shops. The staff politely told the criminal that word from head office was that they were unable to accept bets from him at this time and sorry, there was nothing they could do about it.

On his next call to the bookmakers' head office, Gilligan said he had the full £19,000. But Kenny told him that the board had written off the money already: if he did want to start betting with Paddy Power again, the board would demand that his passport be photo-copied as an assurance that he would not short-change them again, and the hassle just would not be worth it. There are a lot of other bookmakers in Dublin, Kenny told him.

In the High Court case taken by Gilligan in order to challenge the state's seizure of his assets, his gambling was detailed as a cover for his income. During the 2011 case, the reason for Gilligan being barred from Paddy Power was given only as 'a dispute [had] arisen over a cash sum'. As Gilligan saw it, it was an amicable arrangement. He told the court: 'They wouldn't stop me coming in the door because I'm very mannerly, but they wouldn't take a bet.'

In total, Gilligan and his crew placed more than £1 million in bets with Paddy Power between June 1994 and April 1995 as part of more than £5 million laundered in their business along with Ladbrokes, Corals and Boyles. Gilligan's gambling with Paddy Power began years earlier but bookies were only required to keep the paper dockets and records of bets for six months. Kenny retained all his files as soon as he heard from the Garda that Gilligan was involved in drugs. Dealings between bookies and bettors are usually as secretive as those with banks and their customers, but a landmark piece of legislation in Ireland aimed at smashing criminal gangs such as Gilligan's lifted the secrecy. It had come after one of the most heinous crimes in Ireland's criminal history.

On 26 June 1996 a red Opel Calibra had stopped at traffic lights on the Naas dual carriageway when a motorbike with two men pulled up alongside it. One got off and fired six shots into the driver's window. Journalist Veronica Guerin was pronounced dead at the scene.

The next day's *Irish Independent* – part of the same newspaper group for which Guerin worked – bore the headline 'We know who killed her – and he's untouchable.' The assassination of Guerin sparked outrage in Ireland and highlighted how criminal gangs were able to build power bases concealing the true source of their wealth.

The establishment of the Criminal Assets Bureau in 1996 allowed Gardaí to freeze the assets of suspected criminal enterprises and force the owner to prove that they are in fact the fruits of legitimate labour. When Paddy Power got a call from the CAB, they handed over all the dockets and records of bets, which could be cross-referenced by the forensic detectives with cheques issued by Paddy Power and signed on the back by Brian Meehan or other associates of Gilligan.

Kenny signed an affidavit outlining his knowledge of Gilligan's gambling and the nature of bookmaking as an expert witness soon after but was not required to appear in court. That is, until 2009, when Gilligan was appealing the seizure of his properties by CAB. As part of a long line of tactics to delay the process he demanded that Kenny and other bookmakers appear as witnesses for cross-examination. The gangster was fighting the seizure of his assets and claiming that much of his wealth was from gambling, not drug dealing.

As he was called to the witness box, Kenny was taken by how small and wide Gilligan appeared as he sat to the left of Mr Justice Kevin Feeney. After identifying himself as the managing director at the time in question of Power Leisure Limited trading as Paddy Power, Kenny was hit with a question. If Gilligan placed a £100 accumulator on ten even-money horses (meaning that the return on each bet would double the stake for the bet on the next horse so long as each horse won), how much would he win?

Under pressure, Kenny began doing the sums in his head but before he got the answer Mr Justice Feeney, having grown tired of Gilligan's constant attempts to slow down proceedings and waste court time, interrupted and asked the purpose of the question. Feeney also answered the question, having done the calculations on a sheet of paper in front of him. The first bet would return £200, the second £400, the third £800, the fourth £1,600, the fifth £3,200, the sixth £6,400, the seventh £12,800, the eighth £25,600, the ninth £51,200 and the tenth would give a total of £102,400 returned, and a profit of £102,300.

The rest of the line of questioning was more straightforward. In his answers, Kenny outlined how bookmakers monitor certain customers, grouping their bets together and using shop staff to provide all betting slips to build a profile of the punter. This was all part of managing risk and though it was imperfect, Kenny told the court, it did allow Paddy Power to block or restrict customers from placing certain types of bets if they were consistently winning. 'If we didn't do this, Paddy Power wouldn't be here,' Kenny told the court. 'You are assessing the odds and assessing customers and seeing that we come out winning.' By this way of measuring it Paddy Power had come out winning with Gilligan, of course: he had lost £70,000 on £950,000 worth of bets after tax between June 1994 and April 1995.

At the hearing Kenny laid bare the cat-and-mouse game between the bookmaker and big bettors, and detailed how monitoring and screening is used to root out winning gamblers as part of the overall risk-management strategy. It was a far cry from the 'you do the betting – we do the fretting' image he had cultivated in his marketing and it showed how successful bookmakers tightly control their business.

Paddy Power could have sent an accountant to the trial but Kenny told the board that as he was in charge when the bets were taken, he should explain what the process was. Ladbrokes by contrast sent a security analyst and the manager of the firm's shop in Palmerstown to explain its practices and account for a cheque from the firm, which was used as part payment for one of Gilligan's properties frozen by the Criminal Assets Bureau.

It would be easy to see why Kenny – a successful and well-known businessman, not to mention the son of a Supreme Court judge – might have wanted to avoid giving evidence in court of a dispute over cash with a violent drug dealer, and Gilligan seemed to have this in mind when he demanded that representatives of the bookmakers appears in person rather than just giving statements. Kenny felt obliged to attend.

The Gilligan affair had risked dragging Paddy Power's name through the murky world of gangland crime and drug dealers' money laundering but it had managed to pass off with little reputational damage. At this stage it would be all but impossible to unwind the spool of crossed interests between the freedom for people to gamble and the need for criminals to move their money around, but the Criminal Assets Bureau and other arms of law enforcement would monitor them closely in the knowledge that big bookmakers kept good records.

But Paddy Power's system for tracking and tying together the bets of certain customers was not designed as a tool to catch criminals. It was to protect bookies' self-interest and tackle the big problem they face: customers trying to win.

Diarmuid Ring is what is known in betting circles

as an 'each-way scumbag'. That is not a reflection on his personality: in fact, he's actually a doting grandfather in his seventies who goes by the nickname 'Dee' and has a Kerry lilt undiminished by decades living in south Dublin. He spends his mornings poring over the *Racing Post* with his two pet terriers at his feet, trying to figure out where the bookies have got it wrong in that day's races. In the small space on the pages beside the form guide to each horse Ring jots down a percentage, which represents his view of that horse's chances of winning the race. If his calculations are different from the bookies', he backs them.

His designation as an 'each-way scumbag' comes from his exploitation of a rare chink in bookmaker's armour where they are forced to offer odds that are actually in the punter's favour. Each-way betting involves placing two bets, one bet for the selection to win and one for the selection to finish within a predetermined number of places – so depending on the number of runners in the race it means even if your horse finishes second, third or fourth you can get a return on your bet.

The win part of the bet is paid at the full odds you take on your selection, should it win. For the place part, bets are settled at a fraction of the win odds, usually a quarter or a fifth of the full odds. Where this can lead to the so-called scumbaggery is when there is a heavy favourite in a race with a larger number of runners. The bookmaker will be forced to overinflate the odds of the second- and third-best horses in the race and this means that the odds being offered for those horses to place will be greater than the true chance of it happening.

Bookmakers detest these races because they are compromised by the standard-place terms they must offer on horse-racing in Ireland and the United Kingdom, making them pay out on inflated odds for horses that place in races. In order to limit the liabilities for them, a list of 'bad each-ways' is circulated to bookmakers' shops every morning and staff are told to only take small bets on them, or refuse them completely.

Over the years Ring has been doing his best to exploit these bets alongside his other gambling on racing, Gaelic football and cards. Long retired, he has spent much of his time on his hobbies and said that if he were to appear on *Mastermind*, his speciality topic would be either the bookmaker shops or the pubs of Dublin.

He can go back three generations of bookmakers' shops in a street and reel off that the Paddy Power shop at the top of the street used to be a Hackett's and there was a Tully's around the corner before that. He seems to view the entire world in terms of betting odds. When a friend told him he had been diagnosed with a rare form of cancer that luckily had a 90 per cent chance of full recovery a delighted Ring added cautiously that 'sometimes 9/1 shots win'.

Ring is the sort of knowledgeable and considered punter Paddy Power and the other chains don't want in their shops. Bookmakers make it their business to track customers like Ring, who if allowed to bet uncontested would damage profits in the long run.

Of course this position is diametrically opposed to the aims of most gamblers and so bookmakers have to hide the fact. This is the ugly face of bookmaking. It has to be masked with selective lighting so that betting still appears attractive to most customers. For Ring, however, bookmakers are there to be beaten in the same way as opponents around card tables.

Around the same time that Gilligan was pumping money through shops in the mid-1990s, Ring was part of a crew whose bets were being monitored for very different reasons: he was winning money. As can be seen from the risk-management system in place in Paddy Power in the early 1990s, as little as possible was left outside the bookmakers' control, but there were rare gaps in their system that allowed savvy punters to gain an edge: and one was bad each-way bets.

Another was the existence of the 'quadpot', a four-leg pool where punters select a horse to be placed in the third, fourth, fifth and sixth races on a card. The punter could select more than one horse in each race and, if they were successful, win a dividend determined by the level of interest of people betting on-course. The quadpot is offered at every British track and for a time high-street bookmakers in Ireland included them on their coupons.

This system whereby the dividend was determined on-course left high-street bookmakers vulnerable to well-organized customers getting someone on-course to inflate the pool by backing horses with little chance, thus increasing the dividend for more likely horses. In other pool-based pots bookies could lay off some of the liabilities, but this was not available with quadpots, meaning it was ripe for picking. It required a good understanding of horse-racing, an attitude that bookmakers are foes and the ability to organize things in a logical manner. Ring was the perfect man to concoct such a plot.

He became successful enough at winning chunky sums from Paddy Power that on one occasion when he was collecting winnings of a few grand by arrangement at a shop on the northside of Dublin, Stewart Kenny was behind the counter to congratulate him. 'Arrah, I just got lucky,' Ring twanged in his Kerry accent. 'Sometimes you make your own luck,' Kenny responded with a smile.

Ring and his pals continued the quadpot plots for a while until one day they overextended and took Paddy

Power for £30,000 for places at a Kelso meeting in 1995. The on-course pool was £455 and the dividend was £45, which was paid out on dozens of identical bets across the country. The racing room at Paddy Power had collected the betting slips and found out that a series of identical 72-combination bets picking three horses in the third race, two in the fourth, four in the fifth and three in the sixth had been placed around the country. There was no way to gain an edge on punters in this one so a blanket limit on pay-outs for quadpots was imposed. It also marked Ring out as a punter to watch – and though he never did anything illegal or unfair he was not really wanted as a customer by Paddy Power.

When Ring learned that lists of the bad each-way bets are distributed to shops every morning, he started ringing Paddy Power head office and asking for a copy for himself. 'The girl in the shop gave me one yesterday, so I thought you'd give it out today before I went into town,' he would lie on the phone, hoping on the off chance that if Paddy Power management believed the lists were being distributed by careless staff they might stop sending them out altogether.

It was an unlikely thing to happen but Ring enjoyed the cheek of it so every few days he would call Paddy Power's office number in Tallaght, ask to be put through to the racing room and explain that yesterday the girl in the shop, 'she was lovely, she was', had given him the list of the bad each-way races. This went on for a few weeks until one morning he was interrupted before he could get going on his spiel: 'Would you ever fuck off, Diarmuid?' And the line went dead.

Though he never used his name on the call, the racing room knew exactly who it was. Ring didn't mind that – he knew he was a marked customer and he had his bit of craic with the calls so went about his business. What did annoy him was when a gambling buddy of his rang him and said that he had seen Ring's face on the screen behind the counter in Paddy Power. The friend explained that he had been waiting to have a bet cleared by head office when he saw the clerk open a file on her computer and begin scrolling through images of people. He had recognized Ring's bearded face.

This didn't sit right with Ring, who felt like he was on a list of the type of people who bounced checks or shoplifted rather than someone who had pulled a smart stroke within the moral limits of gambling. On the advice of a friend Ring submitted a request for all the information and data held by Paddy Power on him to be released, as he is entitled to under law. Ring found that he was being tracked around shops by Paddy Power staff and a series of instructions were given by the 'risk-viewer' as to how to treat him. *Well-known customer, restrict where necessary, one note read. EW [each-way] – do no favours*, instructed another.

A section of staff notes to help clerks in all Paddy Power shops tried to describe him so that he could be identified quickly and his bets could be restricted or refused. Bray shop staff noted him as 'White hair, white beard. Friendly, mid-50s.' But in Crumlin village he was described as 'Very abrupt.' Staff in Tallaght banned him from placing any each-way bets, while the Shankhill shop just described him as 'Bad e/w punter!!!!!!!!' There was also an email from a person in Paddy Power's head office who said he had received a call from an unnamed shop worker informing them that Ring was in the area. 'Could you get a message up on the screens please?'

Among these notices on his betting behaviour were a picture of Ring taken from a CCTV camera at the counter and a note of his handwriting from a betting slip. This was an effort to stop Ring simply writing out bets and getting other customers to hand them over the counter.

Ring rankles at the fact that he can't place the bets he wants while others can punt with no restrictions. Speaking to me at his house in South Dublin in 2020, with the data file from Paddy Power laid out on top of that day's *Racing Post*, he tells me a story of how in one shop he was told they would not accept his bets and as he was leaving a young woman ran up to the counter and angrily asked for her partner's money back. He had lost his social welfare payment in a betting session and the woman wanted it back. She was crying, pleading for the money, saying that it was all her partner's money for the week. Of course the clerk couldn't give it back and asked her to call head office, where in all likelihood she would be told the exact same thing.

'I remember thinking as I left, I suppose he'll be able to get a bet on when he comes in next week,' Ring tells me, shaking his head.

5

Online from the Bunker

John O'Reilly kicked his legs up onto the desk and lit another Rothman's. Beside the six-foot-six-inch chief operating officer was a shattered IT manager, Paudie O'Connor, who was assisting in moving Paddy Power into the Internet age. On the other side of the desk in the biggest office in the company's Tallaght headquarters was the bright-eyed Cormac Barry, there to apply for a job establishing Paddy Power's digital business.

It was November 1999 and e-commerce was still very much in its infancy, but gambling companies were already alert to the prospect of what would happen if punters could bet from the comfort of their home or office at any time of day. Surfing the web, as it was then known, was still a niche activity and appealed mainly to hobbyists who wanted to discuss and argue over minutiae with other obsessives. In other words, it was perfect for sports bettors, poker players and other gamblers.

O'Reilly may have been unsure about what exactly Paddy Power on the Internet would look like, but in Barry he had someone who had the credentials and vision to make it a reality, even if Barry's family trade was in bookselling, not bookkeeping (his parents ran the Dubray chain of bookshops in Ireland). He had completed a degree in economics and politics in Trinity College before taking a sales job with Iona Technologies, an Irish software giant. Barry had helped the firm set up a US office in Silicon Valley before growing tired of the company culture. He made some cash when Iona IPO'ed and went backpacking around the world before deciding what he wanted to do with the rest of his life. When he returned home to south Dublin, his daily scans of the classifieds in the newspapers did little to inspire him until he spotted an intriguing ad in *The Irish Times*:

'Interested in sport?
Analytically minded?
Team player?
Good communicator?
Race ahead!'

The ad said the role would be multifaceted and outlined how the new gig would involve working as part of the team developing and running Paddy Power's Internet business from technological, risk, marketing and product-enhancement perspectives. It claimed Paddy Power was 'operating at the forefront of technological advancement'. But the reality was very different.

Before the online operation could begin, O'Connor had to climb onto the roof of the main office in the Village Green shopping centre in Tallaght and run a wire over the off-licence below to a smaller building in the car park with a metal shutter for a door. This would be christened 'the bunker'. This wire hooked the two computers in the bunker to the head office's Internet connection, which was thankfully lightly used as most of the staff used fax or phone call instead of email. This did not prevent disruption, though. The Internet servers were regularly unhooked when someone in the main office needed to plug something else in, like a Christmas decoration. It was an inauspicious start to Paddy Power's digital awakening but O'Reilly and Stewart Kenny had seen the growth in telephone betting over the last five years and knew the Internet was the way forward.

Paddy Power's success had been built in bricks and mortar, with smart shop managers and increasing footfall, so there was distrust and sometimes hostility from retail managers at the idea of allowing that customer base to be siphoned off to a digital business. Kenny was adamant that if online gambling was to be a success, Paddy Power would be a success at it. When others raised concerns that the online operation would eat into the takings in shops, Kenny said that if anyone was going to cannibalize the business, it should be themselves.

Kenny had been on the board of Xtra-vision, the video rental business, since 1991, so he knew that home entertainment could complement existing business models. People didn't stop going to the cinema because they could rent movies to watch at home – they simply watched more. If betting followed the gambler home, it would be a true revolution in an industry which had forever been seeking ways to offer more opportunities for its customers to hand over their cash. Paddy Power's bet on going online was not unique and not through any great insight of its own but stemmed from the fact that William Hill and Ladbrokes had announced in the summer of 1999 that they were opening online operations. Paddy Power had a static website showing its offers and odds of the day but the realities of what would be needed to process bets digitally was still unclear. Conor Grant, who had been running the Dial-a-Bet service, believed that once the online operation was up and running it could be staffed by one or two people. This illustrated the conservative estimates of how popular the idea of betting at home or from the office would be for most people.

The initial concern was that smaller bookmakers would be more nimble in offsetting losses from retail stores by operating online or that purely digital firms would undercut the mega-chains, especially as they could locate their servers in tax havens such as the Isle of Man, Gibraltar or the Dominican Republic without any political backlash that they were avoiding paying their fair share into the Irish exchequer. Paddy Power had lobbied hard for reduced betting rates in Ireland to protect the 500 people it employed across 116 shops by 1999 and it would have been a politically sensitive time to follow other operators offshore in order to avoid Irish taxes when its £212 million in turnover was generated mainly through shops on Irish high streets.

Despite its proclamation that it was 'at the forefront of technological advancement', Paddy Power had actually been beaten to the punch of founding Ireland's first online betting website by the one-shop O'Halloran Bookmaker's in Youghal, which had set up luvbet.com as a way of staying afloat when Paddy Power moved into the Co. Cork town in 1999. Hugh O'Reilly, a systems analyst hired by the O'Halloran family, spent £30,000 on developing the website and saw immediate reason to be optimistic that this was the way forward. The first thing that jumped out was the increased turnover on golf betting as 'people who wouldn't like to be seen walking into a bookie's' (i.e. the well-heeled golf-club members) began to open accounts. O'Reilly also noticed that women were opening online accounts. It was clear that 'cyber-punters', as they were referred to in industry analysis, were going to be a different breed to the *Racing Post* readers who frequented bookmakers. They would be younger, wealthier and less interested in horse-racing.

Internal research in Paddy Power was conducted, which offered the first real insight into what its efforts to make betting more accessible and popular had achieved. A Lansdowne Market Research report found that a third of Paddy Power's overall customers were now aged eighteen to thirty-five and many were using the Dial-a-Bet service, which allowed them to gamble without entering bookmaker shops. The British firms had been offering telephone betting and Kenny wanted Paddy Power to follow suit, but by the mid-1990s the company was stretched and it would take time to work out the logistics. This was white noise to Kenny, who wanted everything tomorrow. Frustrated at the answer that it would be months before the operation could be online, he burst into the Village Green office and told John O'Reilly that advertising space had been bought for four weeks so that was the deadline. A phone number hadn't even been secured but O'Reilly was well used to keeping the ship steady while Kenny steered it wildly.

When the pair visited shops together the staff would joke that O'Reilly, towering over Kenny by more than a foot in height, looked like his minder. The reality was not all that different. O'Reilly would warn suppliers offering new products or services not to tell Kenny until he had given them the all-clear or the changes would be expected to be in place tomorrow. Kenny was diagnosed with attention deficit hyperactivity disorder (ADHD) later in life and began coaching other people with the disorder, which includes symptoms of a very short attention span, being easily distracted and struggling to organize things, but at the time O'Reilly only knew that he had to be the steady workhorse to Kenny's wild flights of fancy. From installing screens in shops to launching the Internet business, Kenny trusted O'Reilly to see through his plans, but that didn't mean that there weren't hiccups.

The chaos that ensued around setting up the telephone operation included a problem that did not come to light until weeks after it had been launched. Paddy Power punters were at the shop tills with their wives or girlfriends when their credit cards were declined as being maxed out. Faces red with embarrassment, they called their banks and were told that yes indeed they were at their spending limit and in fact over it, as there had been a number of transactions to Power Leisure Ltd for hundreds of pounds.

This was news to the gamblers who had not placed those sums and had, in fact, won their bets. It turned out that the rush to get Paddy Power's Dial-a-Bet service up and running had led to an error whereby rather than crediting accounts with the winnings, the bookmaker was charging the customers for the amounts they were supposed to have won. It turned out to be an error on the bank's part but it could have scuppered the credibility of the operation if it had been more widespread. O'Reilly had by then established the telephone betting service by employing banks of operators to take calls from all over the country, and this new, easier way of gambling broke down the age barrier as younger men could place bets on the matches they were watching on satellite sport stations, and not just on horse races shown in shops. The internal research was the first of its kind in Ireland and found that 14 per cent of all Paddy Power customers were women, which was largely driven by the Lucky Numbers gambit. Altogether this showed that Kenny's 'if you build it they will come' mentality when offering new products was working. With a plan to float on the stock exchange early in the new millennium, Paddy Power wanted to ensure it was tailoring its services to meet all manner of customers.

Back in the Village Green bunker, Barry was working six days a week and often into the early hours of the morning to get PaddyPower.com live. There was so little structure in place that other than the off-licence-traversing Internet cable when he started, the bunker was empty. Barry had to build his own desk before he could place a computer on it. He and Paudie O'Connor were working in uncharted waters.

Though in the same way that great explorers discovered new lands only to find that others were on the high seas with them, the firms that would turn out to be Paddy Power's main competitors were also starting out in their own silos. In Stoke, Denise Coates had just paid £25,000 on eBay for the rights to the domain name Bet365.com and borrowed £15 million against her father's chain of bookmakers to launch her effort at an online gambling operation. A more curious case was that of Andrew Black and Edward Wray, an odd-couple business team who were putting together a betting exchange that would allow customers to act as bookmakers and take bets against other gamblers. The Betfair model was truly revolutionary and illustrated that online betting would be fundamentally different from shop-based gambling.

Many of the original online operations were not connected to established bookmakers and the early efforts of William Hill, which took its first Internet bet in 1998 as part of a World Cup promotion, were difficult to use even for tech-savvy web surfers. O'Connor had actually deemed

William Hill's effort a flop because it was so unwieldy, but the technology and understanding of user experience had already advanced by 1999, and Paddy Power was determined to get it right so that it did not turn potential customers off using its site. A regional Australian operator called CentreBet was seen as the best in class. The company had pumped money into developing an online operation to capitalize on the interest in the Sydney Games in 2000. It was established in 1997 and took in about AU$100 million a year by offering a sportsbook to gamblers all over the world. This was a figure Paddy Power could only dream of and internally the view was that it would take at least five years before the company would be able to make the Internet business wash its own face.

Kenny and O'Reilly were only finding their way in the digital world. They were also facing dissent from the retail ranks who could not wrap their heads around why a bookmaker's business was hiring middle-class, Trinity College-educated computer brats to waste money on a website. The board and retail managers weren't just a rabble of Luddites; Paddy Power had spent two decades building a retail network of what were effectively social clubs for their customers. They could have a free cup of tea along with the banter and bluster of the other patrons, so why would anyone who wanted to have a bet be interested in doing it alone on a computer in their spare room? Only 228,500 house-holds in Ireland had a computer at the time Barry was hired to launch PaddyPower.com and any office IT manager worth their salt had banned gambling websites from workplace Internet access.

Kenny had looked at the idea of an online operation in 1996 but was not convinced that it would be popular with customers. It would be a struggle to market inter-nationally to make enough profit to be worthwhile, even with the fact that it could be tax-free. He watched Amazon's rise to superpower status in the meantime and knew the opportunity to mimic that as a betting behemoth had been lost – but he was not giving up, even if PaddyPower.com would have to play catch-up.

Ladbrokes and William Hill were already online by the time Paddy Power went live on Good Friday, 21 April 2000. Ladbrokes had announced it was going to invest £100 million in its operation over three years and had already spent a large sum buying the domain name bet.co.uk. Before the days of Google or Facebook allowing companies to target their customers as collec-tions of disembodied data points packaged up by algorithms, the best way to plant your flag on the Internet was to buy a simple domain name. Bet.co.uk was the biggest, brightest flag on the landscape and Barry expressed concern to Kenny and O'Reilly that losing it to Ladbrokes could be game over.

But Kenny knew that the Paddy Power brand was synonymous with betting in Ireland and that his marketing stunts would earn them front-page coverage in newspapers in the UK, such as when the London *Times* covered the decision to pay out on Istabraq for the 2000 Champion Hurdle at Cheltenham the morning before the race. PaddyPower.com would be as strong a name as bet.co.uk for punters, Kenny believed. Within two days of the site going live on Easter weekend it had 2,000 customers, despite there being no advertising or marketing about the launch.

The marketing for the official launch was clearly designed to win over the professional middle classes to the idea of betting by computer. Rather than hiring the Channel 4 racing blowhard John McCririck or a sports star to launch the website as they had done when opening new shops, the notorious rogue trader Nick Leeson was paid around £10,000 to be the face of PaddyPower.com.

Less than a year after his release from Changi Prison in Singapore, Leeson stood in the lobby of the Alexander Hotel near Merrion Square in Dublin city centre touting PaddyPower.com.

Leeson was the world's worst gambler. He had collapsed Britain's oldest bank, Barings, by making a series of increasingly big bets on future markets in a mad effort to recover from losses he had made secretly that when uncovered totalled more than £800 million, twice the trading capital available to Barings. It was a massive news event and his imprisonment in 1995 after a worldwide manhunt had filled the pages of broadsheets and tabloids alike. Leeson's fee was agreed for one television interview and two radio interviews, but when he arrived in Dublin with a pal who Paddy Power had agreed to comp for a night on the town at the bookie's expense, he was told that it would be four television interviews and more than twenty radio interviews. This was Kenny's way in many dealings – asking for extras once the agreement had been made – but Leeson didn't mind as he was not afraid of the limelight.

The first interview was with Rodney Rice in RTÉ, which turned into an evisceration of Leeson's greed, arrogance and recklessness in collapsing a bank for personal gain. Kenny listened outside the studio and feared Leeson would only be fit for bed after the pummelling, but instead the banker strolled out of the studio with a smile on his face. 'That's great, now all the audience will have sympathy for me,' he said. Leeson held court in the Alexander for half an hour to a gaggle of press who had turned up from Ireland and Britain, while the Paddy Power press team flapped around at the failure of the dedicated ISDN line, which refused to work.

The irony of this billion-dollar loser launching a gambling website was a flourish Kenny delighted in and he made sure it did not fail due to any subtlety on the framing of the sponsorship. The disgraced banker posed beside Paddy Power's managing director at the event with a white rabbit and a top hat in pictures that were splashed across the business pages of newspapers in Ireland and the UK. The launch was so successful that due to the number of journalists attending the press event logging onto PaddyPower.com, the website crashed. This was seen as a metric for the launch's success in the days before Google analytics and external agencies offered reports showing the key performance indicators. Still, it meant another late night in the bunker for Barry.

The starting pistol was sounded in a two-decades-long dash in the betting industry to win as many customers as possible as quickly as possible. The online operation was now taking up about 75 per cent of Kenny's time as managing director. His vision was to follow the same strategy as Paddy Power had done in retail: get more people betting small amounts more regularly instead of targeting high rollers. The dot.com business was also to coincide with a faulty mobile phone application and an ill-fated foray into offering a gambling portal on a clunky interactive television set-up that cable providers were rolling out to customers.

Computers, flat screen televisions and mobile phones: Paddy Power was spreading its bet on where gambling would land in the new digital age. While retail-based PLCs in other sectors with long rent contracts and stock pipelines hummed and hawed about the deleterious effects mobile technology and e-commerce would have on their businesses, Paddy Power was keen to invest money trying to get into their customers' pockets.

When Ireland's first mobile Internet service was announced by Denis O'Brien's Esat network in 1999 it was one of the first operators in Europe to offer customers the wireless application protocol (WAP). One of the benefits of this new technology – which even at the time was deemed clunky by most earlier adopters – was that mobile-phone users could read breaking news from RTÉ on the go, check the stocks through an AIB homepage and even scroll through Paddy Power's odds. Paddy Power had already launched SMS text betting, so being on WAP phones was a logical move, and its new online team, led by Barry, was keeping a close eye on advance in mobile technology. The decision to launch a betting service on WAP was ditched after initial trials because it was so slow and unsatisfactory to use that Paddy Power felt it would do more harm than good to the prospects of mobile gambling in the long run.

Paddy Power was Ireland's biggest bookmaker in 2000 and needed to find ways to expand its domestic customer base if its stock-market flotation was to be a success. It also gave the company a chance to pole-vault over all the obstacles that made entering the high street in British cities and town centres such a costly and time-draining prospect. Driven by its position of dominance in Ireland and the long-standing ethos of John Corcoran that the company should always be seeking to increase market share, Paddy Power wholeheartedly embraced technology.

When PaddyPower.com was launched in 2000 the air was already whooshing out of the dot.com bubble but the ubiquity of the Internet and increasing power of chip technology could not be ignored. Mobile phones were a mainstay and while they initially drove the success of the Dial-a-Bet business, as texting became more popular with young people the company offered it as a means of placing bets, and began to invest further in the development of mobile operations.

The appeal was obvious, as noted by Oisín O'Connor, the co-founder of the Dublin-based betting exchange Betmart.com, which also launched an unsuccessful WAP product. 'We think it is as important to be able to bet in the pub on a WAP phone as it is to be able to bet from an Internet link,' he said. Strict prohibition of the mixing of booze and betting had curtailed the natural link between the two vices in Ireland, but there was now nothing to stop you having a flutter from the comfort of a bar stool while you waited for your Guinness to settle – except for the difficulty of getting the bet on before the patchy WAP connection timed out.

For Kenny, mobile betting was an avenue to get younger people interested in gambling, those who didn't want to follow their father into bookmakers' shops and embarrass themselves by not knowing what an each-way bet was. Kenny had always sought to position Paddy Power as an entertainment brand distinct from the rest of the industry. This is what the novelty bets and funny adverts had been about. Mobile gambling would be another string to his bow to achieve this.

It would appeal more to young people and women, who had traditionally eschewed the vice of gambling and were likely to feel unwelcome in betting shops among the seasoned punters circling selections in the *Racing Post*. 'There is a new type of gambler who doesn't spend all day poring over newspapers. He or she is looking for a bit of fun and is not a serious gambler,' Kenny declared in a trade magazine.

WAP was a flop, but a second mobile app was launched in 2004 on the nascent 2G digital cellular network that allowed faster Internet on mobiles.

This was initially hailed as progress and did increase the mobile-betting turnover compared to WAP, but the inklings of concern about the dangers of giving people the ability to bet at any time appeared for the first time. *Mobile Communications International*, the telecoms trade magazine Kenny had spoken to, said that while mobile betting would allow punters who were used to desktop websites to get around the restrictions placed on gambling sites by their employers, it also raised another issue. 'Alternatively, of course, such services can help the hardcore gambling addict get his or her fix when the betting shops are closed.' A user of the new 2G app also told the *Sunday Business Post* newspaper that 'the service was much more "addictive" and user-friendly than traditional telephone betting and that the number of bets per customer were bound to be higher with the new service'.

Just as David Lazer, a data-oriented political scientist at Harvard, had warned about the potential for Facebook to be misused for political interference in 2007, and had been ignored – a decade before that warning became a reality – the early concerns about online gambling leading to addiction issues barely registered in the coverage of the new technology as companies rushed to embrace the profit-boosting fuel of an always-on product.

The appeal of having an online operation was clear: it would allow the brand to attract customers from all over the world with only minimal overheads. Unlike Amazon and eBay – the main Internet success stories at the time – betting did not require warehouses and delivery networks to satisfy customers' demands. And it was plain for anyone to see early on that customers would embrace this new convenience.

By the end of 2000 Paddy Power had 10,000 online customers and senior management decamped to the City of London to lure investors for an initial public offering. It was easy to salivate over the potential profits from expanding Paddy Power's customer base from those who happened to walk past their betting shops to everyone who had access to a computer in the world, but the foundations under Internet-based businesses were still sandy. The dot.com bubble was about to burst as overvalued firms spent too much cash too fast, and with a flotation on the cards, Paddy Power had no intention of getting into a cash-burning exercise.

As chief operating officer, John O'Reilly had grown the Dial-a-Bet business from a small add-on to the shop networks into an operation creating 10 per cent of the company's turnover by 2000 while the aggressive expansion in retail continued. O'Reilly knew that if the online business was to follow the same trajectory it would need specialist expertise.

A year after the website went live Breon Corcoran was hired in April 2001 as managing director of non-retail operations. A no-nonsense former trader from Mullingar, Corcoran had spent his twenties working in the City of London with Bankers Trust and as a derivatives dealer with J.P. Morgan before attempting to scratch his entrepreneurial itch by getting involved with Internet start-ups. There was a language school, a scooter taxi service and a recruitment site, which would pay people for referring friends.

Corcoran was interested in learning about the e-commerce opportunities for the betting industry and had a strong history in risk management, which was a prerequisite for Paddy Power. Corcoran would be the internal voice of the online operation against the nay-sayers in retail and would make sure that they were free to follow a different strategy from the shops. Those who worked closely with him described him as the most intelligent man they had ever worked with – he could see weaknesses and solve them before they became problems. He was exacting in his diagnosis of where improvements were needed in the online division, or non-retail as it was to be known in the still bricks-and-mortar-centred Paddy Power, and he saw many problems compared to rivals.

His first hire was Peter O'Donovan, a recent Trinity College computer science graduate. If Paddy Power was going to be a serious player in the new world of online gambling, it needed new capabilities and that would mean taking on people from outside the traditional pipeline of gambling company recruits.

PUNTERS

Just as Stewart Kenny, John Corcoran and David Power had upturned the Irish gambling sector in the late 1980s, Cormac Barry, Breon Corcoran and Peter O'Donovan would be instrumental in moving Paddy Power into the Internet age. Whereas Paddy Power had grown for its first dozen years on the instinct of the bookmakers as businessmen, its future now lay in the hands of mathematicians and engineers – the people who were to harness the power of the digital age.

6

Let's Make Things More Interesting

Stewart Kenny liked the advert but thought it needed some tweaks. 'Make the bull bar bigger and the grannies more frail-looking,' he told the advertising agency.

The billboard campaign would announce Paddy Power's arrival into the British market as an online operation that was different from the familiar high-street brands punters had grown tired of, Kenny hoped. He and Ken Robertson, the marketing genius recently hired from Xtra-vision, believed strongly that the public was not as politically correct as the media liked to think and that most people got a chuckle out of stereotypical tropes about sex, age, race and gender – or at least most people who would become Paddy Power customers did. The company now had to win over a generation of new online customers in Ireland and, more important, in Britain, where it had never traded before and where the general public had about half as much interest in betting as their Irish neighbours. It needed to be eye-catching, attention-seeking and cause pearl-clutching.

The billboard showed a black-and-white image of an elderly lady hunched over a Zimmer frame, shuffling a few feet ahead of another old woman pushing a shopping basket on a zebra crossing as a four-wheel drive with a bull bar bore down on them. Imposed on the picture were the odds of 2/1 for the leading granny and 4/1 for the chasing octogenarian. 'Let's make things more interesting,' the tagline said. 'PaddyPower.com – Ireland's Biggest Bookmaker.'

For the launch of a new stock-market-listed company in a country which would define its success, they had hired Bartle Bogle Hegarty. The London-based agency had famously launched in 1982 with a campaign for Levi's that didn't feature any denim in it, instead focusing on a black sheep amid a flock of white sheep with the slogan 'When the world zigs, zag.' The agency was not cheap but Paddy Power needed to make a splash to stand out from the crowd and it set aside £5 million for advertising, fresh from the cash injection of the Irish stock-market flotation. This ad made an immediate splash. Help the Aged accused the bookmaker of ageism and devaluing the elderly in society, while the perfectly named Anne Crabtree of the Bristol Senior Citizens'

Bureau labelled them a disgrace. She said she supported the residents who had defaced the billboard near a notorious rat run in the city.

'It's a disgrace. Once again it is pensioners being treated with no respect. Is this what people think about pensioners? I shall be organizing a petition, writing to my MP and campaigning hard against it,' she thundered in an interview. The Advertising Standards Authority agreed with Crabtree's appraisal and ordered the billboards to be taken down, which Paddy Power duly arranged, replacing them with another advert designed by Bartle Bogle Hegarty. A wide-eyed baby stares at the camera in its young mother's arms. Behind the infant are engorged breasts concealed by a nightdress. 2/1 on the right mammary and evens on the left were the odds offered. 'Let's make things more interesting,' said the tagline.

The always cheeky, generally controversial marketing Kenny had initiated in the 1990s was purposefully ramped up after the turn of the millennium when Paddy Power needed to stand out from the crowd. Kenny told the agency that he wanted their edgiest ideas, not the watered-down version of edgy they gave other clients who said they wanted the edgiest ideas.

Barni Evans was hired in the spring of 2001 to introduce the PaddyPower.com brand to the UK audience.

The new marketing chief had worked in e-commerce companies and at Rupert Murdoch's News International where he had launched the digital versions of the mogul's newspapers. Kenny believed that *The Sun* – at the time the most controversial and base tabloid in Britain as well the most popular – was a perfect fit for Paddy Power's entry into the neighbouring country.

Squeezed into the one-room Hammersmith office beside Evans was Adam Perrin, a young digital marketeer who had never heard of Paddy Power when the job to join its new UK office came up. John O'Reilly, who had taken on the role of CEO in 2002 when Kenny decided to 'retire' and travel around Buddhist temples while cashing in his shares, had shared few words during their first meeting and Perrin, like most new recruits to Paddy Power, found the chief executive's size and near-silence imposing. What O'Reilly did tell him was that the Internet was the future of the business and while the company could fall back on its retail network in Ireland, it was banking on digital success.

This impressed Perrin, who had been working for Perform (a digital sports agency that is now DAZN) on building links between English football clubs and gambling companies. He felt that traditional book-makers were too tentative in their approach to online operations and that they failed to understand that they needed to change how they presented themselves to appeal to the new generation of gamblers.

Jimmy Mangan, now chief operating officer, expressed distaste for the way the incumbent firms Ladbrokes, William Hill and Coral advertised their wares. Shopfronts displayed posters with offers for £10 bets on Alan Shearer to score first and Newcastle to win 2-0 with a payout of £700. Why are the ads all driven by winning? Why is it not entertainment? Mangan asked.

This ethos of promoting the entertainment value rather than the earning potential of gambling had also been part of the reason that Kenny had convinced Robertson to join as the Irish marketing boss in 1999, enticing him with the idea that Paddy Power would be a creative and controversial brand rather than purely an odds-offering endeavour.

The culture in Paddy Power was that it could take on the then dominant Ladbrokes by being absolutely nothing *like* Ladbrokes. The first rule in the marketing department was that if it was anything close to what Ladbrokes would do, throw it in the bin. The second rule was that if the campaign doesn't make you nervous, then it doesn't go far enough.

New recruits who moved to work in Paddy Power from other bookmakers and various financial institutions were often taken aback by the force of the ambition to conquer Britain. Some believed initially that the chatter around taking on Ladbrokes, which had profits of £76.5 million in 2000 compared to Paddy Power's £10 million, was little more than an idle boast. How did they think an Irish bookie focused on horse-racing specials could compete with the British firm, which had billions of pounds of property investments and had just bought the rights to the Hilton Hotel brand outside the United States? These new hires soon learned that the culture in Paddy Power fostered by the management team and instilled in their lieutenants was aimed at being the biggest firm in the two islands.

In the Dublin office the nascent online operation was finding its feet and trying to tackle the issues that were cropping up about the limits of PaddyPower.com. There were a lot of unknowns generally around online businesses and specifically around gambling. Would punters want to bet online? Would they even be comfortable with the idea of a gambling company appearing on their credit-card statements? The uncertainties about where the limit for the online arm of Paddy Power lay were outweighed by the potential it offered for scaling the walls into Britain. The stock-market flotation was predicated on the belief that the company would continue to grow, and the neighbouring market was still untouched by the Irish bookmaker.

The risk associated with buying up a string of shops in areas with a strong Irish diaspora in London was high, so it was decided that a ballsy digital strategy would be a way of leaping into England while it built up a high street presence. Without having to maintain a vast retail network, Paddy Power could undercut the opposition online and force them into lowering their margins to compete, if they had the bottle to do so.

As part of the condition for holding an online licence in the UK, Paddy Power had opened a shop near Regent Street in London's West End but its real expansion was initially planned to be based on targeting the Irish diaspora in less salubrious quarters. By shifting its tax base to Britain, Paddy Power would take advantage of more favourable treatment of bookmakers by Her Majesty's Revenue Commissioners than was available in the native isle. The British taxation system was then based on 15 per cent of gross turnover rather than a levy per bet, drawing the Irish bookmakers to its neighbour in a reversal of what had happened back in the 1980s. Paddy Power's entrance into the British market would be brasher than the arrival of Ladbrokes, William Hill and Coral into Ireland.

However, while Paddy Power was hiring new recruits to build its ambitions to take over the century-old British firms, a new generation of start-ups were springing up that would disrupt the bookmaking model entirely. Betfair launched in June 2000 and, to put it plainly, sent the shits up Paddy Power. There was a wave of companies with almost interchangeable names springing up – Betfair, Betmart, Betswap and, more imaginatively, Flutter. From a corporate point of view these companies offered the holy grail: gambling with no risk to the operator. In essence, they were book-makers with no bookmaker. Punters could place bets against each other. If you thought the 2/1 favourite in a race was not going to win you could put £100 up against another exchange user who could bet £50. If the horse lost, you got their fifty quid.

Andrew Black was a bridge-playing, horse-owning stock trader who envisaged a proper technological revo-lution in the betting industry: one that would take advantage of the power of computer systems employed by stock-market exchanges and the increasing preva-lence of high-speed Internet, merged with gamblers' innate desire to bet in ways that don't require the oversight of a racing room or turf accountant. Black joined up with Edward Wray, a J.P. Morgan man, who wanted to do something different in the late 1990s, to bring the idea to life. Within years of its launch Betfair attracted price-savvy customers who were unhappy with bookmakers' increasingly stingy odds as they worked to balance risk with the breadth of their offerings, and international clients who were sick of having their winnings cut by taxes to the state-controlled gambling operators.

It also included a forum where account holders could brag, bemoan and bullshit about their day's betting. Betfair was a social network and peer-to-peer betting platform all in one. This was truly digital.

Cormac Barry, Breon Corcoran and Stewart Kenny were mindful of Betfair's power from the start but after tentative attempts to set up a rival exchange, it was decided that PaddyPower.com would focus on its own model. To stand out from the crowd of online operators, Paddy Power needed to make a name for itself and piggyback on brands that were already successful.

When Kenny stood down as chairman in 2002 to become a non-executive director he departed to pursue his interest in Buddhism by visiting Tibetan temples, studying psychiatry and cycling around West Cork. He did this £2.5 million richer after cashing in some shares but he was still seen internally as the North Star of the company and his influence was still integral to many decisions. The change in title meant that the co-founder was still around the company but he was no longer the face of it. That role went to Paddy Power himself, the son of David, who had been glad-handing big customers in the VIP department. He was the one to go on talkSPORT radio as a betting partner to hammer home the presence of the new brand in the UK.

It was not just his name that made Paddy Power destined to represent the brand. His sense of humour and personality were exactly representative of what Paddy Power, the company, needed to get across to win over the new generation of online gamblers. The fact that there was a real person called Paddy Power allowed the marketing department to push the idea that winning a bet against Paddy Power was like getting one over on a friend. You had been proved right; they were wrong.

William Hill, Ladbrokes and Coral all offered the same products and similar odds to Paddy Power but sold them as an opportunity to win big. The incumbent British brands had failed to attract younger, digital customers because they were afraid to speak to them in a different way from how they spoke to their fathers and uncles who were the current customers. Paddy Power had no such concerns as it didn't have a generation of British customers to protect. Perrin was given the brief to sell the brand as 'pure entertainment': 'We understood the psyche of the gambler and what they are driven by. Most bets lose, don't they? Or there wouldn't be bookmakers. So we had to sell that sweaty palms feeling of when the bet is about to be decided, and the social currency of when your bet lands. That was way ahead of the curve.' The much-repeated mantra is that for marketing to be successful, you don't sell the steak, you sell the sizzle. Paddy Power was selling the sweaty palms, not the chance of money.

The expansion into the UK coincided with bulking up the number of money-back specials and other gimmicks designed to make customers feel appreciated even when they had lost their bet. While many bookies offered enhanced pay-outs to punters who won, Paddy Power paid out to losers instead. The money-back specials were really just a cleverly repackaged way of competing on price. Where previously bookmakers had offered 4/1 as a special when all their rivals were going 3/1, Paddy Power was reducing its gross margin but in a way that benefited losing customers over winning ones.

If other bookies like Ladbrokes and William Hill were doing something, Paddy Power had to do it bigger and bolder. It had begun paying out on bets before the races were even run, such as with Istabraq the day before he ran in the 2000 Gold Cup.

In 2005 they took it even further by settling bets for Chelsea to win the English Premier League two months into the season as the team, pumped with cash by Russian oligarch Roman Abramovich, looked like runaway champions.

From a trading perspective this was reckless. Just seven games of the season had been played and Paddy Power had been stung paying out twice in 2003 when Arsenal looked like they had the league won in March only for Manchester United to beat Arsène Wenger's side to the championship. But Paddy Power had learned a lot from that apparent mistake. Early pay-outs generated massive publicity for the company and Wenger even had to answer questions about it at press conferences, inserting Paddy Power into the discussion about the sport itself. It generated goodwill from customers, who more often than not simply used the early winnings to bet again, recycling them back into the bookie's profits. The media attention the move got also made non-Paddy Power customers more likely to spend with the company on similar bets in the future, and it forced their rivals into making a decision. William Hill, Ladbrokes and the rest could follow suit and pay out as well, making Paddy Power look smarter, but it would not generate the same publicity. All together this was a stroke that cemented the company's position as the 'punter's pal'.

The eponymous marketing man's appearances in the media pushed this further, making himself out to be a figure who represented the brand but also the customers. Paddy Power would appear regularly on talkSPORT – not to push the odds of the markets available, but to talk about the topics that were generating chatter among fans.

This tie-in as a sort of resident bookmaker was a new idea in radio and fit perfectly with talkSPORT, which had recently launched the first commercial sports station to compete with the comparatively staid and safe BBC Radio Five Live. It was blokeish banter that sat perfectly with betting and Paddy Power's efforts to change gambling from something people in the know about horse-racing did to something anyone with an opinion should get involved with. The radio station had won the rights to broadcast Premier League and, chaired by Kelvin McKenzie, the former editor of *The Sun*, it was relentless in its pursuit of laddish listeners. The deal was 'close to the line', according to Perrin, in mixing advertising and editorial content as it gave Paddy Power access to the programme as a guest, but only because the company was paying for ads. Whatever the broadcasting ethics of the deal, it was a perfect fit for Paddy Power that allowed it access to the younger audience it craved in the days before it mastered social media advertising.

The other partnership that elevated PaddyPower.com in Britain was a deal with *The Sun* online. The tabloid was still the most influential newspaper in Britain at the turn of the millennium despite, or maybe because of, regular accusations that its content crossed the line into racism, homophobia and plain bad taste. The Irish bookmaker was already heavily advertising in the most influential paper in Britain, but the online strategy saw value in using the existing digital database of *Sun* customers in an affiliate deal. It was another perfect fit for Paddy Power to build its name in the UK and a partnership deal saw a symbiotic relationship where readers could follow links in *The Sun* through to the bookmaker to open accounts. The bookmaker paid around £250,000 to be linked to the paper's website so that it could turn *Sun* readers into PaddyPower.com customers.

In 2005 Power had also signed a deal to be the exclusive betting partner of the smash-hit reality television programme *Big Brother* and its odds for contestants to be evicted were carried in the daily tabloid articles, regurgitating what had happened in the previous night's instalment. The editorial tie-in also gave Paddy Power scope to grasp the popularity of *The Sun*'s infamous Page Three. On one occasion, after two sisters had appeared topless in the paper, Paddy Power compiled odds on who would appear more often in the paper thereafter.

Perrin and some of *The Sun*'s editorial staff would meet for drinks to discuss what the paper was planning and where Paddy Power could fit in. So when *The Sun* invited young women to take part in the 'Page Three Idol' competition to be featured in the paper, Paddy Power would get the 'runners' and do up its own market. It must have been a strange day for the odds-setter involved to take time away from pricing up Kelso races to ranking the likelihood of amateur topless models to win a tabloid newspaper's 'talent competition'. As well as fulfilling the commercial contract, the articles were popular and gave British tabloid journalists a favourable view of Paddy Power that would help fill column inches and provide fodder for clickbait.

The real market with which Paddy Power needed to associate its brand was English football. The Premier League and Champions League were in hyperdrive by the early 2000s. The dominant clubs known as the Top Four – Arsenal, Chelsea, Liverpool and Manchester United – were pushing financial investment and commercial partnerships to new levels in professional sport. Paddy Power couldn't afford to challenge blue-chip multinational beer, car and airline companies for sponsorship but knew that the football clubs' fans were their customers-in-waiting. The digital marketing team agreed innovative deals in 2005 with Arsenal and Liverpool to be online partners for betting without any associated branding. It was more powerful for Paddy Power to monetize the club's online traffic where the bookmaker paid a retainer to be a partner and a bonus depending on how many new customers signed up to PaddyPower.com through the official Liverpool or Arsenal websites. Betting and English football would soon become so intertwined that Sky Sports would launch its own bookmaker, SkyBet, and rather than allowing bookmakers to buy ad space like other companies, it repackaged slots during breaks in live matches and sold them exclusively to bookmakers in a blind auction, kickstarting years of incessant gambling advertising during live sport that strengthened the link between watching sport at home and betting.

Paddy Power's entry into Britain was advanced. The company had signed deals with *The Times* in 2002, the Cheltenham Gold Cup in 2003, *The Sun* and talk-SPORT in 2004 and *Big Brother*, Arsenal and Liverpool in 2005. This gave the Paddy Power 'challenger' brand an air of credibility and association with market leaders in different fields. The deals are now commonplace between bookmakers, other e-commerce brands and publishers, but at the time they were groundbreaking. And they worked. By 2005 Paddy Power had almost 100,000 customers online and telephone betting, which was a sign of success. But it was also exposing the company to a whole new level of risk.

7

Quants

The way some people tell it, Rob Reck is the most valuable person Paddy Power ever hired. His role in developing a quantitative trading model that mimicked the way Wall Street funds and global investment banks calculated risk gave the bookmaker the power to rake in millions upon millions more from the growing number of online gamblers.

Quantitative trading analysts, known as quants, were at that time in 2004 the richest nerds in the world outside of technology company founders. In the financial markets, quants use publicly available data to develop mathematical models and trading algorithms to determine investing opportunities that when deployed correctly can beat the market, which to investment banks means that they are as good as guaranteeing vast returns. Or at least that was the story up until the financial crash.

In the early 2000s the increasing power of computers and the bullishness of the stock markets meant that the value of a quant had never been higher. Wall Street giants and their offshoots in London, Frankfurt, Tokyo and beyond hired doctoral mathematicians, statisticians, engineers, artificial-intelligence experts and computer coders to skim billions from the financial markets. With the world economy at a rolling boil leading to 5 per cent growth globally in 2004, the share prices of Lehman Brothers, Merrill Lynch and J.P. Morgan Chase doubled. Mathematicians with any trading or risk experience were making massive salaries at investment banks all over the world, or most of them were anyway.

Reck was on a brief hiatus at that time. 'I tend to take long holidays,' he says by way of explanation through a plume of fruit-scented nicotine vape, when I talk to him in a South Dublin park in November 2020. Reck wears his hair past his shoulders, dons a leather jacket and drives a Bentley. If not quite pulling off the demeanour of a 70s rock star, he could pass for the hard-living band's business manager.

When he was first contacted by Dermot Golden, Paddy Power's head of risk, in 2004, Reck had spent time since graduating from University College Dublin in 1994, with a master's degree in actuarial science, working as a risk manager at the National Treasury

Management Agency (NTMA) and then from 2000 deploying his own trading models at small scale in the interest rates and options markets. Having led what he calls a roaming life since leaving the NTMA, Reck knew he only had one more twist in his career before he had to settle down so he approached Golden's invitation with an open mind. 'There were very few quants who were any good sitting on their hands. Things were booming. I was travelling the world, buying convertibles and just going mad. I had nothing else to do, so I said I would take a look,' Reck recalls.

Golden himself had been poached from the trading and risk rooms of investment banks in 2003, as Paddy Power's board was learning the hard way that the company's exposure was growing too fast for the current risk-management processes to handle. The group had 149 retail outlets, which were getting busier due to the marketing increase, and the number of non-retail customers was rising rapidly. The few hundred telephone customers who started using the Dial-a-Bet service in the mid-90s had grown to 18,000 by 2003 and the number of active online customers had jumped from 5,000 to 36,200 since the service was launched at the turn of the millennium. That meant that when Paddy Power had a bad day at the races, it was a really bad day.

In March 2003 half of the races at Cheltenham were

won by favourites, which forced Paddy Power to issue a profit warning to the stock market that its revenue would fall €4 million short of its expectations. The punter-friendly bookmaker had been burned by its own generosity when race after race after race was won by the favourite. The Irish-trained Back In Front won the first race at 3/1 and from there nine more favourites won before Cheltenham closed with another Irish-trained favourite – Sprint Favourite won the final race. It was a disaster for Paddy Power and when the Cork-trained 16/1 shot Monty's Pass won the Aintree Grand National, further hitting the company's profits, a stock note was sent two weeks later.

The market reacted, swiftly wiping €33 million off the company's market capitalization as the shares plunged in value by 13.39 per cent by midday before a slight rally in the afternoon that left them closing at €5.05, a 9.82 per cent fall on the day. With online gambling about to be rocket-charged by the confluence of high-speed broadband, ubiquitous satellite sports in people's homes and the arrival of smartphones, the new risk and quants team would prove to be a cornerstone of Paddy Power's ability to hit oil in the Internet age.

Reck is a man who normally chucks the sports section of the newspaper in the bin as soon as he opens it; he has never had a Sky Sports subscription and boasts that he has never watched a greyhound race in his life (a sport which accounted for an estimated 10 per cent of Paddy Power's €913 million turnover in 2003).

He first agreed to come in for a few Saturdays to observe the risk and trading set-up on Paddy Power's busiest day. Reck was not expecting to be impressed by whatever passed for the trading room in the industrial unit with a corrugated roof in Tallaght, but what he saw sent his brain into overdrive.

Having come from the world of finance where might was right and every point of exploitation was duly exploited, Reck and Golden could not believe the information Paddy Power was wasting. It is almost impossible for a small investor to beat the outcomes of Goldman Sachs or J.P. Morgan because they have bigger and better teams, more computer power and lower latency of execution. Paddy Power had all of these things over their customers and was still struggling to eke out profits on millions of euro in turnover on some sports. Reck was excited by the opportunities provided by the asymmetry between the average punter and Paddy Power. Punters were slower to process data, knew less about the market, couldn't do calculations based on other bookmaker's prices, didn't know what other people were betting on and couldn't respond to the smart money – the industry term for the euros bet by gamblers who win in the long run.

Reck spotted that Paddy Power was awash with raw

data that could be harvested and deployed in models that would in theory sustain profits on markets previously thought to be volatile. He explained:

> We corralled the customers into the models so that we knew what they were betting on once the traders had set the price, and then as they bet the prices changed in line with it automatically so we could keep the book balanced. That could be done on dozens of derivative markets within a single match or race because we had the model set up to take advantage of what would be considered private information in financial markets. The customers didn't know what each other were doing, but we did and that was a fantastic source of information. It was much better than the previous sources of information, which were feeds from racetracks or televised matches, where a trader would literally sit in front of a computer and change the odds as the match went on.

The most valuable information Reck could formalize into a model was the smart money. But he did not limit it to customers who had beaten the bookmaker in the past – he included betting volume and even certain shops where customers had more information about particular sports.

These were all assigned 'IQs' and bets from high IQ sources would flash up in red on traders' screens. For instance, the Paddy Power's busy retail unit at the Northside Shopping Centre in Coolock, Dublin was given a low IQ on horse-racing compared to the outlet in Thurles, Co. Tipperary, near the famous racecourse, where customers were expected to know more about Irish horse-racing. On top of this Reck was amazed to learn that traders swapped information with colleagues in rival firms, tipping them off to smart customers or races where gamblers might be setting up a coup.

'It was a total Wild West compared to finance where any internal information was guarded. Traders were trading all sorts of information, including so that they could bet themselves. When I talk to people from finance about it, they can't believe the level of indiscretion.' For Reck it was a revelation. He was coming from 'a really squeaky, hard-to-make-a-margin industry to a loose-lipped one where the companies have all this private information, the customers are enjoying themselves while I have all this firepower in terms of computers'. *This is a place where a quant can make hay*, he thought to himself.

But first there was a more immediate problem to be solved, right in the middle of the shed. The fishbowl office in the centre of the unit was where betting in-running was handled. This form of gambling allowed punters to keep betting on the outcome of races or matches even after they had started. Betting in-running had been developed by rival Internet firm Betfair, which had high-powered computational models to handle different odds, and little to lose since it operated a betting exchange where punters played against each other rather than against traders.

Breon Corcoran knew there was big potential in this as a new form of gambling but Reck recoiled at the inefficiency of the way it was managed. Right in the middle of the room, which was to be home to risk management, frantic traders were on full display hammering at their keyboards in a seemingly endless state of panic, updating the odds based on what was happening in the race, which was being streamed into the glass-walled office directly from the track. On busy days they were reduced to data-entry clerks while more senior traders barked instructions at them.

'Sweating in-running,' Simon Moore christened it when he joined as Golden's second quant in early 2005. Moore had taken an eight-week summer internship with Paddy Power as a statistician in 2003 after responding to a handwritten note that had been pinned to a noticeboard in the maths department at Trinity College, where Moore was studying management science and information system studies.

After graduating with first-class honours he went

off to work for the multinational professional services company Accenture because he had been told by lecturers that he needed to get a 'blue chip' on his CV. Within a year he'd had enough of the pressures of the consultancy world. He rang Breon Corcoran. 'I don't care that clients are paying us €500 a day, I'm not a waffler. I want my work to speak for itself,' he said.

Unlike Reck, Moore is a sports nut. He will play or watch anything, and he loved pitting his wits against Paddy Power's traders who he believed were driven too often by their guts rather than their brains. With him on board, the die had been cast. Golden was a banker who had brought in another banker and a maths whizz. It was clear to the traders that things would be different.

But initially there was no grand strategy. The idea was that risk would be tightened up by having a model close to that which worked in financial services and since the guys who were hired were smart, they'd figure out what to do. First and foremost they were problem-solvers, using their computational skills to make the current structures more efficient.

Paddy Power's IT system was built mainly on a stack of bits from outside providers and papered over with Excel sheets to keep it up and running as new elements were dreamed up to entice more customers. This created a logjam for traders, who would in many cases have to enter the same data into multiple Excel sheets for it to be used in different ways. Reck and Moore asked the traders if it would help if they could design a system where it just required one input to be redirected. This was referred to by the pair as 'linking the Luas lines', referencing the typical Dublin complaint at the time that the city's two tram lines didn't connect.

Previously up to four hours a day could be spent typing into spreadsheets and physically writing out odds to be faxed to shops. Reck and Moore were about to save a ton of admin work every week. It showed that the new team was not there to replace the human traders with machines (well, not yet, anyway) and that if the traders worked with them they could ultimately improve turnover on their own books and get the bonuses that came with that. While there would have been an existential clash between the brains of the quants and the balls of the testosterone-driven traders, the new set-up worked well as they swapped ideas over smoke breaks and fed each other titbits that had trickled down from management meetings that could help them impress their bosses.

To a man – and it was all men – traders were sports nuts. Many of them came from racing families or were the sons of on-course bookmakers; others were the sorts of boys who pored over sports annuals and could recite backwards by rote the winning captains of All-Ireland finals, goal scorers in FA Cup finals and Tour de France Yellow Jersey holders. They were not cut from the same cloth as the quants and risk recruits but they were mathematically minded and had the self-belief to back their own opinions. A 5/1 shot in a horse race was so because the trader had determined it using their own internal model. Others might have landed on 7/2 or 4/1 but the trader lived by his own opinion and he put it on the line. (It is one of the great frustrations of serious gamblers on horse-racing nowadays that most bookmakers share the same odds on each race, as the amount of data available and existence of betting exchanges have shaved out the opinions, leading to monotony on odds.)

One thing Golden insisted on early as head of risk was that the traders be given better pay – this helped with relations between the new quants team and the trading staff. But it was not an attempt to win them over: sports traders were by nature gamblers who had cut their teeth betting against other bookmakers. When they believed another bookmaker had got their price wrong, they usually bet it. This was all well and good to earn some drinking money on the side, but it was a distraction. Following an €8 million investment in a new electric point of sale (EPOS) system throughout the retail network in 2004 and a bit of clever hacking of it for internal systems by Reck's team, the systems were tightened up and the real fun for the quants could begin.

One telephone room in the risk department was used to take calls from retail clerks who wanted advice from traders when high-staking punters tried to get suspiciously large amounts on particular prices. It was another inefficiency in the system that Reck abhorred so he fixed the problem by working with the IT team to divert files containing scanned dockets on their way to central servers. The dockets could be flagged by shop staff to appear on traders' screens where the approval, or not, of the bet could be done electronically. The phone staff were redeployed to the Dial-a-Bet centre and Reck, who was now head of quants, had emptied a room, which he could now fill with more quants and computer servers.

Under Golden's guidance, Reck and Moore began approaching the traders and asking if there were ways that mathematical computer programs could serve them better. They stood outside the 'sweating in-running' office, scratching their chins and watching as football traders sat in the middle of the room watching Sky Sports coverage of Chelsea and Manchester United while calculating new odds in their heads for various in-play markets.

The job consisted of manually updating a spreadsheet

to change the win and next-goal odds as the match progressed. So when Chelsea winger Joe Cole let the ball run out for an attacking corner in the fourth minute of play, the trader had to pause the in-running market and update the odds on Chelsea scoring. When William Gallas headed in Frank Lampard's cross from the resulting corner, the trader had to pause the betting market and adjust his odds again. This meant that each trader could only oversee one event at a time, and the number of matches the in-running bets could be offered on was constrained by resources.

'Where are those numbers coming from in your head?' was the gist of the approach from the quants boys. They believed that they could design a mathematical model which could predict how any football match would play out and the resultant odds changes that should be made as events occurred within the match. The traders would still draw up the main markets on a race or match but a model designed by Reck, Moore and the rest of the quants team would be able to offer derivatives of those markets. For example, it could automatically translate the main market odds on how many goals would be scored when Manchester United were playing Barcelona into a derivative in-running market based on the current score, expected goals and time left to play at a given moment of the match. 'Sweating in-running,' was suddenly no sweat. This was all sweetened by the fact that the derivative markets were typically higher margin than the main markets so for no extra work traders were getting higher returns and bigger bonuses.

Since its flotation on the stock market in 2000, Paddy Power had become increasingly stretched as it attempted to diversify its offerings, retain its existing customers and grow its presence in the UK, which was then seen as the main growth opportunity for the company. It was a delicate act of plate-spinning that led to a lot of broken delph in the first years, but Golden's team were about to prove themselves as important and innovative as the company's much-celebrated marketing team. They would never get the credit publicly of course, because the arrival of quants and ex-bankers at Paddy Power led to the development of a corporate gambling firm that was the antithesis of the brand that had been carefully curated over the previous twenty years.

Staying true to Stewart Kenny's idea that gambling was purely entertainment for punters, Paddy Power was always presented as a seat-of-the-pants operation that would regularly be caught on the hop by a clever gamble, or would bumble into big losses on a favourite. This did not sit with the fact that the engine room of the company was a crew of cold-hearted mathematical savants who were implementing the same tactics as

Wall Street investment funds to protect Paddy Power's share price.

The branding of Paddy Power and marketing strategy to attract young punters to online betting, coupled with the high-powered quants system protecting the company from risk was a market-leading combination that allowed the company to set itself apart from its competitors as Internet gambling became ubiquitous in the early 2010s. But back in 2005, the new quants-based approach was in its infancy and only being used to complement the idea that traders had been taught how to set odds by their fathers, who had been taught by their fathers.

'The mindset was that gambling was innate,' Moore remembers. 'People would actually say in the trading room, "I can *feel* a goal coming on here." How do you explain that you can codify that "feeling"? Or we would hear things like "that horse has *class*", so how could you convince someone that you had put a mathematical model around it?'

Moore and Reck began building models for football and tennis, which were both relatively simple to distil down to their mathematical principles. A few key traders who were active on the Betfair exchange for their personal betting habits had seen what computing power could bring to bookmaking and got on board with the idea, so the introduction of derivative markets progressed.

Two young traders, Johnny Hartnett and Alan Quinn, contributed to modelling teams that built robots that priced up greyhound races by scraping data from the betting markets so that the odds would change related to the amount being bet on each dog in a race. There was also proprietary trading where other companies were bet against in order to cover bets, and make profit for the Paddy Power team. It was clear that this holistic system could sustain a new depth and range of markets, which would grow to be a crucial differentiator for PaddyPower.com over other bookmakers and it was felt by many in the company that Tallaght housed the best trading team in the industry.

The arrival of data feeds from a third-party company called Bet Radar in 2007 allowed Reck and Moore's models to be run across dozens of simultaneous live events. The traders would have access to more matches and as such could trade them in-running more easily. Reck and his team found a way to hack the feeds so the information could bypass the trader and run directly into the model. This would allow the model's algorithm to change prices in reaction to the data from Bet Radar without any human intervention. It also allowed models for new products to be developed and kick-started a 'build it and they will come' era of innovation at Paddy Power.

The quants team was being asked to develop increasingly obscure markets in an effort to deepen the pool of bets gamblers could wade into with Paddy Power. *Who is going to bet on whether there will be four yellow cards in the second half?* Moore thought as sat at his computer.

But he knew that the markets were carrots to the punters who were becoming accustomed to being able to bet on almost any event within a match. The bets were marketed as things the customers had been asking for but really they were designed internally and pushed out. The quants models were so complex that they could rake in stable margins from abstruse markets, such as the chance of a team being behind at half-time and going on to win the match.

Since the early days, Paddy Power believed it knew what its customers wanted before they did. And if other bookmakers offered something more attractive, Paddy Power was never too proud to just rip the idea off. In the early 90s, when other bookmakers offered bonus pay-outs on accumulators that won, Paddy Power offered money back if a punter's horse beat the favourite but didn't win the race. It was one of many money-back specials that the company offered over the years to enhance its image as the punter-friendly bookmakers, but Reck and Moore's work on the in-running markets had led them to think more about how their models could support those concessions. As Reck says, 'The psychology of the gambler is fascinating because the near misses are as important as the wins. We were trying to generate products that could work with that and fit in with the money-back specials or concessions around that. When you're close to a win, you think "next time, man". People brag about their winners, say nothing about bad losers and probably remember the close ones forever.'

They began modelling ways of giving money back to gamblers who had hit three of the four bets in an accumulator without losing the company any profit. The competitiveness of other prices would be affected, so that if the four-fold was truly 80/1 in the odds, it would be offered at 70/1 with a money-back special if three legs won and one lost. The ideas were generated ad hoc by the online product developers, traders and quants chatting outside the shed while on their frequent smoke breaks.

As the quants team became more embedded into the online operation they began developing more derivative markets on more sports, generating models for handball, volleyball and European basketball to appeal to Eastern European customers. But horse-racing was still about 80 per cent of Paddy Power's turnover and the quants had been struggling to innovate on what new markets it could offer.

As Reck was building out his quants team, he emailed

a recently graduated Trinity College student who was friends with a trader. Budget had been made available for a sports-modelling position and Reck was seeking the right candidate. He emailed Kevin Cunningham in the summer of 2008 and started to outline projects that were being considered in Paddy Power, referencing research done by South Korean economic theorist Hyun Song Shin who has published a number of papers on a subset of game theory that looks into games where there is incomplete information. It is a deeply academic subject that can be applied equally to global market crises or horse races. Cunningham had little interest in leaving the master's in statistics he had begun at Oxford to take on the sports modelling role in the shed. But, impressed by Reck's email, he agreed to work with Paddy Power over the summer as a research project.

Reck had been thinking about how quants could offer more to horse-racing markets, so he sent Cunningham a 1999 paper by two Trinity economists who had looked at how accurate bookmakers odds were in determining the true probability of a race outcome. It was an analysis of Shin's theory of longshot bias, which states that the odds offered on favourites are actually more generous than those with longer odds when compared to the probability that the favourite will actually win. It didn't really have much practical application for Paddy Power but Reck suggested a question that had been perplexing bookmakers for years. How can you predict why a horse might fall in a jumps race?

For years Paddy Power and other firms had offered money-back specials if a gambler's selection fell or threw its jockey off in the middle of a race. Cunningham arrived in the shed and set about looking into what factors might be at play.

The potentials were multiple and many traders suggested it was down to bad training or poor handling by jockeys, or the fact that some horses favour different types of ground. Cunningham began the arduous task of collecting data for every hurdle and chase in the UK and Ireland since 1 January 2000. He looked at the variables in the races: distance, number of runners, horse's age, horse's weight, the extra weight given to the jockey as part of the handicapping system, whether the race took place in Ireland or the UK, the prize money on offer and the bookmakers' odds on the horse winning the race.

He sought to find correlations between the factors and employed models previously used by researchers attempting to predict rare events. Cunningham found that the most significant variable was the age of the horse at the time of the race. For every year older a horse gets, the odds of it falling decreased by 10.6 per cent over easier fences and 7.7 per cent over harder fences. If a horse is five years older, this decreased the probability by 43 per cent. He also found that if a horse was a favourite the odds of it falling increased by 18 per cent and that the weight allowance of the jockey and the country in which the race was run were contributing factors.

Cunningham plotted his findings into a model and submitted it as his master's, being awarded a distinction from Oriel College, Oxford. He went on to work for the United Nations and as a campaign analyst for the British Labour Party before returning to Ireland to start his own polling company and work as a lecturer in Technical University Dublin. And Paddy Power got a new product to launch: faller's insurance.

Faller's insurance would apply Cunningham's model and offer punters slightly shorter odds on a race with the assurance that they would get their wager back if the horse fell. The model allowed the marketing department's money-back special promotion to be offered on all jumps races without any hit to profit.

Reck still poses the question, 'What makes a horse more likely to fall in any given race?' when talking to people about the applications for quantitative analysis in sports betting. Rarely does anyone say age, instead echoing the traders' theories about bad jockey-handling or racing too fast. But even when they hear the answer, few people can understand the appeal to Paddy Power's customers.

'The ethos we had was that customers want to express their opinions. They put their money where their mouth is and say: this horse will win. But what if it falls? Well, then their opinion is: if the bastard stays up it will win. So now we have something for them,' Reck says.

Although the quants were thriving in Paddy Power in 2008 the team was still small, and it was hard to attract young graduates who had dreams of working on Wall Street into the shed. Moore went to events in Dublin and London where companies pitched their culture and salaries to the smartest graduates, giving presentations after the recruiters from Goldman Sachs and Deutsche Bank had finished theirs. 'People would be sniggering. They might come up to me after and ask what I was doing there. I'd explain what we were doing and they would just say they wanted to go work for a bank. Yeah, go work for a bank – that sounds like great craic,' Moore recalls.

The financial crash – caused in part by the craic at the banks people were snubbing Paddy Power for – created more opportunities for the quants team. Up until then a particular type agreed to work for them. As Reck put it, they were as smart as anyone else in their fields but usually had 'a personality defect a mile wide'. He would go through CVs from recruitment firms and focus on people who had fallen off in the second year of their placements:

You had to be very good to do quants; we needed people who would come in and do their own research because there was no academic research to rely on. Anyone we needed had to be damned bright, inventive and be able to figure it out for themselves. But why would they come out to a shed in Tallaght? We ended up finding the guys who were unacceptable to J.P. Morgan or Goldman Sachs for whatever reason – 'personal issues' as they called them.

The quants team were the geniuses who powered Paddy Power, but sometimes they stood on other people's toes by overestimating their value to the company. Some pissed off the traders with their approach to betting: one junior member of the risk team even applied for the role of chief executive officer when it came up in 2013, apparently unaware of the power structure of the corporation. In fact, the savant-like ability of many of the quants led to discussions among management about whether the company should approach a charity to explore if the company could be more welcoming to people on the autism spectrum. The idea never materialized and although the team expanded to more than forty by 2010, the recruitment process remained tough.

Moore found that this diminished pool of talent was actually a benefit to the quants team in the early days.

'It wasn't a sexy company to work for, it was out in Tallaght and conditions weren't very nice. So the people who actually turned up for the interview, having got the 77A out with someone smoking marijuana down the back of the bus the whole way, they wanted to be there and nothing would deter them from the work.'

Reck says that this created a Hotel California effect on the quants team even as it began to grow, where 'you can check out but you can never leave'. The all-in culture was bolstered by the fact that senior management took an active interest in the trading-room floor. John Corcoran, the founder of the company and owner of several champion horses, would spend the Cheltenham Festival every year in the shed among the staff, who were worried sick that some small error would cost Paddy Power millions. For Corcoran, though, it was all good fun and he'd delight in hearing about the revenue generated when some well-fancied favourite failed to win. The bright young things coming out of college with quants pedigrees had had their investment-bank dreams shattered by the financial crash and the imploding economy. Paddy Power was suddenly a safe bet in the corporate landscape of Ireland.

The influx of technology multinational companies also led to a state-supported ecosystem of degrees pushing innovation in computer science. Advances in chip technology meant that the near-smoking servers that were running the simulations for in-running markets in the old telephone room in the shed could be replaced with much smaller computers. This meant more complex sports could be modelled effectively and match outcomes could be simulated tens of thousands of times before a price was set.

American football had been a nightmare in this regard because unlike soccer, with its low-scoring tendencies and slow-moving ball, NFL matches needed to be re-simulated depending on thousands of different potential scenarios from each play. Cracking this would not just prove the strength of Paddy Power's models, but would be a vital component of appealing to US gamblers if the opportunity arose in future. The quants IT team worked with researchers in Trinity who used powerful graphics-processing units similar to those in PlayStations to perform thousands of calculations a second. 'We thought then that if we had the power to do that then we could do all sorts of things, we could simulate all of the different paths from any event. So we could look at who is going to score first, who is going to score next, who is going to score last. We can calculate who is going to get sent off,' Reck says. 'When we had all these up and running we were powering each market the same way a PlayStation game is powered. That is a scary level of power.'

8

The Kennedy Era

'What did you think of us being chased out of St Peter's Square last week?' is not the sort of question that comes up in the interview process for the new chief executive of a listed company, but Patrick Kennedy must have answered correctly.

In 2004 Fintan Drury recruited the Dubliner to lead Paddy Power's audit team as early institutional investors stood down from the board while selling off their shares and taking with them the financial expertise required by a company with global ambitions. Soon after, John O'Reilly announced that he was following through on his plans to depart at the start of 2006 after five years as chief executive and Drury appointed the global head hunter Spencer Stewart to find twelve suitable candidates for the gig, including six from Ireland.

One of the names that was returned was Kennedy.

At the time of his interviewing process Paddy Power was in the news for its latest Pope-related high jinks. Power, the brand ambassador, and Ken Robertson, the PR chief, had been treating St Peter's Square like the betting ring of a greyhound track, displaying a signpost of odds in view of news cameras from around the world when they were run out by the police. Pope John Paul II had just died and the bookmaker was offering odds on his successor, lapping up coverage from the BBC and other outlets who embraced the soft-news distraction as the slow process of selecting a new pontiff dragged on.

Kennedy got what the Paddy Power brand was about and saw the potential explosion in online gambling. If Paddy Power could get that right, then it would be a global leader in a new era of technology-powered bookmaking. The international gambling market was worth $300 billion but only 5 per cent of that was online. An accountant by background, Kennedy was impressed by the strengths of the quants and risk department that was being built by Dermot Golden and his sense of humour fit with the marketing company's vision. Crucially, he took to heart John Corcoran's mantra that while rivals were focusing on the short term, the long-term market was free. This would prove crucial for the success of Paddy Power as the economic recession took hold two years into Kennedy's reign as chief executive

As the global financial system was collapsing and Ireland was staring into the abyss of a generational recession, the 38-year-old chief executive announced that Paddy Power would not be cutting jobs and would instead offer more value to punters – the opposite of what most firms were doing. Kennedy reacted to the loss in customers coming into betting shops with a best-price guarantee on all horse and dog races in Ireland and the UK. If you place a bet at certain odds and the starting price (SP) is better, Paddy Power will pay the longer odds. So if a punter bets at 3/1 and the SP is 2/1, he gets paid 3/1. If he bets at 3/1 and the SP is 4/1, he gets 4/1.

The cost of this guarantee was estimated to be as much as €8 million, but the Paddy Power chief executive, who was drawing a salary of €1.3 million, ploughed ahead. He said the company would continue to advance into the British retail market and pump money into the online operation. The market reacted by dumping shares in the bookmaker, causing the price to fall by 40 per cent from the previous year. This was chastening for the young CEO and some obsevers wondered if his appointment was a blunder, but Kennedy knew there were long-term investors who would pick up the slack over the coming years, however – it was just a matter of finding them. Kennedy embarked on a roadshow of investment houses to explain the strategy.

Potential investors were particularly enamoured by the state of the Tallaght headquarters as it showed that the bookmaker was not wasting money on high-spec offices; in fact it barely had enough desks for all the staff in some departments. Kennedy's strategy of cutting the company's margin also squeezed its competitors, many of whom were already struggling to cope with Paddy Power's money-back specials and other offers even before the recession. But the real schism between the Irish mega-chain and its compatriots was only starting to emerge.

While the bookmakers in the UK were raking in hundreds of millions in profits from fixed-odds betting terminals (FOBTs) throughout the 2000s, gambling in Ireland was still regulated by laws going back to the 1930s and 50s. It was high time for reform and the Fianna Fáil government led by Brian Cowen committed to a consultation on updating the laws and bringing in regulation that would allow 'super casinos' and book-makers to expand their offerings.

FOBTs had proliferated in bookmakers across Britain with the blessing of Tony Blair's Labour government in 2001. They allowed punters to stake up to £300 a minute on video games such as roulette and blackjack that guaranteed returns of up to 7 per cent for the bookies who hosted the machines in their shops. They had been blamed for a rise in gambling addiction, antisocial behaviour and money laundering for drug gangs, but they guaranteed fast and easy profits for retail bookmakers who were already feeling pressure from online operators when the recession hit.

The Irish Bookmakers Association (IBA) and Ivan Yates, the former Fine Gael minister who had left politics in 2002 to make hay in the gambling sector during the Celtic Tiger boom, were pushing for FOBTs to be introduced in Ireland as a way of giving the smaller operators a fighting chance against their competitors who had established large online businesses. The IBA employed Davy stockbrokers to conduct research: they estimated FOBTs would generate €50 million in profits for Irish shops with Paddy Power taking in €8 million, Ladbrokes around the same, BoyleSports €5 million, William Hill €3 million and around €25 million being spread across the 930 independent operators.

Yates had bought out the Joe Molloy chain of shops to give him forty-nine outlets in the country. He would be a big winner if the FOBTs were introduced, allowing him to fuel further expansion. In politics Yates was from the more libertarian wing of Fine Gael and was sceptical about the rhetoric that FOBTs were invitations for people to gamble their lives away. He pointed out, not unreasonably, that online casino games allowed people to bet without limit from the comfort and secrecy of their home PCs. Paddy Power was a member of the IBA alongside Ladbrokes, William Hill, Irish family firm BoyleSports, Yates's Celtic Bookmakers,

Hackett's, Bruce Betting and over thirty other independent firms.

The association had been pushing since 2006 to introduce FOBTs in Ireland, with Yates declaring that he had legal advice that the machines complied with Irish law as they were not technically slot machines, which the archaic legislation prohibited. Any early plan to introduce them without a change in the law was scuppered when Michael McDowell, the justice minister, said the machines would be seized if they were found. When the IBA began its push, Paddy Power walked away from the association and Kenny began pulling the old levers of his media and political network to highlight the link between the machines and gambling addiction.

Kenny believed he was going on a solo run and when word got back to Drury and Kennedy about his supposedly secret lobbying, he questioned whether he could remain on the board if Paddy Power backed the introduction of FOBTs. But Kennedy, Drury and other board members believed they would tarnish the reputation of bookmaking in Ireland if they were introduced and agreed to support the campaign against them. They somehow squared away the hypocrisy of filling their UK shops with the very same machines by writing that off as a cost of doing business in Britain. However, in March 2008, Kenny called up his old friend John Martin and gave him a full breakdown of the lobbying efforts going on behind the scenes as he saw them. The IBA and Ladbrokes had written to Brian Lenihan, the Fianna Fáil minister for finance, and offered him an increased cut of taxes from the betting in exchange for allowing bookies to plug in FOBTs at the 800 shops around the country. Yates and John Boyle of BoyleSports were also pushing for FOBTs on the high street. Horse-racing Ireland wanted the machines at tracks so they could hoover up some of the money too. Funding for the horse and greyhound industries were state-funded to the tune of €50 million at the time, and any prospect of increasing tax take from gambling to sustain this would have been welcome to the government.

An article appeared in the satirical magazine *Phoenix* on 21 March 2008 in the usual style of the publication, which is read mainly by politicos, journalists, lawyers and business people looking for some gossip on their rivals. With no byline other than 'Goldhawk', the nom de plume of all contributors which allowed them to spill the beans without exposing their own interests, the article detailed all the lobbying going on and included some extra factoids, such as a mention that Yates 'might well be tempted' to sell his chain of shops to William Hill if the 'one-armed bandits' became a feature of Irish bookmakers.

In a truly Trumpian stroke, the article also included

a reference to the machines being dubbed the 'crack cocaine of gambling' in Britain – four years before a British anti-FOBT campaign popularized the phrase. It was actually Donald Trump, who had coined the term comparing video gambling machines to street drugs in 1995 when he was lobbying against the introduction of video bingo machines to New York, which would pose a threat to his New Jersey casinos. The rhetorical flourish was catnip – even crack cocaine – to tabloid newspaper editors, and when it was taken up again by campaigners against FOBTs it framed the debate as one in which the bookies became pushers and their customers vulnerable. The *Phoenix* article ended with an insight that left no illusions that its source came from someone close to the centre of the discussions in Ireland. 'Wouldn't Seán Barrett be the ideal chairman for the all-party committee?' it asked, naming the as-yet unan-nounced appointment of the Fine Gael TD to the as-yet unconfirmed committee.

There was no doubt among the bookies about who had broken ranks with the industry to air their tactics and supposed motives for fighting to get FOBTs intro-duced into Ireland, but Kenny now had cover for framing the debate his way. Labour justice spokesman Pat Rabbitte indicated that he would not take part in a cross-party committee to examine the wider issues with Irish gambling laws if the review would allow

FOBTs to be brought in. Aping the language of the *Phoenix* article, he described them as 'the crack cocaine of gambling' and 'turbo-charged one-arm bandits'. With Kenny secretly in his ear, Rabbitte said he had heard that finance minister Brian Cowen had 'given the nod' to bookies that the machines would be allowed. 'It's a straight transfer of money from the poorest to the wealthiest of our society. Transferring tax levied on the backs of feckless youths to the racing industry is not socially responsible,' Rabbitte said.

Rabbitte began to take Dermot Ahern, the justice minister, to task for his handling of the matter. In harsh language he painted the picture that the government was seeking to use the all-party group as cover to introduce the machines to Ireland. He claimed that a report from a previous committee looking into casinos had been suppressed after it advised against introducing FOBTs but it appeared that the industry was gearing up for their introduction under future legislation when Rabbitte and Paddy Power teamed up to crusade against them. Ahern bristled at Rabbitte's characterization of the government using the committee as cover and said the Labour TD was 'being fed something by someone'.

Kenny flew into the fight with gusto, using his position within the industry to be an ally to those outside it. It was viewed by some in the industry as duplicitous and self-serving in a way rarely seen in Irish business, where industry networks tend to lobby in concert. More frustrating for the IBA members, it was clear that Kenny had backed a winner. While Labour and Rabbitte could be ignored to a degree by the coalition government of Fianna Fáil, the Progressive Democrats and the Green Party, Kenny's success in getting Enda Kenny, the Fine Gael leader, on board, doomed the prospect of FOBTs in Ireland. By October 2008, when the all-party committee was formed, Barrett was indeed appointed as chairman but before its first meeting he announced that the introduction of FOBTs was 'not on the agenda'. Ahern himself even conceded that he 'could not countenance' the machines.

That distaste seemed well grounded, as research by the UK Gambling Commission found that while those gambling on FOBTs represented just 3 per cent of the overall market, they made up 11.2 per cent of those who exhibited problem gambling behaviour. This was a concerning insight that supported Paddy Power's opposition to the machines in Ireland, but that supposed concern was undermined by the fact that they had almost 500 of the machines in operation in the UK when they were likening them to 'crack cocaine' at home. People who worked in the company at the time knew Kenny's position on the machines but had various interpretations of his motives. One senior figure said they believed Kenny was acting on his keen political instinct that FOBTs would be regulated tightly within a few years and that over-leveraging on them at the expense of making Paddy Power shops entertainment hubs would be damaging in the long run. Another source said that they believed he was opposed to them morally but that he was also driven by the belief that there would be a regulatory crackdown, which would ruin the gambling reputation of bookmakers in Ireland. Kenny had pointed out that while Irish politicians were happy to pose for photographs in betting shops during general election campaigns to appear to have the common touch, this would have been self-sabotage in the UK where the political debate about bookies was one of addiction and public health concerns, not the fun of having a flutter.

When asked for their view, another senior source at Paddy Power said simply, 'Ask Ivan Yates what he thinks.' Of course, Yates was happy to speak on the record about his old foe. 'I found it very hypocritical that Paddy Power had the maximum number of FOBTs in UK shops, and had no, shall we say, moral problems or ethical problems with them there,' he said, starting slow and revving up to make a point – as he has done throughout his political and broadcast career:

The real reason they weren't in favour of them was because they wanted 500 betting shops in Ireland, they wanted massive rationalization and consolidation. They wanted every independent wiped out. They wanted the Brits gone and they wanted it all to themselves. What they felt about FOBTs was not a moral issue, don't make me laugh. The only moral issue they had was that FOBTs would keep independents in business and that was what they were really and truly morally opposed to.

Whatever their motives, Paddy Power's lobbying was successful in preventing the introduction of FOBTs into Ireland. And, for a few more years at least, politicians were happy to cosy up to the controversial bookmaker.

9

We Hear You

Taoiseach Enda Kenny smiled widely as he was greeted by Patrick Kennedy when he got out of his state car outside Paddy Power's new offices in October 2012. Finally, a good news story.

The first two years of the Fine Gael leader's tenure had seen public patience fraying as the terms of the European Union International Monetary Fund debt deal started to become clearer. Ireland had been lauded as the poster boy for austerity after imposing €24 billion worth of cuts since the financial crisis. But a new euro-zone debt crisis had caused the country to slip back into recession.

The government was at a deadlock in talks with unions about reining in public sector pay, which had ballooned in the boom times. The Celtic Tiger was now well and truly over, however, and Ireland's international reputation and domestic confidence was in ruins. Public patience had frayed: there was a growing feeling that the country's economy was being hollowed out as memories of the 1980s recession were turning to reality. A record 87,000 people emigrated in 2012 and international newspapers were reporting that young Irish workers were sending remittance payments home to their families. The unravelling of the economy had caused the unemployment rate to soar to 15 per cent, the fifth highest in the EU and well above the EU average of 10 per cent. One in five men and one in ten women were out of work.

Happily, Kenny was at Power Tower to announce 800 new jobs at the most Irish of Irish companies' swanky new headquarters in Dublin 4. Paddy Power had outgrown the shed and moved to a new four-storey office called Power Tower in the leafy suburb of Clonskeagh. Instead of the industrial units housing pet-food distributors and driving schools on Airton Road in Tallaght, the company was now beside University College Dublin, where graduates were only too keen to work for the company their predecessors had turned up their noses at. Paddy Power was still known mostly as the marketing circus that could be hammered by a bad run at Cheltenham, but under Kennedy its image had changed markedly. At investor days in Dublin and London, Paddy Power was pitching itself as a company powered by big data in a way that was impressing even Google and Facebook. Its marketing claimed it was flying by the seat of its pants, more concerned with causing a stir than making a mint, but in reality it was as successful as any indigenous Irish online operation at the time. By 2010 three-quarters of the company's €143 million global profits were from the Internet arm, powered by 643,000 customers. That was the same year that the bookmaker became the financial institution with the highest value in Ireland as the banks collapsed – a symbol of who had placed better bets during the Celtic Tiger. Paddy Power had also achieved the original aim of its founders in 2011, when it became the biggest listed gambling company in Europe by surpassing Ladbrokes, which had failed to adapt to the Internet age with the same success as the Irish firm. The group founded by Kenny, Corcoran and Power as the last throw of the dice against the British firms taking over Irish high streets was now worth €2 billion, making it the biggest bookmaker on the stock exchange.

Enda Kenny's visit was designed to show that the betting company was no longer just a cheeky chappie having a bit of craic, it was a bona fide technology company. It was still Paddy Power of course, so there was the ceremonial presentation of a Lycra suit in the firm's trademark Kelly green for the 53-year-old cycling enthusiast Taoiseach, emblazoned with the marketing slogan for Paddy Power's mobile app, *We Hear You*, along with *The Coronary Club* where the team name should have been. Kennedy then led Kenny and a gaggle of photographers and political reporters through the trading room where young men in casual shirts sat in front of six screens each displaying graphs, raw computer code and, of course, live horse-racing.

The Taoiseach was introduced to traders and members of the risk and quant teams, where the intricacies of Paddy Power's model were explained. Kenny was clearly blown away by the technological advancements in the betting industry. 'My God, I heard language here from some of the people that I met which was quite incredible,' he told workers and the assembled press in the top floor restaurant of Power Tower. 'In fact I never knew, as one who used to throw darts at the old board, that there was a formula for hitting the treble-twenty three times. I didn't understand that. I thought you had the dart, hand to eye, let fly and hoped for the best.'

The *Irish Independent* colour writer Lise Hand was trailing the Taoiseach on his visit and was clearly also taken by the computational power of Paddy Power's operation. She wrote that:

anyone who innocently thinks that the placing and taking of wagers is a ramshackle, haphazard business is sorely mistaken. For the bookmaker's main office is more akin to NASA Control, with several floors stuffed with traders, analysts, geeks, mathematicians and technological wizards. They even have, as one tour guide around this hi-tech HQ informed the bamboozled posse, staff whose job it is to 'understand customers' needs and emotions'.

This may have been the first mention in the national press that Paddy Power had a quants-powered engine at the heart of the company's operation, as the fact was purposefully hidden behind the well-crafted marketing schtick portraying the firm as a bit of fun. 'Several floors stuffed with traders, analysts, geeks, mathematicians and technological wizards' did not fit the company's image but this was a rare time when Paddy Power was desperate to show that it deserved a place in the Irish corporate landscape alongside the multinational technology giants such as Facebook, Google and Amazon that were taking over Dublin's office blocks.

The message was impressed upon the Taoiseach and the official government press release announcing the trip to Power Tower said the announcement of the new jobs and office 'highlights the strides Irish companies are taking in e-commerce and technology . . . I commend the company on its commitment to Ireland and in particular its commitment to retaining and developing Irish graduates.'

Paddy Power was not just interested in attracting young people to work for them; they wanted them as customers too. Since launching its website in 2000 the company knew it had to lower the age profile of its customer base. Market research conducted following the launch of PaddyPower.com showed that 84 per cent of adults in Ireland were aware of the brand and 60 per cent would name the company unprompted. The problem was that the average age of the people who were actually Paddy Power customers was older, and 18- to 34-year-olds were less likely to gamble with them, or anyone else.

The investment in the first ten years of the website had allowed Paddy Power to take a leading position, but by the mid-2000s the generation of millennials who had grown up on satellite sports channels and the Internet were coming of age. They were more likely to watch Wrestlemania than the Galway Races.

When Kennedy was appointed chief executive in 2006 there was a realization that the new generation needed to be attracted in a different way. And so, over the next four years, Kennedy doubled down on a strategy of ever-edgier marketing and a start-up attitude to innovation. Paddy Power would be bigger, brasher and better than the competition.

In 2010 Paddy Power became the first gambling company to launch an iPhone app. There was initially reticence about the prospects for yet another foray, after the WAP flop and 2G dud, into putting technology on phones, but the board knew they needed to go to their customers. Along with Breon Corcoran, who had grown the online operation by following the models of Silicon Valley e-commerce giants, Kennedy was clear in his vision that the company needed to get a leash around the Internet as part of its approach to capturing the lucrative youth market.

When he was selected as the Irish Marketing Institute's All Ireland Champion for 2010, the chief executive was blunt about what the company was trying to do. 'We are consumed with trying to ensure that our brand is relevant to 18- to 25-year-olds, as they are tomorrow's consumers,' he said.

The brand that had been developed by Stewart Kenny and Ken Robertson was perfectly pitched to the young men who spent their days scrolling the Internet for cheap and crude gags. Gambling was becoming increasingly corporatized but despite having been subject to shareholders' sensibilities for a decade since flotation, there was no sign that Paddy Power's brand needed to mature. In order to stay afloat in the social media churn of Facebook and Twitter, on which by 2010 young people were increasingly spending their days, Paddy Power needed to be even edgier.

'Here's the challenge. If your brand has been successful for ten or twenty years, it's a brand that the parents of the 18- to 25-year-old associate with, which has the inevitable default consequence of driving away their children. No sooner do we drive an industry-leading position on Facebook when signs emerge that the younger market is moving on because their parents are on it,' Kennedy told the Marketing Institute in 2010.

In the role that came to be known as 'Head of Mischief', Ken Robertson had been poached from Xtra-vision by Stewart Kenny in 1999, and they, along with David Power's son Paddy, had built a brand that was perfectly suited to the social media age. Paddy Power's brand was young, fun and dumb. Ladbrokes, William Hill, BoyleSports and the rest were *on* the Internet but they were not *for* the Internet in the same way Paddy Power was. Even though his experience was as an accountant, Kennedy was close to Kenny and had an involvement in the day-to-day high jinks of the marketing department. He wanted to know what the plans were before big events and seemed to delight as much as 'the mischief team' or mischief department – as the marketing executives who concentrated on the company's wilder stunts became formally known in 2011 – did in the potential for controversy.

Past campaigns had been carried out for controversy's sake and the only way of measuring their success had been by counting the clippings of the tut-tutting newspaper articles they generated. With Facebook, Twitter, YouTube and a whole ecosystem of digital media companies dependent on clicks for their survival, as well as third-party marketing firms who knew how to turn those clicks into profits, it was now possible to use controversy as a direct pipeline to new business. If an ad campaign resulted in 80,000 Google searches for Paddy Power, the data teams worked to make sure that as many people as possible clicked through to sign up using a range of new digital marketing techniques. But it also needed to keep people searching for the brand by being as ballsy in its marketing as possible.

In Kennedy's first year as chief executive in 2006, Paddy Power's annual report for shareholders was a take on the cheekily chauvinist lads' mags such as *Nuts* and *Zoo* that were then selling more than 300,000 copies each week in the UK and Ireland. Aping these publications, the Paddy Power annual report featured a young woman on the front cover covering her breasts and pubic area with her hands. *Go to page 4 for more great figures* it read, directing shareholders to the key metrics for the fiscal year. The number that stood out was that the amounts staked online had grown by 60 per cent to €525.4 million. This meant the online arm of the company was now generating more than half of that which was staked in the retail network. It also showed that the company's efforts to cross-sell customers into the lucrative gaming options on its online casino site was 30 per cent of the profits from the Internet. These games were bought in from outisde firms who gave sales pitches boasting about how they were faster, more lucrative, and designed to trigger joy in gamblers even as they were losing.

The lads' mag theme for the annual report was not just a chance to titillate shareholders but a play on the fact that 2006 was Paddy Power's eighteenth birthday, when the company's Internet operation was about to come of age. Paddy Power's office was full of Ireland's brightest mathematicians and marketers, the head and the heart of the company. Peter O'Donovan, the computer engineer hired out of Trinity College by Breon Corcoran, had worked directly with Cormac Barry to flip the switch in Paddy Power, turning it from a retail bookmaker with an Internet arm into an e-commerce giant with a legacy retail network.

Kennedy, Corcoran, Barry and O'Donovan achieved this by hiring the brightest youngsters they could find, depending on the ramped-up risk operation as a safety net and using generous promotions as a way of attracting new customers.

The culture of Paddy Power under Kennedy was described as 'highly aligned and loosely coupled'. Everyone knew what the strategy was (more customers, more margin and more fun), but how this was achieved was by allowing each division to take its own risks. Kennedy, Corcoran, Barry, O'Donovan and the rest of the decision-makers were all from mathematical, analytical and quantitative backgrounds so they really understood risk. Not just in terms of financials or betting markets, but in the opportunities that taking risks in new areas could bring.

That was why Paddy Power had always invested in new platforms such as WAP betting, interactive television portals and social media marketing. There was no one with a crystal ball who knew which platform would ultimately succeed but the risk appetite among the team was such that they moved quickly – and way before their competitors – to find out what would work. This agility meant that they could innovate where possible and adapt competitors' ideas so that Paddy Power customers weren't missing out on anything that Ladbrokes or Betfair was offering. It was common for Robertson to call O'Donovan or someone else in the online team late on a Saturday or Sunday night to tell them that a news event required a new betting market to be drawn up. It could be a Premier League manager who was about to be sacked or a politician who was on the brink of resigning. If Paddy Power moved fast enough their odds would be part of the news cycle.

For example, when the Eyjafjallajökull volcano in Iceland erupted in April 2010, sending an apocalyptically thick cloud of ash and smoke over Western Europe and causing unprecedented disruption to air travel, Robertson presented it as a way for Paddy Power customers to insure against their summer holidays being cancelled by betting on specific airports being closed on particular days in June and August. So a £1,000 holiday could be covered on a £20 bet at 50–1 that Heathrow would be closed on 18 July. Ultimately, the bets all lost as the cloud cleared by mid-May and travel resumed as normal.

This agile and innovative culture set them apart from the likes of Ladbrokes and William Hill in Britain and Celtic Bookmakers or Boylesports in Ireland, but Paddy Power was an e-commerce business now. It had a range of products – sports bets, casino games, poker – to sell and a cross-over into retail operations, including a growing number of FOBTs in the UK.

O'Donovan moved Johnny Devitt, an engineer who had been working on a failing product offering spread betting on the financial markets (this was another punt by Paddy Power to attract new gamblers by allowing them to speculate on price movements in financial markets), into a new role overseeing the company's use of marketing technology. The new world of digital advertising allowed every interaction with a potential customer to be indexed and evaluated. Devitt and O'Donovan took engineers' mindsets to marketing and Paddy Power became a leader not just in betting but across all e-commerce platforms.

Google and Facebook invited the bookmaker's heads to speak at events as a way of illustrating the power of their platforms for using personal data and targeted campaigns to power commerce. Stock-market analysts pored over the data from Paddy Power and positioned it among the top firms using digital marketing technology. They employed 100 people in the department by 2010, which would have put them ahead of most marketing agencies in Dublin at the time and the level of detail they generated around customer acquisition, retention and relationship management was far above what any betting competitors – and other firms of Paddy Power's size –were doing at the time. They were spending more than most Irish businesses, over €20–30 million annually, and targeting it towards mobile phone users, which was also where Google and Facebook were pushing the market towards. The tech giants cosied up to Paddy Power and involved their digital teams in the deployment of new technology platforms and tools.

Facebook was hoovering up any and all data it could from users who had downloaded its apps and Paddy Power was at the forefront of linking that with its own internal profiling. This supercharged the expansion of mobile gambling, particularly in Britain, where the cost per acquisition was the metric that would determine success. Paddy Power's internal teams cut through the data to maximize the conversion of Facebook users who saw their ads or displayed an interest in sports into new customers. Once they were in and had bet, the retention programmes kicked in to prevent them 'churning' – logging out and never returning. The analysis and tracking of customer activity led to Paddy Power increasing the amount of money it made (i.e. the amount gamblers lost) over the lifetime of any account. The website was designed to make depositing as seamless as possible. Analysis by stockbrokers looking at the firm found Paddy Power to have among the highest return on investment in new customers and the lowest rate of churn.

But it was not just a science for engineers – there was also an art of sorts to the digital marketing.

The Paddy Power brand sat easily on the trollish, bawdy social media stream of Twitter. In 2016 Mícheál Nagle, Paddy Power's social media manager, gave a presentation in Twitter's Dublin headquarters to show how he used the platform to interact with customers and develop a strong voice for the brand.

On the screen behind the Corkman was a tweet he had fired off in 2013 at rival Ladbrokes, which was aping Paddy Power's schtick too closely by posting Premier League memes and off-colour jokes about sports presenters. The British firm had just tweeted a picture of a gangly, middle-aged woman who bore an unfortunate resemblance to Arsène Wenger, the then Arsenal manager. Nagle and the Paddy Power team had grown weary of Ladbrokes copying jokes, so under the picture of the woman Nagle had written *Your mum!* The playground insult aimed at the bigger rival was perfectly in tune with Paddy Power's other output, and in the days when a few hundred retweets was seen as going viral, the *Your mum!* message got thousands. It was the most puerile, juvenile thing that had come into Nagle's mind but it worked.

Paddy Power's use of social media platforms was not just to push out maternal insults; it was a way of harvesting information about their potential customers and reaping the rewards in new accounts and increased deposits. It paid for advertising but also analysed the jokes that worked well and tried to repeat them and this kept their voice fresh and engaged with customers.

The internal Facebook ranking of Paddy Power's page, which fed into the algorithm that determines what to show in users' newsfeeds, was nine out of ten because it didn't just push followers to its own site; it tried to make them fans of the brand on Facebook. By contrast, Betfair's ranking was two out of ten. Paddy Power was the first bookmaker to reach a million followers on Facebook as O'Donovan and Devitt analysed what worked and what didn't. Customers who downloaded

Paddy Power mobile apps or landed on PaddyPower.com by following links from Facebook were tagged. The analytics Mark Zuckerberg's platform used showed what worked and what didn't, but Paddy Power's extra layers ensured they were tailored to the company's needs.

Paddy Power was far from being the first bookmaker or e-commerce platform on the social network, but it was ahead of most in having dedicated content teams. While other brands used paid ads, following the old business mantra 'sell, sell, sell', Paddy Power followed 'tell, tell, sell'.

It knew what its customers were interested in beyond just betting and interacted with them by posting jokes or news updates and would only then try to get them to log into the website. It was costly employing teams of young college graduates to think of *Your mum!* jokes, but they more than paid for themselves – it was clear from the data showing how effective social media was in generating new accounts or getting existing customers to place a bet. The success did not go unnoticed in Facebook's Dublin headquarters either. O'Donovan was invited to present at Facebook's marketing consultants programme to show other advertisers on the platform how to maximize returns from the new tools.

Devitt was a master of ad technology in its early

days, overseeing maximum return from the paid campaigns and jocular posts. O'Donovan's mantra was that it was an aggregation of small things that created a competitive advantage, not just one big idea. Every Facebook post, mobile app download and customer sign-in was analysed with a view to learning as much as possible about what worked. This was gambling fuelled by the glowing coals of Silicon Valley's new data-burning smokestacks.

The real-time data fed every decision made, from what horses to include in offers at Cheltenham to where to open a shop in London. The feeds of information could allow marketing, trading and risk staff to drill down into particular bets and respond. If mobile customers were taking an offer but desktop users were not, the marketing team could change where the social media ads displayed to correct this. If a horse was being backed more heavily than the traders had appetite for, the profile of the customers betting could be examined to determine why this was the case: was there a coup in the offing or had they simply followed a bogus tip from a website? It also worked for retail. If one shop appeared to be operating at a lower margin than expected the data would show that there were more horse-racing bets being taken than anticipated and offers on football or golf could be promoted to redress the balance.

Internal analysis of customers was done on a continuous basis and automated systems highlighted where profits might be hit by punters backing less profitable events. In the horse-racing division limits were imposed on accounts that might be profitable in the long run. These do not necessarily need to be winning accounts – it is just as likely to be a punter who backed a horse at bigger odds than it goes off at when the race starts. This is viewed as a sign that the punter is savvy and taking advantage of prices before the influx of bets moves the odds to their more likely outcomes.

Savvy customers were restricted in line with a system of secret 'stake factors' that categorized customers based on their past bets. The risk team routinely restricted accounts to the point that managers began to complain that they were being too heavy-handed and that this was shedding customers who would lose in the long run.

An insider described the stake factors as such:

1.00 – A standard or new customer who would be allowed to bet freely.

0.80 – A customer who was being monitored because they had bet in a way that aroused suspicion that they might win in the long run.

0.50 – A customer who bet overnight to take advantage of early prices on horse races that were generally more generous than the odds when the race began.

0.30 – An unprofitable customer who was winning in the long run and who was likely to be restricted in how much they could bet on a given race.

0.10 – A 'warm' customer who was likely to have insider knowledge or be betting for people who did.

0.05 – A 'rat' who engaged in arbitrage to guarantee a return. Rats are the bane of online operators. The practice of placing a series of bets with different operators to ensure a return is done to take advantage of inefficient markets in stocks and retail, but in bookmaking it is a mortal sin. Their accounts were closed completely.

0.01 – Effectively an account which was closed because it was so heavily restricted based on the likelihood that the gambler would win in the long run. They could still bet, but only pennies.

This strategy of risk management was imperfect and needed constant monitoring from a team within the trading department, but it meant that Paddy Power was not exposed to large losses from savvy customers. The bookmaker argued that this was to ensure that the average customer was still able to bet freely, but it is hard not to see it as rigging the game in a way that roots out winners while populating a customer base full of losers without being upfront about the nature of the operation. Flutter declined to comment when approached prior to publication.

Those losers did not escape Paddy Power's attention, however – they were cross-sold, using targeted social media advertising and email promotions offering free bets, to high-profit casino games where they were free to pump whatever amounts they wanted into digital roulette games with no interruption and no loss limits.

The heaviest losers on sports betting were deemed VIPs and the handling of their accounts was handed over to a team of agents whose job it was to increase turnover on these accounts by offering incentives such as large free bets, or taking the customers out to a day at the races or to the Paddy Power seats at major football matches. Using third-party software from Qlik, a Swedish company, staff could monitor betting data in real time and carry out in-depth analysis on accounts to determine if they were likely to be profitable for the company, or if they should be restricted.

The rapid growth of new accounts meant that it was no longer possible for risk managers to efficiently review them without doubling the number of such staff, which would not have been cost-effective.

Instead, the quants team developed software based on early accounting computational systems that calculated each new customer's 'future expected margin' (FEM). Just as the quants wonks had been able to develop an algorithm that calculated which horse might fall in a race, now they could read into a few bets from new customers and identify who might be more likely to take a few quid off the company – and how they should be stopped.

FEM was a clever calculation that graded each customer's bets against a demarginated SP or odds on a horse based on the on-course bookmakers that was viewed as being a fair price and sent to Paddy Power through a data agreement. If, for example, you bet on a horse at 7/2 with Paddy Power and the SP is 7/2 then the true price will be considered 4/1, so you have taken lower than the true odds. If the SP is 5/2 for your 7/2 bet with Paddy Power, the system calculated that you had bet on a 3/1 shot at the larger price of 7/2. The FEM system could then calculate the margin Paddy Power expects to make off that customer over the lifetime of their account and when they reached a certain threshold of bets it would automatically impose a stake factor.

An analysis of data collected on the accounts which had been assigned stake factors by the human risk managers in the trading team found big inconsistencies. Some customers were given harsh factors despite only deserving to be monitored, while some clever customers who had a clear edge on Paddy Power were betting too freely.

Only a small fraction of Paddy Power's customers were affected, less than 5 per cent, but then again only a tiny percentage had ever been able to win anyway. The new technological power of the company was able to stop even these punters in their tracks before they had a chance to take a chunk of profits.

This FEM model could be applied to varying degrees of accuracy to all punters who used Paddy Power online, which, coupled with the tracking power of the data-grabbing and website mechanics, would nudge new users towards more profitable (and many say more addictive) casino games.

This was the brave new world of data-driven book-making in Paddy Power. It was innovative, incisive and analytical. It was also wholly unknown to the hundreds of thousands of gamblers who were walking around with the Paddy Power app's full suite of sports betting and casino gambling software in their jeans pockets. As Paddy Power's slogan on social media ads pushing the new app said: 'We hear you!'

10

Future Expected Margin

Stewart Kenny had always been explicit about it: bookmakers promoting the idea that everybody was able to make money from gambling were selling a lie. The value of gambling to the average punter is the thrill; the moments when the skin on your palms heats up and the sweat begins to form while your mouth gets that little bit drier.

That was what Paddy Power was selling. And although they did promote the rare events when a punter had a touch that led to a few thousand in winnings as a way of highlighting that the bookie doesn't always win, as they saw it they were really in the entertainment business. But the entertainment business is notoriously expensive. By the middle of the second decade of the 2000s, though, Paddy Power had it sussed. By the time a punter places fifteen bets on

FUTURE EXPECTED MARGIN

horse-racing or turns over €500 on their account, the firm has a strong knowledge of how much it could expect to win off them. A punter's past behaviour was processed through the FEM equation to predict the profit margin Paddy Power could expect to make from the customer in the long run.

This FEM system was refined over the years as the quants and data analysts filled out rooms in Power Tower with growing teams in specialized areas.

The system was kept secret for obvious reasons – it would be hard to sell the cheeky punter's pal image of the brand if everyone knew that their bets were being filtered through equations to determine how much value they were. Internal training documents from 2018 reveal the FEM of Paddy Power's customers. An analysis of 100,000 randomly selected customers showed that just under 14,000 would give Paddy Power 12 per cent margin on all their bets, slightly fewer would give 11 per cent, just under 12,000 would give 13 per cent, about 11,000 would give 10 per cent, just over 8,000 would give 14 per cent, just under 8,000 would give 9 per cent, and the rest would be spread out over other values.

The graph illustrating the FEM of the 100,000 punters goes up to the handful of customers who would lose 39 per cent of the amount they gambled with Paddy Power, but for those who might win the FEM

191

fades to nil after −3 per cent. That is because the FEM system is designed in part to restrict customers who bet on horse-racing and win in the long run.

To achieve this, the brains in Paddy Power's quants and risk departments developed an equation for 'shrewdness', which attempted to differentiate between people who might have a low FEM because they tended to back short-priced favourites, and those who were likely to beat the bookmaker in the long run. This was calculated based on the punter betting at a price which was more generous than the one offered when the race started – a sign that they were an intelligent gambler. If punters were deemed to be shrewder by the automated system, then the risk traders would give more weight to their business and might cut the odds of horses based on their future bets.

The power of the maths driving the risk at Paddy Power meant it could instantly take in variables such as the time the bet was placed, whether those bets were the best available price compared to other bookmakers, the FEM from past bets and the shrewdness factor, itself determined by a number of variables. In the long run, if racing punters were determined to have a negative FEM (that is, they might make money) and their account was in profit, then they were given a stake factor, which limited how much they could bet.

By 2018 this process had been largely automated. After fifteen racing bets or €500 turnover on racing, the automatic stake-factor algorithm had enough information to begin assessing a punter's value to Paddy Power. As all customers already had stake factors assigned, the new automated system started cleaning up the work of the human risk managers who had lowered or increased the factors in the past.

If the automated system deemed a customer needed a lower stake factor, which meant the punter was not able to bet as much because they might win, it would tag the customer's account with a note that said they should be assessed by the risk managers. The internal documents from 2018 show that 'warm' customers (deemed as such because their information could be of value to the business due to their closeness to the events they were betting on) were treated differently by the system and required a manual review. Risk managers would look out for traders in other bookmakers, people connected to the sport, or journalists.

No matter the equation in Paddy Power, public relations always had to be factored in. So when the algorithm found an account that should have been restricted because of a low or negative FEM, it would be overridden if that account belonged to a journalist who covered horse-racing. It was not unknown for connections of journalists, who were aware of this gap in Paddy Power's risk management, to get their own bets on through the intrepid hack's account.

A more regular source of frustration was the Eastern European and Asian bot networks, which engaged in arbitrage to take advantage of different prices offered by bookmakers and those available on exchanges such as Betfair. These arbitrage traders or 'arbsters' were guaranteed small profits by backing multiple horses in a race at odds from different suppliers. The amounts won on each bet were tiny, and it was too tedious to be worth most people's time until bad-minded punters realized they could get dozens of bets on at the same time by creating bots that opened accounts and placed bets at the odds. The risk management found ways to disrupt these bot networks when they appeared but they were a constant nuisance.

For real-life customers, the risk analysts drew up a list of indicators that would determine whether the racing-risk managers should clear large bets from customers. Gender, method of deposit, stake type, likely socioeconomic profile, length the account had been open, links to other people, username style and lifestyle of the person as determined by social media were all considered.

The internal training documents for the risk managers gave examples of a customer who would likely generate a high margin for the company. A female who deposits money into her online account in shops, has a betting pattern fitting others of her age and address, lives in the regulated Irish market, has had the account for six months, has no known links to anyone in the industry, has the username of a favourite horse, and whose social media reveals no links to any warm sources was listed as a good profile that would likely result in long-term profits of a reasonable degree if treated correctly.

A bad profile might be a male who deposits using a third-party payments system such as PayPal, has a sharp rise in stakes after a period of inactivity, is based in the UK, has had the account for two years, was recently flagged by a third-party cookie-tracking system known as Iovation, has a regular user name and whose social media search reveals Facebook friends with industry employees.

This profiling of racing customers was designed to prevent smart gamblers getting one over on Paddy Power, but the use of social media checks and third-party cookies was potentially a data protection issue. It also raised the question: if Paddy Power was willing to invest so much in technological innovation to root out winning customers and build profiles, which determined how much they could make from losers, could they not do the same for people who were spiralling into addiction?

11

The First Europeans

Across from the Chanel store on Flinders Lane in the middle of Melbourne's chic business district there is a basement restaurant called Coda where chefs with tattooed knuckles serve up French-Vietnamese fusion featuring Hervey Bay scallops, spinner crab and sustainable caviar. The wine list is 'interactive' – you have to talk to a sommelier to order a glass of red, or cough up the equivalent of €9 for a bottle of Japanese beer.

In 2009 Coda's owner, Matt Tripp, was celebrating his thirty-fifth birthday party. Like most millionaires at their own parties, he was being introduced to his own guests.

Among the crowd filling the industrial-chic eatery was a jetlagged Cormac Barry, who had just been on the other side of a deal that had made Tripp yet another fortune. Paddy Power had successfully negotiated a

€27.2 million deal with the young businessman for 51 per cent of Sportsbet, an online gambling company he had turned into a regional power since buying it for $250,000 in 2005. As is the way when Australians and Irish meet, the conversation soon turned to genealogy and it turned out that Barry's Melbourne-born wife's uncle Vincent Murphy was a close friend of Tripp's father, Alan. Barry was immediately rechristened 'Murph's nephew' and spent the night in easy conversation, enjoying the food, the drink and sharing stories about life in the trenches at Paddy Power.

In the hotel room the next morning he opened the book Breon Corcoran had given him when sending him to oversee the integration of Sportsbet into Paddy Power. It was a business management guidebook outlining how to ensure your success in the first hundred days in a new company. Its first two pieces of advice were simple enough: don't get drunk and don't talk about your old company.

But it didn't matter as within days Barry knew he wanted to stay in Australia. The Sportsbet deal was truly transformational: it was the biggest move Paddy Power had made and it was a steal at the price. It paid back the outlay within three years, but more than that it gave the whole management team a new confidence that they were leading a company that was about to take on the world. Paddy Power was going global.

Since Patrick Kennedy's appointment as chief executive Paddy Power had begun to outgrow its dominance of the Irish market, and while it was still strategizing its entry into Britain against the might of the incumbents and speed of the start-ups, it began to look for new international opportunities. One of his first hires was Andrew Algeo, who had worked at Goldman Sachs and as an investment manager for Irish billionaire Dermot Desmond. A champion yachtsman from the Royal Irish Yacht Club in Dun Laoghaire, Algeo took to the seas for his new employer as well, mapping out where there would be opportunities for acquisitions or to partner with other firms in countries where the state controlled gambling.

Algeo was an old Trinity College friend of Breon Corcoran's and had been looking for a new opportunity since leaving Desmond's International Investment and Underwriting. He wanted to find a fledgling e-commerce company that had big ambitions. Flicking through the *Irish Times* list of the top 100 companies in Ireland there were few that fit his aims, but Paddy Power stuck out and he recalled being impressed at the company's showings at investor conferences. 'Do things that the business does not do today,' was the brief Kennedy gave Algeo when he joined.

Algeo started a business-to-business arm that sold to the French government, the British Columbia government in Canada, Niké bookmaker in Slovakia and the New Zealand Racing Board. There were markets where Paddy Power could not operate for regulatory or commercial reasons but it could offer its services from the trading room and quants division in Dublin. The deals allowed the local gambling operators to offer sportsbooks themselves without any start-up fees, and avoid getting dragged into grey markets across Europe where online betting was taking place despite being unregulated. The business-to-business arm was also a clever way of generating more income from the risk and trading operation set up by Dermot Golden.

Once the traders in Dublin had drawn up the odds for an event, the prices were pushed out to the business partners with different margins applied to match the local operator's particular needs. So a 2/1 shot for Paddy Power's punter-friendly strategy could be offered as 5/4 in British Columbia where customers were less price sensitive, or evens (1/1) in France to take into account the local tax regime. It was a hub-and-spokes set-up that generated income for Paddy Power without exposure to the different markets or the cost of trying to launch in those regions, if the regulations permitted it.

Algeo understood that Paddy Power was a customer-centred brand though, and while his deals with other businesses opened up new revenue streams, a deal he concluded for Kennedy encapsulated the company culture.

In 2007 Ireland was awash with money and book-making was a vibrant industry with confident business owners competing with each other on price and product. But there was also a sense of solidarity in the trade, with the high-street rivals looking out for each other and acting as one when it came to regulation. All except for one.

The horse-racing industry was also enjoying the fruits of the economic boom and the advent of satellite sports, which meant it could capitalize on the broadcast rights to its events. Joe Lewis, the billionaire currency trader, was part of a new group called TurfTV, which bought the rights to races and intended to sell them to book-makers' shops, breaking the monopoly of the SIS and adding a new bill for bookmakers to pay every month. But Irish bookies felt they were already overpaying to the horse-racing industry and even Ladbrokes refused to take up the new service, which would give the book-makers a strong hand in negotiations. An annual levy on the bookies funded the upkeep of racecourses and provided prize money in return for the sport producing the fodder for punters to bet on. This was the deal that had existed for decades, so the efforts of the racing industry to charge the bookies more fees for the races they were already paying for was unacceptable. It was further complicated by the fact that the SIS, which had been the exclusive channel for streaming races into shops, was part-owned by Ladbrokes and William Hill.

As the stand-off rumbled on, audio-only coverage of races was streamed into shops while the bookmakers held rank, but behind the scenes Algeo had been sent by Kennedy to do a deal – Paddy Power would defect from the industry line. Alan Morcombe, chief executive of the Alphameric Group which owned Turf TV, met Algeo and they agreed a multi-million-pound deal that shot up Alphameric's share price by 19 per cent.

The real joy was in Paddy Power's head office, though, where they had managed to get a cut-price deal of around a million a year and hurt their rivals at the same time. Adverts were drawn up to say that Paddy Power was the only high-street bookie where punters could watch every race and the company's name was cursed by executives in Ladbrokes and William Hill and at every independent in Ireland.

It was a dirty thing to do, the competitors felt, but it was too good for Paddy Power to ignore: the deal would make them stand out in the eyes of punters, weaken the bigger brands' offering, and add strain to independents. Ladbrokes and William Hill had been sure that no second-tier bookmaker in the British high street would do a deal with Turf TV and that they would all demur to the bigger corporations' negotiating tactics. Paddy Power had just sixty-two shops in the

UK at the time but breaking rank had caused a major schism in the industry. Ladbrokes withdrew its £100,000 sponsorship of a handicap race at the Glorious Goodwood festival over the row with the industry, but it was replaced by Alphameric.

Meanwhile Paddy Power began its ad campaign to alert customers that they could watch every British race in Paddy Power shops – and rub their rivals' noses in it. Paddy Power, the spokesman, donned a top hat and tails to parade up the King's Road in Chelsea to promote the fact that punters could watch the Royal Ascot meeting in his brand's store but not in their neighbouring William Hill's. Former jockey Willie Carson stood outside the Hill's with a megaphone to tell the punters inside that they could watch the racing next door. They soon followed in line, with Ladbrokes, BoyleSports, the UK Tote and independents cutting their own deals over the following months.

Kennedy knew that the deal would be done eventually but Paddy Power's culture was such that he knew it would be a lost opportunity to wait for the rest to act. And so he engineered an outcome where his firm got the praise, a cheaper deal and was seen by punters as having their best interests in mind. But that was just for the shops. Paddy Power was by now a technology company as much as anything and the investment in risk and quants meant there was significant monetary value in the information its trading room produced. Under Kennedy it started to maximize its returns from this while supercharging the core business through rapid, relentless online growth.

Every couple of months Kennedy and Corcoran would get a call from a sporting organization or blue-chip company that sponsored a team, enquiring if Paddy Power would take a bet for them. The companies and clubs had signed contracts that gave bonuses depending on the success of teams in certain competitions. For example, if a county won the All-Ireland football championship its sponsor might be on the hook for bonuses and its marketing budget for the year would live in uncertainty until the third Sunday in September when the final is traditionally held.

A novel way of achieving some certainty for those sponsors and of tapping into the information Paddy Power was already generating was devised in 2008 with the establishment of Airton Risk Management, named for the Airton Road office in Tallaght where 'the shed' which housed the quants and rest of Paddy Power's team was located. This company was effectively an insurance broker that allowed sporting organizations and their commercial partners to hedge against their financial liabilities on the outcome of future events.

Its clients were fully confidential and Paddy Power did not sing about its existence either, as the idea of the punter's pal having such a strong grasp on the potential outcome of events that it would underwrite sports companies did not exactly sit comfortably with the slogan 'Winging it since 1988.' Two decades later Paddy Power was offering services to eliminate the risk of football clubs offering their players bonuses contingent on success in particular tournaments.

For example, a national rugby union paid Airton Risk €1.93 million to cover their possible bonus pay-outs of €7.7 million if they won the 2019 Rugby World Cup in Japan. Smaller deals were done with pizza companies and electric shops who offered free slices or vouchers for each goal scored in the 2012 European Football Championships.

Multinational companies that sponsor high-profile sporting teams are also clients of Airton Risk, and are hedging against bonuses in their deals with clubs should they qualify for major finals or win domestic tournaments. In 2019 more than €100 million was hedged through Airton Risk. If the Airton Risk managers had £5 million to hedge on an event, they could try to see if a Paddy Power trader would take a portion of it and then go to other bookies or even hedge funds and lay it off. It was an interesting and innovative business but it would not be the next brand under the Paddy Power banner to take the group forward.

*

All eyes were always on America in European gambling firms. Any potential entry into the market (which was highly regulated, to the point of prohibition in most states) was explored. Kennedy and his lieutenants had met with the pinkie-ringed owners of Las Vegas and other Nevada casinos and Native American leaders who owned betting establishments in other states as part of their reconnaissance on the US market, but nothing ever came to pass.

It was a much luckier set of circumstances that gave Paddy Power the edge in a lucrative new market, stealing a march on their British rivals and launching the Irish company as a global force.

In March 2008 a constitutional case in Australia was decided that blew the gambling market wide open in the country and provided the perfect opportunity for Paddy Power to go truly international. Betfair had sued the state of Western Australia for what it said were unconstitutional protectionist policies preventing it from offering its services in the province, despite it having a licence in the state of Tasmania. The case ruled that Internet and telephone-gambling operators were not confined to the geographic region of their licence and customers in other states could use them, even if state law forbade it.

Within weeks of the decision landing Algeo was on a flight to Australia arranging to meet with every gambling company that was operating online. The luck of the Irish was that Paddy Power was already well briefed on the Australian market before the deregulation because Cormac Barry and Barni Evans were both married to Australian women and had pushed their bosses to pursue opportunities in the market they saw on family trips as the perfect environment for Paddy Power to land on new shores. It had already launched in Italy, Spain and Germany with little success, but Australia, they promised, would be different.

After the Betfair case, Algeo expected to be part of a wave of European speculators looking to strike it rich in the outback; instead, the former investment banker informed his Dublin colleagues that he was alone on his voyage. 'I'm the first European they've seen,' he said cheekily, noting that there appeared to be little interest from Ladbrokes, William Hill or the other UK operators. 'They must be concentrating on opening a second shop in Bromford [a rough part of Birmingham],' he joked.

Soon after Algeo, Barry and Barni Evans met with the top four Australian online operators Sportsbet, SportingBet, CentreBet and IASBet. They were amazed at the figures and the potential for growth. Aussies are the biggest gamblers in the world, losing about €15 billion every year (compared to the Irish who lose €1.8 billion) making them the most prolific punters on earth

– followed by Singapore and then Ireland. That's the equivalent of €800 per person per year in Australian and €500 per person in Ireland.

Entering a large competitive market was a big gamble, but Kennedy and the board were eager to make their move. However, they needed to hedge their bets. Sportsbet was the top prize and Matt's father, Alan Tripp, and Grant Griffiths, a major shareholder and adviser to the Tripps, had made their own approaches for a European superpower who could help the Australian company reach their potential.

Barry had spent two weeks in the office of IASBet over Christmas 2008 looking into the figures and how it might fit into Paddy Power. The Tripps and Grant Griffiths, who also had a small stake in IASBet, agreed to meet the Paddy Power team in London. The plan was for Paddy Power to buy IASBet and then IASBet to buy a 51 per cent stake in Sportsbet so it could be easily consolidated into one entity.

By May 2009 Kennedy and Corcoran were on a flight to Melbourne with their wives to finalize the deal and celebrate in the city's great restaurants. The plan was to sign on the dotted line and fly back to Dublin for the announcement at the 2009 AGM on Thursday. But before they sat down to eat on Saturday night, Alan Tripp told the visitors over a drink that he was worried about the deal. Mark Reed of IASBet had realized he was the kingmaker in the deal and due to Paddy Power's requirement that he sell off a small bookmaker, which had taken bets from the US in previous years, he was kicking off.

What was supposed to be a celebratory meal turned into the start of strategizing that continued on into the Sunday with Algeo and Griffiths re-cutting the deal to be a straight purchase of 51 per cent of Sportsbet by Paddy Power. IASBet and Reed were out, for the time being at least. Griffiths and the Tripps agreed to sell 51 per cent of Sportsbet to Paddy Power – and the smarts on the part of the Australians was that they wanted a buyer who could supercharge the growth of the company in a short space of time and would then buy out the remaining stake at a higher market value in a few years. Kennedy and Algeo were impressed with how the Australians operated. It was a finely cut thing – Kennedy needed the announcement before the AGM so as not to delay the deal and the midnight flight from Melbourne didn't allow for much rest as he and Corcoran had to prepare the slides to present the proposal to shareholders.

In Dermot Golden's office in Tallaght, the rest of the management team waited for the flight to land at 7 a.m. still unsure of what sort of deal could be struck. There was some concern that they had lost an opportunity and would have to go back to the drawing board. And then, around midday, the arrivals strolled in and announced that the deal was done.

There was a buzz in the office. Kennedy, Corcoran and Barry believed they could build a company in Australia that would be as strong as the Paddy Power brand. Corcoran told Barry to get down there for a few weeks and get a feel for the place. Tripp would be staying on as chief executive but Barry would be the Paddy Power man on the ground. A deal for IASBet was finalized and Paddy Power landed in Australia as the market leader.

The difference between the management styles in Paddy Power and Sportsbet were as striking as the difference between the grey Dublin weather and bright Melbourne sun. Upon his arrival in Australia Barry needed to change his own management style to suit the laid-back natives. Paddy Power was about arguments, competition and pushing each other hard, but the Sportsbet crew wanted work to be fun.

Paddy Power had grown from an all-hands-on-deck culture into a more adversarial one where the intensity of the office was rising week to week. The constant drive for growth and new opportunities was invigorating, but it also became tiresome.

Down in Australia there was an opportunity to recreate some of that but with a more balanced approach to life outside the office; something rarely considered in Paddy Power at the time. Tripp believed in relationships and only hired people he trusted and the people they trusted. There was no recruitment process led by headhunters dragging the best candidates through three sets of interviews. There were few management meetings either – he ran the company on momentum and Barry needed to adapt to that.

The culture was laid-back but the business was serious. There were 93,000 online customers by the end of 2009, staking AU$450 million. This was a 40 per cent increase in online wagers in 2008 and further proof that Paddy Power could grow Internet gambling. Paddy Power bought Sportsbet outright in 2011 for AU$338 million in total, marking a stratospheric return on Tripp's original payment of AU$250,000. It wasn't a bad deal for Barry either, who joked that he convinced Paddy Power to pay a few hundred million so he could fulfil his dream of living in Melbourne.

With two years under Tripp, Barry had adjusted the Paddy Power formula to suit Australia. Barni Evans came down and took over the marketing for Australia as he had done with the entry in the United Kingdom at the start of the millennium. The marketing push and suite of new betting markets hooked into Sportsbet from Dublin were a new advent for Australian bettors and the competitors SportingBet and CentreBet struggled to match the new entity.

Barry and his team were using all the lessons Paddy Power had learned in the previous decade in a new market and the results were convincing. With Barry in charge this was to be the purest experiment for the new model of data-powered Internet gambling.

With Breon Corcoran and Peter O'Donovan working on the same systems in Dublin, Luke Rattigan employed a data-analysis approach to Sportsbet that allowed it to supercharge its growth.

Part of this included fostering a culture in the company that encouraged innovation and decision-making that would result in more customers, more products, more profits: growth, growth, growth. Outside business consultancies Korn Ferry, Human Synergistics and DDI were hired to give the management team a common purpose that could be transferred to the staff to achieve the brand's internal drive 'to give excitement to life'.

Powered by the quants team in Dublin, the products had more depth and breadth than the competitors could offer and could run 10,000 simulations per a match to generate all manner of bets on different outcomes on the more than 5,000 markets it offered every day.

The company soon became a magnet for highly educated scientists in Australia and Rattigan gave a speech at the World Disrupt Forum in Sydney in 2016 in which he boasted of the neuroscientists, econometricians, statisticians, doctors of machine learning, mathematicians and chemists who worked for the gambling company.

Rattigan said that Sportsbet was driven by the purpose of being 'gamechangers' and spoke of Elon Musk, the Tesla founder who was now selling services to NASA as part of his own space exploration project.

'While we are not yet at Elon Musk levels of innovation, we are still doing some pretty cool things,' Rattigan told the crowd of technology workers and business leaders.

'We have been on a journey with tech and data. As an e-commerce business, we have always had a significant amount of transaction data – what people bet on, how much they bet, when they bet, what device they use, etc. In fact, over the Melbourne Cup we processed more than 12,500 transactions per second,' he added.

Rattigan outlined how every interaction with a gambler generates data to be analysed and used to encourage more use of Sportsbet products. He illustrated how punters who set up the iPhone's system that enables them to use their fingerprint instead of a password generated three times more logins a month. He detailed how the company had used a technological workaround to get over the Australian law banning bets from being placed during live events unless they were done in person or by phone. The regulation was designed to protect shop betting and had the added benefit of slowing gamblers down. Sportsbet had enabled customers to select their bets on the app as normal and then input the selection over a phone call with an automated system, which did not require the punter to speak to anyone but simply used interactive voice-response technology to state how much they wanted to bet. It was a legal way of using the online app to place a telephone bet. He displayed images that showed the level of testing the gambling company did on the layout of its adverts for its mobile app and website to encourage people to follow through and open accounts. A simple yellow box in the top right-hand corner of an advert generated five times more people to click through and open accounts than similar adverts with the same main text.

Sportsbet and Paddy Power were using every trick of the trade available to them to ensure that they took advantage of the new digital tools that drove e-commerce platforms. Rattigan also revealed the sort of data analysis that had won O'Donovan and the digital marketing team in Dublin kudos with social media giants Google and Facebook. Paddy Power was ranked the seventh highest brand globally for social mentions during the 2014 World Cup in Brazil, behind

McDonald's in sixth place but ahead of Budweiser in eighth – not bad for a company that couldn't even trade in the United States. But Paddy Power was using the social media networks for more than brand building – it was a powerful conveyor belt of directly acquiring new customers. It generated clicks by causing outrage using a prank marketing campaign that tricked people into thinking swathes of the Amazon rainforest had been felled to create a clearing that spelled out C'MON ENGLAND. The controversy created headlines and social media chatter that fed into Paddy Power attracting almost 150,000 new online customers during the tournament.

The real-time targeting of the most profitable customers was refined to a science that made sure Paddy Power always got the return on its investment in digital marketing. While others employed a scattergun approach, Paddy Power was precise.

When the Australian operation came under Paddy Power's ownership its turnover was $1.8 billion and profit was $31 million. By 2015 Sportsbet recorded a $117 million operating profit in Australia for the full 2015 calendar year, up 54 per cent compared with the previous year, on a turnover of $4.19 billion, of which $3.85 billion was from online operations. In human terms, 3 per cent of Australia had a Sportsbet account. The Australian operation now accounted for 44 per cent of Paddy Power's profits, making it the single biggest source of profit for what was now a global giant.

This massive turnover and customer growth was powered by Barry and his team's firm grasp on the fundamentals of how to grow an online business. While Paddy Power had permeated the culture around sports in Ireland, and the United Kingdom to some degree, Sportsbet was absolutely dominating the Australian market as it opened up to allow more Internet gambling. Up until then Aussie punters had enjoyed few options for sports betting, usually limited to match results and tournament winners, but now they could bet on anything from the first player to be stretchered off in an Australian rules match to how long the summer drought would last in Melbourne.

Ken Robertson had migrated for nine months from August 2014 to help build the brand in the same politically incorrect, stereotype-goading manner that the Paddy Power brand had pushed. Australia has a strong connection to Britain and Ireland and the political incorrectness of the brand translated well. When Bruce (now Caitlyn) Jenner announced he was transitioning to a woman in 2015, Sportsbet opened a market offering gamblers 'the chance to have a punt on what name he/she will choose' and sent out a press release which included the line: 'Fair play to Bruce, it takes a lot of balls to em . . . cut off your balls.'

The expected controversy and criticisms ensued and a spokesman for Sportsbet issued a non-apology statement, saying that, 'If you did take offence, we obviously apologize. We didn't do this to put anyone off. We don't want to offend anyone. And it's not our intention. We bet on things like this. We bet on the royal baby's name. We see this as another scenario like that.'

This was straight out of the Paddy Power playbook and began a series of controversy-baiting adverts by Sportsbet, but the real marketing power of the firm would only be revealed in the hundreds of millions it spent to build its brand as the dominant one in Australian gambling.

A 2018 investigation by the Australian Broadcasting Corporation's flagship current affairs programme 7.30 found that Sportsbet paid $490 million in marketing between 2013 and 2018, with $62 million spent on Google, $19 million on Facebook, $43 million with the TCN-9 (the broadcaster of the National Rugby League) and $21.2 million with the Fox Footy Channel.

That is all part and parcel of advertising spend for online corporations, but more curiously the investigation also uncovered that Sportsbet had paid fees to Quantium, a data analytics firm that National Australia Bank supplies with de-identified customer transaction data from all its account holders. The company is part-owned by Woolworths and uses the NAB data to analyse spending habits for all kinds of sectors, including online gambling. A Sportsbet spokesman confirmed to the broadcaster that the company 'uses data and analytics to understand our market share and make informed business decisions'.

A spokesman from Quantium told the investigative journalists that it had actually ended its deals with gambling firms in 2018 'following an update to our data ethics and usage policy' and that it provided a 'high-level breakdown of the sports-betting market' that could not be used for individually targeted marketing. What the investigation did reveal was the sophistication of Sportsbet's approach to customer acquisition by blanket sponsorship deals with broadcasters and targeted social media and online advertising tools from Google and Facebook, all bolstered by in-depth profiling of the behaviours of potential customers. That was yet another example of how online gambling operations were in lockstep with the new data-fuelled tools and how this amounts to near surveillance of online consumers. Sportsbet had even advertised on dating platforms, paying $41,000 to Tinder and $10,000 to Grindr. Flutter declined to comment when approached prior to publication.

In the same way that potential customers' existing associations with media brands and football teams were leveraged by Paddy Power to break into the UK in the early 2000s, a similar strategy with affiliate marketing amounted to $111 million of Sportsbet's marketing spend. The beauty of these deals for the gambling firm is that they redirect followers of bloggers, tipsters and social media influencers to the gambling website and the affiliate that refers the new customer gets a percentage of the money lost through that account. Of course, what is not clear to the prospective punter who follows a tip from a blogger through the affiliate link to Sportsbet is the bare bones of the deal: the more the gambler loses, the more the 'tipster' wins.

In response to the revelations Samantha Thomas, an associate professor of public health at Deakin University who specializes in understanding the impact of gambling industry strategies, said gambling advertising warranted a similar approach to the restrictions placed on tobacco: 'What we had with tobacco – that was clearly incredibly influential in preventing the next generation of smokers – was a comprehensive framework that regulated all types of advertising.'

This was the kind of language that led to sharp intakes of breath in the boardrooms of gambling corporations. Sportsbet had been faced with accusations that it was preying on the Australian love of sport to entangle gambling with sport. The millions upon millions it spent on different marketing avenues around sport was testament to its efforts to link its products to watching live sport in the minds of fans, and the irreverent nature of its brand tone, which goaded politically correct sensibilities, gave the sense that it was an uncaring corporation.

Harsher regulation was looming as headlines about a public health crisis caused by gambling mounted, and the company knew it had to move. Barry had developed a reputation in the Paddy Power group as an executive 'who could see around corners' and Sportsbet launched its own ad campaign to temper the addiction issue.

The Australian Association of National Advertising had just issued a new code that prohibited gambling corporations from targeting children and young adults as part of a range of new rules for gambling adverts. Sportsbet's next ad campaign was one that no one would have expected from the company.

In 2015 the company spent $1.5 million on an advertising campaign aimed at helping customers to break down the psychological barriers that prevent compulsive gamblers from seeking help. The IT team had designed a system in the Sportsbet app that would allow customers to force the mobile betting app to block them from gambling for a set number of hours or days.

A blokey but serious advertising campaign accompanying the new tool aired during prime-time television including cricket coverage, the evening news, *Top Gear* and *The Big Bang Theory*. One ad showed an increasingly exasperated gambler watching sport in a pub with two pals. With a manly voice-over stating that 'good mates can see when their buddies need a break from the punt', the gambler tears up a beer mat, punches the air in celebration, then claws his nails across the table and falls off his bar stool. 'Righto, that's enough,' the voice-over says as the friend shows him how to 'take a break' for twenty-four hours by using the new option in his mobile app. 'Yep, good call!' the voice-over says encouragingly as the gambler relaxes and turns to his friends with a sigh of relief.

It was a simple but radical use of Sportsbet's technology and marketing prowess. It also allowed people who felt they were losing control to exclude themselves from gambling without having to explain to customer-service reps why they wanted their accounts closed. No other company had yet used their own advertising spend in this way to warn about the dangers of their own products, but Barry and Evans were facing increasing scrutiny from the regulators and politicians in Australia and wanted to show that Sportsbet was committed to a sustainable model. They were also among a small but vocal number of people in the group who were growing frustrated that gambling addiction was not being taken seriously enough.

The move to play up the dangers of gambling was controversial internally in the Paddy Power group but the board ultimately adopted a view that they were 'scared but supportive'.

The 'take a break' campaign worked up to a point. About 2,000 customers a month used the feature in the first year, giving Sportsbet cover in political hearings about the allegations that gambling companies were failing in their social responsibility. It resulted in an immediate hit to profits – as was intended – but by 2016 Sportsbet was reducing its marketing spend and the campaign's roll-out was stalled.

Stewart Kenny would later tell campaigners who were calling for reform of the gambling industry that this was the reason he walked away from the company he had co-founded and been the face of. He said he felt he was a lone voice in the industry looking to move towards a more 'ethical' model, as he called it, and that he could no longer work with the company if it was failing to promote tools that it had developed to protect addicts and compulsive gamblers.

But the warning signs that Paddy Power was not alive to the dangers of its own products had been there for years.

12

Tony10

The higher-ups usually only visited the trading room during the Cheltenham Festival when the buzz of the biggest week in Paddy Power's year electrified the cramped offices on Airton Road. Staff were gripped by fever as traders' and risk managers' screens filled with data showing the thousands of bets being processed every second while everyone watched the races on the televisions mounted on the walls around the room. The mid-March week was always high stakes for Paddy Power with millions spent on marketing and sweaty palms among traders who knew that a run of Irish winners could send the share price tumbling.

But this wasn't Cheltenham. It was a supposedly normal Thursday in June 2011 with a run-of-the-mill racing itinerary at Leopardstown, Yarmouth and Haydock. Nothing to get excited about really, so there was confusion among the racing trading staff about why manager Colm Sevastopulo's office was crammed with people from the other side of the building. Dermot Golden, the head of risk, looked tenser than usual. It was becoming increasingly clear that the visit from board members and other senior figures from the corporate side of the business was due to something serious. And it was.

Tony10 had gone missing.

Tony O'Reilly, the biggest gambler on Paddy Power's books, had been a figure of fascination among traders because of his massive stakes on an increasingly random range of markets from Norwegian women's football to obscure Eastern European tennis tournaments. Tony10's modus operandi seemed to be driven only by backing the favourite in the next event that was coming up. It didn't matter if it was televised or if the sport was covered in the Irish press – in fact it usually wasn't.

On some days Tony10's betting could account for more than half of the turnover on Paddy Power's sportsbook, more than any other single gambler in the company's client list, which was quite an achievement for the man they knew to be a post office worker with a modest home just outside Carlow town.

It was decided that alerts would be sent to shop staff with a picture of Paddy Power's biggest customer along with an order that they contact head office immediately if he was spotted in-store. Back in Tallaght, the IT staff were told to monitor his account for any activity, and anyone in customer service or any other department who got a call from O'Reilly was told to act normally and not to spook him in any way. Under no circumstances should anyone alter or erase his account – the Gardaí had served a search warrant.

The desks for traders were arranged in a square with so little room between them that if two traders pushed their chairs out to get up at the same time they might crash into each other. The rumours of what was going on filtered out fast.

As Tony10's reputation as a high-staking punter grew in the previous months, the fascination with him grew across Paddy Power and curious traders decided to search for the address on his account to see where he lived. This revealed a three-bed semi-detached house. It sat in the middle of a quiet cul-de-sac looking out onto a large green for the children of the young families who populated the Sandhills estate to play in. The saloon cars of the commuting families were parked in the driveways with smaller second cars pulled up on the verge of the path. The estate, just five minutes outside Carlow town, was typical of the type that had sprung up around Ireland during the boom years. And this is what was fascinating to the Paddy Power traders and risk managers gathered around the screen. The house was entirely unremarkable.

So how did the biggest gambler on Paddy Power's books come to live there? A guy punting tens of thousands in single bets, losing more than €164,000 in a 24-hour gambling session, and with an eight-figure turnover on his account, lived in a €350,000 house?

O'Reilly's own story was told in quease-inducing detail in the book he wrote with Declan Lynch in 2018, *Tony 10: The Astonishing Story of the Postman who Gambled €10,000,000 . . . and Lost it All*. It shows how O'Reilly began with a £1 bet on Patrick Kluivert to score first and for the Netherlands to win 2–1 against Argentina in the quarter-finals of the 1998 World Cup. Over the course of the next twelve years, O'Reilly falls into a brutal gambling addiction, stealing €1.75 million from his job as a postmaster with An Post and ending up in prison having lost everything – his family, career and that three-bed semi-detached house in the unremarkable estate in Carlow.

Here is that story from inside Paddy Power, based on interviews with people who were working at various levels of the company during the time of Tony10's activity.

The list of Paddy Power's highest-staking customers includes English Premier League footballers, Formula One drivers, race-horse owners, golfers, broadcasters, rugby players and blue-chip businessmen – basically the typical high-rolling client list of a major bookmaker. But from 2009 to 2011, at the top of that list was a post office worker.

By late 2009 Tony10 had achieved almost legendary status in the Paddy Power trading room. Here was a guy losing £10,000 to £40,000 overnight on streams of chunky bets on horse-racing in Ireland, England and America, first-goal scorers in UEFA Champions League fixtures, accumulators on Belgian cup matches, tennis matches, ice hockey and some €1,000 hands in black-jack and casino games.

Racing and sports trading are separated in Paddy Power, allowing traders with specialist areas of expertise to deal with their particular sport or game. The appetite for risk in these different areas is partly down to traders' individual tastes but is also part of the overall corporate strategy to limit exposure to winning bettors and increase the potential for profits off losing customers.

Tony10 was a losing customer in a way few others on Paddy Power's books even came close to, so the risk managers and traders talked about him regularly as his stakes increased. His gambling was so intense that it had to be removed from the performance reviews of traders as it caused such swings in their profit and losses on particular events that it did not give a fair reflection of how well they were pricing them. As one trading room insider at the time said:

> If a guy comes out of nowhere and is doing five grand in one race and ten grand in the next, and then putting five grand again on random football accumulators, you wanted to know who it was. There were the people with connections to racing or those you would guess were big football players or whatever, but Tony10's address was just some random village. We looked up his address and saw it was just your average house. The reaction was, 'What the fuck is going on?' but it was more curiosity than anything else. But look, everyone who was connected to risk knew it was a guy in a normal house with a normal job.

Flutter declined to comment when approached prior to publication.

For the most part of the early days of O'Reilly's gambling with Paddy Power the discussion amounted to little more than that: who is this guy and how is he betting so much? Little was known about him other than that his account was registered to the nondescript house in Carlow, which allowed some information to be gleaned from Google Maps and property websites that showed it was not the house of some multimillionaire.

Discreet questions were asked of traders in other betting companies if they knew about him, but O'Reilly didn't register with other bookmakers so it was initially presumed he might have got a lot of money in an inheritance, or maybe even won the Lotto.

The degrees of separation between people in Ireland are often so minimal that it seems that everyone knows everyone else in some way, and in 2009, while O'Reilly was falling further into his addiction and pumping hundreds of thousands of euro into Paddy Power, a junior sports trader recognized the man everyone was talking about. He was a postman of some sort, and he used to work in Scragg's Alley (a local pub in Carlow town where both the trader and O'Reilly drank) and he was a handy soccer player back in the day. These factoids painted the picture of a normal, humdrum life outside the massive gambling stakes, and only added to the intrigue within the trading room around Paddy Power's biggest customer.

When the corporate bigwigs crammed into the trading room in June 2011, O'Reilly's family and friends were searching the Wicklow Mountains, with the grim understanding that they might find his body. The sports trader who drank in Scragg's Alley took it upon himself to contact the owner of the bar – O'Reilly's best friend – to alert him to activity on the Tony10 account, which at least allowed the distraught family to know their missing son and husband was still alive. It is clear by now that Tony10's disappearance was linked to a €1.7 million fraud at an An Post branch in Gorey.

'Fuck. That must be Tony10,' was the nature of the conversation between the men who had handled his bets in Paddy Power's head office. The next day rumours spread in the office that O'Reilly had been seen in a shop in Belfast after attempting to collect cash for a docket with bets worth €10,000. The Northern Irish shop manager called his counterpart in the Gorey Paddy Power shop where the bets had been placed and the Gardaí were informed soon after of the wanted man's whereabouts.

O'Reilly's family rerouted their search for him from the Wicklow Mountains to Northern Ireland, and while crime journalists converged on Carlow town to cover the story of the postmaster who had stolen a fortune to gamble away, the newspaper articles were being passed around Paddy Power's trading room in Tallaght.

In the days following O'Reilly's arrest, Paddy Power the spokesman downplayed the idea that the company's online operation was awash with people blowing large sums of money on bets.

'Last year we took over 60 million individual bets,' Power told *The Sunday Times*, claiming that the average stake was €15. 'Of course you hear of the big losses and winners in the papers, but five-figure bets at Paddy Power are as rare as hen's teeth.' Power added that his company would only accept large wagers from customers 'with whom we have a relationship'.

What Power didn't say was that he was the man developing that relationship along with a team of staff whose role was to increase the turnover on high-staking losing customers' accounts and to stop them being poached by another bookmaker. Protecting the prized assets, in other words. When a technological snafu knocked PaddyPower.com offline in April 2011, Power himself called O'Reilly and assured him if he needed to have any bets on, he could do so through him personally. This was what you got as a Paddy Power VIP.

O'Reilly was an unassuming postmaster but Tony10 was a VIP – Paddy Power's designation for high-staking customers. Tony10 would not have been able to have such large bets if Paddy Power's risk systems had not ascertained first that he was likely to be a loser. The decision to assign him VIP status meant that his stake factor was increased to a multiple of what the average customer could win on an event.

For example, in a decent-quality Irish horse race Paddy Power will allow customers to win €15,000 or so on a single bet. So if the horse is a 3/1 shot, the maximum stake they will be allowed is €5,000. If that customer has shown some sign that they are savvy on racing, their stake factor will be cut to less than that, so they may only be allowed a few hundred quid, or in the case of some customers, they will be restricted to pennies. O'Reilly's stake factor was increased to forty, according to one insider at the time the Tony10 account was active. So he could bet 4,000 per cent more than the average customer on the basis that Paddy Power wanted to keep him sweet enough that he would not seek his gambling thrills with a rival.

Paddy Power the spokesman's phone call to O'Reilly turned out to be unnecessary as the website was live again by the afternoon and the prized punter could bet online through his account. The horrible mania of compulsive gambling on the very day of that phone call makes you wonder what would have happened if O'Reilly had needed to phone in his bets. Would the company have been able to answer to the nature of the bets it took from the post office worker on that Monday in April 2011?

Bets flowed from the Gorey post office's Internet connection through Tony10's account and onto the risk managers and traders' screens in Paddy Power's head office. O'Reilly and Lynch's book details the punts on Negeri Sembilan, a Malaysian football team, Balestier Khalsa FC in Singapore, Breiðablik Kópavogur in Iceland, Trenkwalder Admira in Austria, Kasımpaşa's under-20s outfit in Turkey, Belarus's national under-19s team, tennis players named Charalampos Kapogiannis, Daniel Muñoz de la Nava and Thales Turini, and a horse named Shouldhaveknownbetter.

Are these the bets of a man having a bit of fun and enjoying sports – particularly when these matches and races were not televised? Now consider that the sizes of the bets were €20,000 and €30,000 and amounted to a loss of €462,000 in a little over twelve hours. There was no phone call from anyone in Paddy Power the next day.

As part of the traders' curiosity about Tony10, a call had been placed by a staff member to a garda they knew personally about whether there was any criminal investigation into a man by O'Reilly's name in Carlow, and they were told that there wasn't.

The trading staff in Paddy Power at the time the Tony10 account was active said they didn't have any reason to believe he was stealing the money – and some didn't even consider that – though they now believe they should have been aware that the patterns of his betting indicated a compulsive gambler. It was clear that he was attempting to win certain amounts of money by adding odds-on favourites in events into accumulators. But this was before the company touted 'responsible gambling' initiatives and when the limits on how much a punter could lose amounted to how much they had in the bank.

Still, it was not as if Paddy Power as a corporation was not aware it was dealing with an individual who did not display the means to place bets of almost half a million euro on a Monday afternoon (Flutter declined to comment when approached prior to publication).

The systems of quants and risk coupled with the data harvesting of the technology that powers the Paddy Power online operation allowed for detailed analysis of customers. If analysts wanted to see how a new product such as a market on the number of yellow cards in a half of football was being taken up by customers they could pull up the data and see what types of punters were betting on it. Other customers like them could then be nudged to bet on that market too with targeted advertising, incentives such as free bets or a more prominent display on the website.

The staff at the company were not ignorant of gambling addiction or the potential for money laundering, but it was not part of the culture in the company at the time to focus on it too much for the rank-and-file workers. One insider with access to cross-company data put it quite succinctly, referring to the fashion in Ireland for working-class and social housing areas to have religious names in their addresses: 'Every so often you would pull up data and see that the most active customers in a market had addresses with the names of patron saints or Catholic priests in them. You had to think that there was something not right there. It might have been money laundering, drugs or addiction but you had the sense there was some level of misery going on.'

The main concern for risk managers, though, was not about addiction, but that O'Reilly would take them for a large chunk on one of his bets. This could potentially have affected their bonuses but was probably unlikely – such was the extent of O'Reilly's gambling that his bets had to be cleared with senior figures in the risk department.

In fact, one junior risk manager was assigned a late shift to specifically deal with the Tony10 account; to manually clear O'Reilly's bets as they came late into the night. While the rest of the staff would put their coats on and watch the 9.20 p.m. race with one eye as they headed out the door, one risk manager was required to stay behind and monitor O'Reilly's betting as some of the accumulators he put together would potentially result in pay-outs of more than €200,000. Even with the heightened stake factor this required clearance from a superior, though of course O'Reilly rarely managed to land his six-figure pay-outs and the bets were always cleared.

As the legend of Tony10 the high-staking everyman grew in the Paddy Power head office, his value to the company did too and was reflected by his treatment as a VIP, though it was remarked at the time that he was an extremely low-maintenance customer given the amount of money he pumped into the website. Other more seasoned and traditionally wealthy gamblers knew their worth to bookmakers and would take advantage of the offers made available to them, such as free tickets and nights out in executive boxes at high-profile sporting events. O'Reilly, however, only availed of an invitation to Paddy Power's executive box at the Aviva Stadium for the Europa League final between Portuguese sides Barga and Porto in May 2011 and the Dubai Duty Free Irish Derby in the Curragh on 27 June of that year.

By the end of the following week the legend of Tony10 came to a screeching halt as the staff handling his account were told by senior management that they should not close it under any circumstances – a strange request given that they had no intention of blocking out their best customer. But it soon dawned on them that all was not right. The IT team were told to keep an eye on any activity on Tony10's account and alert their manager. Gardaí were now involved.

O'Reilly had gone missing on Wednesday 29 June after being told that a routine audit of his post office was to be conducted that morning. Gardaí sent a notice to newsrooms around the country that there was a blackout on reporting of the missing postmaster, but within Paddy Power news of Tony10's disappearance was being passed around as office gossip. Then they just got back to work.

The week before Christmas 2012, O'Reilly was sentenced to four years in prison for stealing €1.75 million from An Post over a 14-month period to feed his gambling habit.

Judge Pauline Codd suspended the final year of O'Reilly's sentence because he had cooperated with the Garda investigation and had taken steps to address his addiction. It was not mentioned in court, but O'Reilly had also agreed to cooperate with An Post and its insurer Ace Insurance in attempting to get the money back from Paddy Power. He had been called to a meeting in a hotel room with his former employer and its insurer before his court case to discuss the matter, but there was no subsequent follow-up.

When asked the obvious question by journalists – will Paddy Power pay the money back given that it has now been proven to be the proceeds of crime – the only response given was: 'Paddy Power's policy is not to comment on any individual cases or on any investigation with which we have been involved.'

But they did pay it back, according to two people with knowledge of the board's decisions at the time who spoke to me on the condition that they would not be named. Patrick Kennedy wrote the cheque for €1.75 million and arranged a meeting with the chief executive of An Post, Donal Connell, to deliver it along with a non-disclosure agreement.

Ten years after he was caught, O'Reilly believes he got away easy in terms of his prison sentence. When I speak to him while researching this book in the summer of 2021 and tell him that Paddy Power paid the money back he says he doesn't know how to feel. He wonders if he might have got a shorter stint in jail, but he can't put into words the emotions he feels about the money being paid back in secret. However, he believes that if it was done publicly it would have shown that Paddy Power does accept responsibility for their role in what happened, even if it may have opened the company up to paying back the proceeds of crime in other cases.

It probably doesn't mean all that much at this stage of O'Reilly's recovery. Since leaving prison, O'Reilly has obtained a BSc in Counselling and Psychotherapy with Middlesex University and now works as an addiction counsellor specializing in gambling and internet addiction.

The publicity around his story and the success of the book about his addiction, which has been optioned for a Hollywood film, have made him a well-known figure in Ireland and in gambling industry circles abroad. When he was at an event in Malta, where many gambling companies are based for tax purposes, he got word that a former Paddy Power employee had wanted to speak to him.

Susan Lawson trained Paddy Power staff at the time of Tony10's activity and was head of responsible gambling operations when she left the company in 2018. At the event in Malta in 2019 O'Reilly got on well with her. She told him how much she was affected by his story and frustrated by the industry response to addiction so they discussed the possibility of starting something in the field together.

It never came to pass and O'Reilly joined up with Barry Grant, the head of Problem Gambling Ireland, to lobby against inaction on addiction problems and provide counselling services. Lawson introduced O'Reilly and Grant to Stewart Kenny in 2019, and the man who had lost it all at Paddy Power received an apology from the man who founded the company. 'Listen, we got it wrong. Sorry,' is what O'Reilly recalls was said.

Kenny had agreed to meet O'Reilly and Grant to discuss fundraising for their problem gambling charity and O'Reilly expected to face a multimillionaire gambling tycoon displaying the trappings of his wealth, so he was taken aback by Kenny.

'I had to laugh when he pulled out these reading glasses that were the sort you get in petrol stations. The man is worth I don't know how many millions and he pulled out these glasses that cost about €4,' O'Reilly remembers. 'There were no airs and graces about him, he was down to earth, which made it easier to be forgiving. A few other people who worked there at the time have reached out to apologize but no one who is high up still will do that. They still just see it as a money-making machine.' Flutter declined to comment when approached prior to publication.

O'Reilly accepts the apology from Kenny as an individual but he doesn't believe Paddy Power or the wider industry has done much to address people in similar positions as he found himself in during the depths of his addiction. Through his counselling practice, O'Reilly is at the coalface of gambling addiction and still speaks to people in their late teens and early twenties who have found themselves in debt or with suicidal feelings because of their gambling:

I don't harbour any resentment or blame towards their failings with me, but I do for their failings with everyone else since. At the time with me, maybe problem gambling as an issue wasn't as prevalent as it is now, but we're ten years on from that and I'm still seeing the same cases. That's the bit that gets to me. That's the bit that keeps me talking about it. I can take what happened with me on the chin. But when a lad who is coming in now tells me that the same thing has happened to him – that just shows me that they're only paying lip service.

13

Vanguard

Ronan Wall braced himself before showing Patrick Kennedy the figures.

Wall is a handsome, red-haired Corkman who had been head of operations in Paddy Power after joining as a founding member of Matchbook, a sports-betting exchange. Kennedy had assigned him to a new project in 2013 that would be a departure for Paddy Power, and like nothing ever attempted in the gambling sector before. It was to be called the Vanguard Project. Wall had crunched the numbers with the data analytics team and presented what it was going to cost the firm to Kennedy: 15 to 20 per cent of profits.

That would be the price of making Paddy Power's digital gambling operations free from the scourge of misery caused by sucking in money from addicts. In the wake of Tony10, the senior management at Paddy

Power could see that the public perception of betting and gambling corporations was shifting towards a view that would result in closer regulation. As with many new Internet services, there was a distrust and distaste for online gambling that was intensifying with the revelation that an otherwise respectable member of society had fallen into an addiction which led him to steal more than a million euro.

Paddy Power had grasped technology, data and marketing by the balls to create the conditions that enabled Tony10 and was raking in millions every month from people in similar states of vulnerability. Kennedy's view was that if Paddy Power's teams of statisticians and analysts could find the patterns in how people gamble and nudge them towards betting more, then surely if they could spot when the conditions were forming for people to spiral out of control, those same teams might be able to protect those people. Project Vanguard was an attempt to reverse-engineer addiction.

Wall had been working on Paddy Power's existing responsible gambling programme, which had just followed the light-touch standards of the rest of the industry of only stepping in when a punter had extremely heavy losses in a short period of time, but Kennedy wanted a much more pro-active system to be put in place. Stewart Kenny was also supportive of the plan, and others on the board and in the management committee believed it would be good morally, and also fend off more intense regulation from the government.

The gambling industry in Ireland was happily self-regulated and as the biggest brand Paddy Power knew they would face the brunt of media and political criticism over their practices, so they should act first to show they did not want problem gamblers on their books. Wall sought the input and expertise of Professor Jeffrey Derevensky, a co-director of the International Centre for Youth Gambling Problems.

Derevensky is a forceful scientist who was spearheading research into what he said was an epidemic of problem gambling among young people, facilitated by the new easy access to 24/7 online operators such as Paddy Power. Derevensky travelled to Power Tower from McGill University in Montreal to hear from Kennedy, Wall and the rest of the Paddy Power management council.

He was not like other academics who doled out certifications as part of paid consultancy with gambling corporations, but he was open to working with Paddy Power, though he indicated that if he didn't think the outcome of the project was worthy, he wouldn't sign off on it. Paddy Power's legal team had him sign a non-disclosure agreement in any case, from which he has never been released.

The only public utterance about the Vanguard Project did not refer to the name, and was in the company's annual report to shareholders in 2014 where Derevensky said: 'This research is congruent with Paddy Power's commitment for leadership in the harm minimization of its customers and provides an excellent example of the types of practical research that can be used to enhance its Responsible Gambling program.' Project Vanguard was spread across the departments of operations, online, quants, compliance and marketing, to give it a global view over the entire Paddy Power group.

In 2013 gambling addiction had just been included in the *Diagnostic and Statistical Manual of Mental Disorders* as a disorder similar to alcohol and drug addictions. It was still poorly understood generally and especially within the gambling industry, where workers grossly underestimated the prevalence of addicts using their shops, websites and apps. But the people working in Paddy Power's online operations knew that the data they were seeing about e-gaming players was evidence that there was something serious going on for many people. In fact, when Project Vanguard began the general estimate of what problem gamblers in Paddy Power's customer base contributed to profits was around 1 per cent, or maybe 2 per cent if you gave a more liberal definition.

The 15 to 20 per cent figures shocked them. They related to people who could be categorized as problem gamblers and those who were underage and gaining access to the website. This scared the hell out of those involved (in fact a later study by the Centre for Social Justice found that this figure may have been an under-estimate, and stated that 25 per cent of profits come from addicts).

As Vanguard's data started to play out, it showed that the percentage of Paddy Power customers who could be classified as exhibiting addictive behaviours was about 1 per cent, which was in line with the popu-lation prevalence. It was the amount that they were contributing to the company's coffers that shocked. Project Vanguard reverse-engineered addiction by analysing all the customers who had closed their accounts and cited problem gambling as the reason. A model was built using the data of the patterns of gambling over the lifetime of those accounts.

It showed that it was not just losing large sums of money that foretold a descent into addiction. Many were depositing higher amounts than their usual top-ups, and winning, then increasing their bet sizes as their winning racked up. It also showed that many younger gamblers had closed their accounts and cited addiction concerns, but they were in fact not sticking out as high-staking losers – they were actually just spending huge amounts of time on the website, pushing small stakes around on bets from the morning to late at night. This caused some in the Vanguard group to pause for thought; perhaps addiction to gambling was not just about the loss of money, but the loss of time. Éamonn Toland, who was head of Dial-a-Bet and went on to be a president of the US operation before leaving to work as a consultant for other firms looking to establish in the US, believes now that there is enough data to identify addiction at this level but that the industry is too nervous to confront the issue of obsessive behaviour when it does not relate to large losses.

The model that deployed in 2013 was based on the initial customers who had closed their accounts over addiction and when it was applied to all active customers it began pulling out about 50–100 people with potential problems a week. The responsible gambling team first tried to determine if there was any publicly available information on these customers that could help give some insight into whether or not they were gambling within their means.

This was an imperfect method, to say the least, especially as many people posted pictures of themselves on holidays on social media, enjoying fancy cocktails or bottle service in foreign nightclubs, not when they were in supermarket uniforms. It was decided that when people triggered the different issues identified by the model, there should be a soft intervention such as an email alerting them to the increase in activity on their accounts and alerting them to cooling-off periods, or self-exclusion tools, which allow punters to block themselves from accessing their account for a set period.

The most serious breaches identified in the model would result in requests for information to show that the customers could afford the amounts they were betting on the website. This was an awkward and unscientific process, where customers could complain of the intrusion into their personal lives by the cheeky-chappie bookmaker, or refuse to engage in the process altogether.

If Paddy Power simply closed the account, it would probably just lead to the person identified as an addict moving on to another gambling firm, so the interventions were designed with language not to scare them away. There is a marked difference in telling someone you think they've had enough to drink for the night versus accusing them of being an alcoholic, so the emails sent to people identified as losing control of their gambling were crafted to be friendly rather than alarming.

The internal fanfare around Project Vanguard also got the staff talking about what responsible gambling was in a way they hadn't before.

As one staff member at the time put it, when Tony10 was active it was clear he was gambling recklessly but there was no real system around how to deal with that:

> It would be like if calling someone a muppet became a racial slur, and you'd been going around for years calling people muppets with no idea about that. We just were not aware of it as an issue [in 2011] in the same way we would be today. That's not an excuse, it's just the way it was in the industry at the time. You were fascinated by an account like Tony10 but you didn't know what it really meant.

Vanguard was also a way of legitimizing Paddy Power as a socially responsible company when Kennedy was bolstering the staff at the company and trying to attract the best and brightest to the firm. Young graduates, or the best techies, were less likely to dedicate themselves to a company if they believed it was part of a social ill.

Paddy Power was maturing under Kennedy from a pesky outsider in the United Kingdom into a major player, and along with William Hill and Ladbrokes it was part of an industry attempt at self-policing called the Senet Group, which was working out the best way to manoeuvre through the increasing scrutiny of online gambling without being hit by harsher regulation or sin taxes – those levies placed on specific activities deemed harmful and designed to reduce demand. Around the time of Project Vanguard, the 'When the Fun Stops, Stop!' marketing slogan was being devised to be included in an industry-wide advertising campaign.

As the Vanguard model was deployed it gave Paddy Power an increased understanding of their customers' behaviours. If a punter appeared on a report, their betting was analysed against their past behaviours. So if a customer who only bet on horse-racing suddenly started backing darts players late at night, that could be seen as an indication that they were chasing losses, or if the darts world championships was being televised it might just mean they were having a punt in the pub.

This idea of measuring gamblers against their norm was clever, as it allowed Project Vanguard to catch people who might not be betting massive amounts but might be increasing their bet sizes in a way that needed intervention. So if a customer usually only wagered in fivers suddenly went to €100 they could be caught in the same way as a guy who typically bet €100 and started placing €1,000 bets.

Depending how much a gambler was changing their behaviour they could be targeted with an automated response. Some would be emails, or they could get an overlay on the website alerting them to the responsible gambling tools the company wanted them to use, and they could also be directed towards addiction services. Kennedy was supportive of Vanguard but was concerned that if Paddy Power led with their chin on promoting it, it would look like self-praise and would lead to increased scrutiny of the downside of the industry.

Kenny had seen what was happening in Britain to the bookmaking industry's reputation and he wanted something to be done in Ireland so that the fun of betting would be seen above everything else – and politicians would still be happy to pose for photos backing themselves in Paddy Power shops at the start of general election campaigns. In a way, the efforts to curtail the level of addiction among customers could be seen as following John Corcoran's vision that Paddy Power should be concerned with long-term strategies over short-term profits, such as the easy money from problem gamblers.

Project Vanguard was initially pushed internally with great fanfare. It definitely changed how Paddy Power handled people who it identified as problem gamblers, but it was watered down as the drive for more innovation and market share continued. As a high-level response to the problems addiction posed it reordered how the company thought, but for those dealing with customers day to day in risk management and trading it was soon forgotten. It is still common for people who trigger Vanguard's alert system to be made VIPs.

Its success is hard to quantify: Vanguard was certainly ahead of its time as other gambling companies and third-party firms have since started working on similar models using machine learning to identify problem gamblers. But whatever Project Vanguard did achieve, it never resulted in a drop of profits of 15 per cent to 20 per cent and Paddy Power would continue to attract addicts.

14

Spot the Stallions from the Mares

Imagine the commentary. It is a late September night in the Parc des Princes, Paris and England are facing Tonga in their last pool game in the 2007 Rugby World Cup. The unfancied Pacific Islanders are in possession.

'Tevita Tu'ifua does well there, and the ball is inside. Ephraim Taukafa carries it forward, he's held up, but Tonga are still in possession . . . Taukafa to . . . Seilala Mapusua to . . . Eliota Fuimaono-Sapolu to . . . Paddy Power.'

That was the kernel of the idea. Imagine the craic of a player lining out among the Tongans with the name Paddy Power. The idea was first floated in the weeks before the 2007 tournament when it was being reported that Tonga might have to sit out the tournament because they couldn't afford the expenses associated with it.

Every day in Paddy Power's marketing department

began with a morning conference similar to the one held in newsrooms at papers and broadcasters to decide on the day's coverage. When the news that a team in England's group was in financial turmoil, Barni Evans, Ken Robertson, Paddy Power and Perrin knew they had the marketing equivalent of a scoop. They got in contact with the Tongan Rugby Federation through rugby player Epi Taoine, who had spent much of his career in England and had even been a housemate of Perrin's during a spell when he was based in London.

The pitch was simple. Paddy Power would cover the five-figure costs of Tonga's tournament in exchange for the team being a vehicle for the betting company to hijack World Rugby's premier event without paying the huge sums official sponsors such as Heineken, Coca-Cola, McDonald's, Toshiba and other multinational super-corporations had paid.

The marketing department was being built on increasingly attritional guerrilla marketing as a way to insert Paddy Power into anything and everything its potential customers might be watching. In 2003 Robertson was delighted when the company branded the hurleys of Wexford's Damien Fitzhenry and Paul Codd and Cork's Seán Óg Ó hAilpín, much to the disgust of the suits in the Gaelic Athletic Association's headquarters. Paddy Power was told to relinquish its corporate box in Croke Park and was accused of using the players as 'pawns' for its own aims. The three players were funded to the tune of €750 each, which was paid back in spades as the controversy around the branding, which breached the association's regulations, lasted for weeks and became a talking point about the increasingly commercial nature of the amateur game.

Since then, Robertson and the rest of the Paddy Power team were always looking to create mischief – the internal term for ambushing events, upsetting vocal minority-interest groups and generally making light of world events.

The opportunity to ambush the 2007 Rugby World Cup was too good to pass up. As part of the sponsorship Taoine changed his name to Paddy Power by deed poll the week before the tournament and a hairdresser was sent to the team's Montpellier camp to dye their hair green before the match with England. But World Rugby had other ideas and Taoine was not permitted to use his new name for the tournament because he had already registered under his previous name – even the hair dye had to be washed out after the tournament officials intervened. 'The Tongan team and officials have agreed that they will appear normally and have been reminded of the importance of the match,' said a statement confirming the hair dye being shampooed away. Instead Paddy Power bought a couple of thousand bright green curly-haired wigs and handed them out to fans around the stadium. These were enthusiastically donned by those who had turned up to support anybody but England.

For the less than £100,000 in sponsorship, the £42.44 fee for changing a name by deed poll and the price of some plastic wigs from a joke-shop supplier, Paddy Power had inserted itself into the build-up of an England World Cup match in a way that no other sponsor had.

But not everyone was happy. Was it not humiliating for a team – on the biggest days of the players' careers, representing their proud island nation – to become marketing gimmicks for a bookmaker? Perrin recalls one article in particular, published in *The Guardian* in September 2007, which accused Paddy Power of demeaning the Tongans. The sports writer Barry Glendenning condemned Paddy Power for turning the Tongan team into a 'freak show' and eviscerated the stunt. He said Paddy Power had made 'eejits' of the Tongans and displayed a 'dead-eyed opportunism at the expense of a poverty-stricken rugby team willing to do anything, no matter how demeaning, to please the sponsors'.

Paddy Power had expected some blowback but for Perrin this was only proof that the Tongan prank had worked. 'One of the rules in the rulebook was that if you piss off a small vocal minority that is not in your customer base, then so be it. That Tongan stuff was 95 per cent, almost universally, liked, but there are always snippets of negativity.'

Perrin and Taoine are still friends, and he has visited Tonga where the former rugby player is now a member of the royal family through marriage. After Perrin left Paddy Power he made a touching documentary about Pacific Island rugby and some of the social problems in the nations, but what he gained from the World Cup stunt was an insight into how far Paddy Power would push things. This was amplified by the rivalry between the people in the marketing departments to be the ones to come up with the next big stunt, and to push it further than the previous one. Robertson was usually the instigator of the big-ticket stunts. He was the soul of the mischief department, constantly making off-colour jokes and coming out with the most outrageous ideas in the morning conferences. But it was not just the marketing department who pushed things forward. Patrick Kennedy, as chief executive, valued the mischief department as an integral part of what made Paddy Power successful and allowed them to retain an edge that other corporate bookmakers did not have.

There was a paranoia in Kennedy, inherited from Stewart Kenny, that Paddy Power would lose its soul by becoming just another corporate bookmaker. The company had always mocked its competitors as 'corporates who take bank holiday Mondays off'. In fact, Paddy

Power always preferred to launch attention-seeking offers and marketing campaigns on bank holiday weekends as they knew their rivals' decision-makers would not be working and by the time they responded Paddy Power would already have won all the credit. That top-down culture of making the brand as outrageous and controversial as possible led to Paddy Power becoming one of the most recognized companies in Ireland and England, far outstripping its rivals in betting and being closer to Ryanair or Guinness in brand recognition despite spending a fraction of their budgets on marketing.

The Paddy Power marketing team was made up of Paddy Power customers. They were mainly men in their twenties, thirties and forties who had grown up on lad mags and Internet humour, so if they thought an idea was funny, the chances were Paddy Power's customers would too.

By 2010 gambling advertising on television was no longer prohibited, triggering a splurge of spending around sporting events by the likes of William Hill and Ladbrokes. But Robertson, Christian Woolfenden (the head of marketing, who had been talked out of a job with Bacardi in Miami by Kennedy and Kenny on a night out in Dublin that included a test to see if Woolfenden could taste the difference between four different types of gins) and the Paddy Power team wanted to use the new opportunity not just to get Paddy Power more closely associated with live football or golf;

they wanted to push the idea of the company as an entertainment brand.

The marketing team knew that if they could get complaints into the Advertising Standards Agency, they were on to a good idea. The more complaints, the more publicity; the more publicity, the more customers. So they cynically gamed the outrage, ensuring it was ratcheted up enough to have the Paddy Power name in the spotlight for as long a time as possible.

The ads were designed to aggravate those vocal groups who were outside Paddy Power's customer base. One of the most successful was the first, featuring Tiddles the cat and the Blind Wanderers FC five-a-side team. The 30-second spot showed Tiddles running onto the pitch only to be apparently hoofed into a tree by a player mistaking the feline for the ball. A suited man then walks over to the shocked player waving a wad of cash. 'Paddy Power can't get Tiddles back. There's nothing we can do about that,' he says soberly before cheering up and adding: 'But we can get you our money back with our money-back specials. Check 'em out at PaddyPower.com.'

The ad immediately drew complaints, as Robertson had intended, but it was on the right side of the regulations and had been approved by a pre-screening group to go on air. The ad did genuinely upset some people who said it was likely to promote animal cruelty (though Tiddles was shown unscathed at the end of the spot) and was demeaning to blind people. Perrin remembers that when the letter from the Advertising Standards Authority arrived announcing that it had started an investigation but that the ad could remain on air for the time being, the media-buying companies were contacted and told to find programmes to feature the ad which would generate more complaints:

> We wanted to get the complaints up basically, from people outside our target audiences. We were running TGI reports [an industry term, Target Group Index analysis, which finds the customers best suited to a brand] to find what programmes had the biggest amount of cat lovers so we could then run the spots on them. We would then run spots on shows that indexed well against cat lovers, so I supposed they would have been the same spots Whiskas the cat food was going for. It was all very much a case of harmless fun with people who are not in our target audience, as long as the target audience absolutely loves it.

The ad featuring Tiddles' unfortunate wander onto the Blind Wanderers' Astroturf would have generated no more than a few dozen complaints if it wasn't for the targeting at cat lovers. Instead it generated such upset that it was the most complained-about ad of 2010, causing more objections to the watchdog than the second most complained-about content: the first-ever television spot in Britain advertising abortion services. The advert was the subject of a letter-writing campaign by anti-abortion groups but even that could not generate as much upset as Paddy Power's ad.

Pissing off cat lovers was one thing, but Robertson and Christian Woolfenden, the chief marketing officer, always wanted to do more to embed the Paddy Power brand into the public consciousness.

In 2014 it began running an innovative 'We Hear You' campaign where Paddy Power responded to social media comments from its customers, but of course what was heard was only fuel for the politically incorrect ideas to be shoehorned into a new feature. The first television advert for the campaign opened with a Facebook comment, 'Can't wait to see some beauties at Cheltenham Ladies Day' before an excited voice-over declares: 'We're going to make Ladies' Day even more exciting by sending in some beautiful transgendered ladies. Spot the stallions from the mares.'

Beginning with a woman smiling at the camera while a hot-dog vendor holds up a flopping, foot-long Frankfurter sausage behind her, a series of brief shots of people at a racetrack are shown while the voice-over tries to guess their gender. In the big punchline of the ad, the camera pans slowly down a woman while the voice-over guesses 'woman' then hesitates as the camera shows the woman is holding a dog for a brief second before the shot switches to another woman walking out of the male toilet. 'Dog, I mean man!' the voice-over declares.

It caused an instant storm online, with LGBT groups claiming that it was harmful and discriminatory. Paddy Power the spokesman responded to media requests and seemed shocked at the outrage. 'A bit of mild-mannered fun,' was how he described it, claiming the company was surprised that it had received such a hostile reaction since it had actually been pre-approved for broadcast. He rejected the suggestion that the ad mocked transgender women, saying it depicted transgender women as 'beautiful'. 'You wouldn't be able to tell the difference,' Power added.

This fake naivety was one of the mischief department's cleverest tactics. The ads were of course designed to needle the politically correct and cause offence at the expense of transgender people, but by feigning confusion at the inevitable reaction it ensured Paddy Power was positioned on the same side as the people who saw it all as a joke. 'We Hear You' indeed. The mischief department's old foe, the British Advertising Standards Authority, was damning in its assessment of the advert. It upheld complaints from interest groups and the public that the suggestion that trans people could be segregated into the equine genders of stallion or mare trivialized a complex issue and objectified a minority group in a serious way. The ruling said that:

> By suggesting that trans women would look like men in drag and that their gender could be speculated on as part of a game, the ad irresponsibly reinforced those negative stereotypes and, particularly by framing the game in a way that involved a member of the public who had commented on Paddy Power's Facebook page, the ad condoned and encouraged harmful discriminatory behaviour and treatment.

The ad is still viewed by alumni of the mischief department as their finest work, particularly as it got a reaction that ensured the bookmaker was being talked about in every newspaper and on every radio station as the Cheltenham Festival began.

Kennedy and the executive team accepted the controversy and backlash around the company not just because it was good fun, but because it drove new online accounts and the number of bets placed with Paddy Power – the two metrics that really mattered, much more than the number of complaints an ad got.

15

Vatican City to Pyongyang, via Tallaght

Rory Scott was in Paddy Power's Hammersmith office when a hired fixer with connections to the highest officials in North Korea got word back: Kim Jong-un wants bows and arrows.

It was September 2013 and the gambling company's recently hired head of PR had spent most of his first year working at Paddy Power on an outlandish plan to have Dennis Rodman lead a team of former NBA players on a trip to the most isolated country in the world as part of a marketing stunt. Having immersed himself in the murky bureaucracy of the Democratic People's Republic through the local fixer and an international crisis group, he was becoming used to absurdity in his working life. But Scott knew he should alert his higher-ups to this latest development.

He sent a one-sentence email to Ken Robertson, Paddy Power's advertising director – and head of mischief – and Christian Woolfenden, the global marketing officer at the stock-market-listed company. 'Send £50,000 for bows and arrows,' Scott wrote, only half joking.

This is the world of Paddy Power's mischief department, which was formed in 2011 as part of the marketing team, where attention-seeking is a virtue beyond all others and not being talked about is a high crime. Since the mid-1990s it had always played close to the line, which usually entailed starting on the far side of the line and walking back towards acceptability. The company's attention-seeking stunts celebrated every shade of eejitry and crudity imaginable and delighted in the finger-wagging from opinion pages and special-interest groups.

Even still, the prospect of sending arrows to a country named by George W. Bush as being in the 'axis of evil' was something that required pause for thought. In an effort to bolster the claim that the marketing stunt involving the UN-blacklisted country was for 'basketball diplomacy', Scott had been cleared to provide funding for the building of courts and provision of some branded basketballs and jerseys in Pyongyang.

Kim Jong-un, however, had recently inspected the North Korean archery team and deemed their equipment sub-par for his aim of defeating South Korea in the upcoming Asian Games. He wanted to change his demand from asphalt courts, hoops and nets to tungsten-tipped arrows and high-velocity bows.

Scott had joined Paddy Power in September 2012 after a summer spent with the Coca-Cola-sponsored travelling roadshow bringing the eagerly awaited Olympic torch to cities, towns and hamlets around Britain ahead of the London Games. One of the stand-out incidents on that tour was when a man was spotted with a bucket of water in the crowd as the Olympic flame passed through the Leeds suburb of Headingley. He was tackled by security before he could douse the torchbearer and the flame moved on to nearby Potternewton. Life was different at Paddy Power and Scott was now considering whether he should attempt to source Olympic-grade archery equipment for North Korea and if that would fit with Paddy Power's brand.

Marketing men are by their nature mythmakers and bullshit artists so it is not clear how much effort was put into securing arrows for a despot's archery team. Rumours within the company were that the equipment was sourced but that the logistical problems of getting bows and arrows into North Korea scuppered the plans, while others say it was never given serious consideration. Some say they were actually sent through South Korea, which was hosting the 2014 Asian Games and where the North Korean archery team would be training. No one would comment on the record for fear of reopening a rare time in Paddy Power's history of attention-seeking where it bit off more than it could chew.

In any event the North Korea trip did result in a reprimand from the United Nations Security Council. A panel of experts initiated an investigation and in March 2014 a report found that the five bottles of vodka given to Kim Jong-un by Rodman, and Paddy Power's gifts of a bottle of Jameson, Waterford Crystal decanter-and-glass set and Mulberry handbag for Kim's wife were on the banned list of items. Thankfully for Paddy Power, the UN officials in Ireland who investigated the gifts said that the total value of the goods at $3,000 was low and that it constituted a 'once-off' arrangement so was not considered commercial trade. But it did cause a sweat in Power Tower.

The organizers of the gifts for the North Korea trip had been unaware that they might breach any rules, but the fact that using a hostile despot to push the Paddy Power brand had caused international consternation was lapped up. It was a singularly unique event in the company's history but the North Korea trip perfectly encapsulated the sort of 'two fingers to the politically correct' stunt that earned Paddy Power the status of one of the most recognized brands in Ireland and the UK.

Over the years deliberately controversial ads had led to the company being accused of being racist, blasphemous, ageist, transphobic, classist, ableist, and of making light of animal abuse.

These complaints were usually met gleefully by those in the mischief department and there was no concern of wider reputational damage to the business. They knew Paddy Power customers were not the type to get upset by letter-writing campaigns from special interest groups, and they definitely didn't share the sensibilities of opinion writers in broadsheet newspapers.

A pope's power to capture the imagination of punters was a long-standing obsession in the Dublin offices of Paddy Power, stretching back to the 1994 posters about John Paul II signing for Glasgow Rangers. So when Joseph Aloisius Ratzinger resigned in February 2013, Scott and the firm's eponymous spokesman were on flights to Rome within hours to generate attention towards their brand in the middle of the world media's coverage of a historic event.

The only idea they had with them was a crude one Robertson had given them before they left Dublin: 'Money back if the Pope is black.' It was exactly the sort of punchy, devoid-of-nuance slogan Robertson had pulled out of brainstorming sessions since joining Paddy Power in 1999. Paddy Power was unapologetic in its attempts at 'newsjacking' serious current events to push its own brand. Its strategy was driven by 'talkability', a marketing term for the practice of seeking to insert a brand into public consciousness by making it part of a wider discussion, so their customers are talking about them to each other. Paddy Power's brand building was an effort to make sure its customers talked about its stunts to their pals when having a pint. The louder and lewder Paddy Power's newsjacking was, the more likely it was to become part of the news itself.

The mischief department had become masters of this method and a pope resigning was sure to be a big talking point. So when Robertson noticed that two front runners to replace Pope Benedict XVI were black, adverts were drawn up showing Nigerian Cardinal Francis Arinze as a 6/1 shot and Ghanaian Cardinal Peter Turkson at shorter odds of 4/1.

Power and Scott treated St Peter's Square like the betting ring of a greyhound track, displaying a signpost of odds in view of news cameras from around the world. This was actually Power's second time standing in the middle of the Vatican hawking odds on the next Pope, as he had done the same in 2005 after John Paul II died. That time he was the subject of BBC coverage and attracted the attention of security guards, who quickly moved him on, so in 2013, Power was determined to make an even bigger splash.

The PR men were again embraced as a soft news

distraction and this gave Paddy Power ample opportunity to fill the void. Robertson and Scott were searching for a way to retain the curiosity of the international press when they remembered the pictures in the newspapers the week before of Dennis Rodman and Kim Jong-un smiling courtside at a basketball game in Pyongyang as part of a Vice Media documentary. It was the sort of absurdity that Paddy Power's marketing had thrived on and Scott was now standing in the middle of Vatican City, on the phone with Rodman's agent Darren Prince, trying to convince him to send his star client from Pyongyang to the Holy See.

Prince is a no-nonsense New Jersey sports agent who overcame opioid addiction to build a multi-million-dollar business in the strange area overlapping celebrity and sport. Alongside Rodman and other NBA stars, his client list has included disgraced professional wrestling icon Hulk Hogan, legendary stuntman Evel Knievel and Baywatch star turned Playboy model Carmen Electra. Prince agreed a hefty price to send Rodman to the Vatican, but with the condition that 'he's gotta have a limo'. Scott's parents live in Rome so he was familiar with the terrain and attempted to use his local knowledge to dissuade Prince from this demand, given the fact that any car bigger than a Fiat Punto is not particularly suited to narrow, cobble-stoned streets of the 2,000-year-old city. 'He's gotta have a fuckin' limo,' Prince said as a punctuation to the conversation.

The next day Scott stood outside Rome airport beside a white stretch limousine, waiting for Rodman to arrive. The affable English lad with soap-star good looks has designer stubble and loosely slicked-back, sandy-coloured hair. When one colleague from the Irish office was having dinner with Scott on a working trip to London a waiter approached their table and asked if he would be interested in having a drink with a woman at the bar who looked like a model neither of them could recognize at the time. That was the sort of thing that happened to Scott.

Scott was only in Rome because the rest of the marketing department was working on Cheltenham, the biggest horse-racing event in Paddy Power's calendar, and his ability to speak Italian might be useful for getting out of a bind with the *polizia*. His language skills were of little interest to Rodman, who completely ignored Scott on the ride from the airport to the hotel, sitting in silence beneath sunglasses, headphones, base-ball cap and scarf wrapped around his hung-over head. The only sign that there would be any break in the silence at some stage was a knowing look to Scott from Rodman's bodyguard and right-hand man Christopher 'Vo' Volo, a former MMA fighter.

After a shower and a meal at the hotel, the 6ft 7in

NBA legend and cultural oddity finally agreed to hear the briefing for why he had been hired to promote a gambling website in the middle of the Vatican while cardinals had begun the process of electing a new Pope – a scenario about which Rodman had an unnerving lack of curiosity. 'Three things you need to know, Dennis,' Scott said with enthusiasm. 'We're called Paddy Power. We've got an offer on: money back if the Pope is black. And you're going to be asked who you've got your money on so just say "Cardinal Turkson of Ghana".'

'Yeah, yeah,' Rodman responded in a sub-baritone drawl that did not inspire confidence in his interest in the election of a new supreme pontiff, Bishop of Rome, and chief pastor of the worldwide Catholic Church. But that didn't really matter as Rodman was swapping his own baseball cap for one bearing the Kelly-green font of the Paddy Power logo. He insisted, however, on wearing a garish floral sport coat, which largely covered the T-shirt he was given with the company's insignia.

Back into the limo and off to the media throng at the Vatican, Scott felt like he was settling into his new job. There was now a day's worth of media lined up around the most tabloid-magnetic basketball player in history, which was sure to maximize brand exposure for Paddy Power. The first interviewer of the day from the internationally syndicated Reuters TV approached Rodman and asked why he was in Rome. 'Uh, Paddydotcom. Online poker,' Rodman barked.

Newswires carried stories of a frenzy around Rodman in St Peter's Square as pilgrims and reporters swarmed around him. 'It don't matter what colour this other guy is, I mean if he's black or white, yellow, green, who cares? As long as he goes out and does what he has to do and blesses people,' Rodman declared.

Reuters reported that rather than pumping the betting for Cardinal Turkson as he had been asked to do as one of this three briefing points, 'He admitted he did not know the names of any of the candidates for Pope but said his favourite pontiff had been John Paul II, who was "just so cool".' With Rodman and Power (the spokesman) all over the international media it actually worked out despite Rodman's failure to stick to his brief. The remit was to create as much chatter around the company in as many unlikely places as possible. It didn't really matter that Rodman was the main story so long as Paddy Power was a subplot.

Over an expense account's worth of champagne after pizzas and steaks with Rodman later that evening, the naturally curious Scott asked about the North Korea trip he had just returned from.

Rodman had been roundly denounced in the American media for referring to the despot as a 'friend for life'

and 'awesome guy' and he genuinely couldn't understand why it was such a serious issue.

Having spent the night before reading about the
geopolitical importance of the trip, Scott enthusiastically gave Rodman a history lesson about the significance
of his audience with Kim Jong-un. Jimmy Carter, the
former US president, Eric Schmidt, the executive
chairman of Google, and Ban Ki-Moon, the former UN
secretary general, had all recently visited North Korea
without being granted an audience with the Supreme
Leader. In contrast, Rodman was given five-star communist treatment with a palatial hotel suite, dancing girls
at state banquets, an endless stock of cigars and a seat
beside Kim at the basketball game. Rodman still
displayed no recognition of the enormity of what his
trip meant but shared that Kim Jong-un thought the
exhibition match featuring the Harlem Globetrotters
'sucked'.

The wheels in Scott's head started turning and he
began to think about a 'peace game' between a North
Korean team and former NBA players. He thought
a venue in a neutral country would work best –
Zurich maybe, or, better yet, Dublin. A Paddy
Power-hosted match between North Korea and the
USA in the basketball arena in Tallaght, the suburb
of the bookmaker's first headquarters, would be
perfect. Rodman was on board with the idea, and

seemed to genuinely believe in the benefits of 'basketball diplomacy'.

When the buzz faded the next day, so too did Scott's belief in the feasibility of the idea, but he couldn't quite shake thinking about it. He began researching the Ping-Pong Diplomacy of the 1970s, which used table-tennis to thaw hostilities between China and the US, leading to the lifting of an embargo and resulting in the visit of Richard Nixon and Henry Kissinger to Shanghai in 1972.

Back at his office in London, Scott had almost dismissed the North Korean idea as too preposterous but he mentioned it in passing when he was giving a debrief of his Rome trip to Woolfenden over a pint in a pub. 'You need to tell Stewart,' Woolfenden said. 'Phone Stewart right now.'

Scott's last contact with Stewart Kenny had been a phone call during the Rome trip when word got back to Dublin that Scott had been put in the back of a police van as the authorities tried to stem some of the frenzy around Rodman. Scott didn't let on to the police that he spoke Italian so he could hear them talking about how they had no reason to arrest or charge him and would have to let him go after half an hour. When he shared this detail with his boss Kenny erupted in high-pitched laughter and in his nasal Dublin accent roared, 'Amazing! Brilliant!'

Scott regarded Kenny as 'the evil genius' behind the Paddy Power brand. He had overseen the likes of Robertson in ensuring it continued to push the boundaries and eat up column inches even as it became a stock-market-listed corporation, with shareholders' sensibilities to consider. Still, Scott was somewhat apprehensive about calling Kenny and suggesting they put part of the marketing budget into a deal with North Korea. But he made the call, introducing himself as the guy who had been put in the police van in Rome, and outlined his idea, asking if this was something that should be considered.

He was met with a familiar laugh and proclamation. 'Fucking brilliant. Amazing. Let's do it!'

Scott circled back to Prince, who was equally enthusiastic about the idea. His 'yes', however, seemed to have the punctuation of the 'ka-ching' of a cash register. Prince made the introduction with Michael Spavor, a Canadian consultant who promotes investment and tourism in North Korea and who had organized the Vice trip. He also gave details to contact Charles Smith, a former NBA player who had been organizing exhibition matches around the world and would be able to corral a team of retired pros who might be willing to take part.

Outside of Rodman and Prince, Spavor would be one of the few people to know what Paddy Power had planned. The mischief department's so-called guerrilla-marketing campaigns have been partly responsible for new laws being introduced around large sporting events to ensure official sponsors with much larger budgets are not ambushed. This just meant Paddy Power's marketing department had to find new ways to insert the brand into the public consciousness. Woolfenden (who now works for the tobacco firm Philip Morris International) described the mischief team at the time as being like a 'black ops team on nitrous oxide'.

Ideas and early stages of organization about the mischief department's bigger plans were kept secret from the rest of the company. It was not unknown for complaints to arrive from colleagues in other departments after controversial stunts, with Paddy Power employees saying they disapproved of them. But of course this was usually taken as a sign that the stunt had worked.

Erecting a 50ft-high 270ft-wide Paddy Power sign in the style of the Hollywood Hills landmark on the hill overlooking Cheltenham race track during the biggest racing festival in the world without the organizers' knowledge, as had been done in 2010, was one thing. Liaising with the North Korean regime was a different matter.

On the phone to Spavor, Scott made clear that it

would be a real match – not an exhibition – in Dublin or Zurich with former NBA players led by Rodman, and that it should be presented to the sports ministry as Rodman's idea. Kim, Spavor said soon after, was on board but wanted to discuss it with Rodman again.

In an effort to calm his conscience and square off any accusation that the company was ignoring the starvation and state violence in North Korea, Scott wrote to Dr Daniel Pinkston. He explained to the Seoul-based director with the International Crisis Group, an NGO committed to preventing and resolving deadly conflict, what was planned, and asked tentatively, 'Are we crazy?'

Pinkston had written an opinion piece in *The Guardian* following Rodman's trip to North Korea, which was also founded on the idea of basketball diplomacy. In the article Pinkston set out a caveated support for the idea of using sport to bridge the gap between North Korea and the West. The former US Air Force man said that while Rodman might well be used in state propaganda, it was also likely to be subversive because it showed Kim Jong-un embracing something different. 'If Kim wants basketball diplomacy, I say: "Bring it on!"' Pinkston wrote.

He even agreed to come on board to take some of the flak that was sure to come from the media and politicians if the idea went ahead.

On 3 September 2013 footage of Rodman walking down the steps of a plane in Pyongyang with a Paddy Power-branded baseball cap atop his head was broadcast by DPRK state television along with a denial from Rodman that he was being sent to secure the release of Kenneth Bae. Bae was a Korean-American missionary who had been detained in North Korea since 2012 after being sentenced to fifteen years' hard labour on bogus charges of attempting to overthrow the government. Bae had written to his family and complained that he was suffering serious medical problems, including going blind and other complications of diabetes. Back in Dublin Paddy Power the spokesman told the UK media that the stunt was 'all a bit bonkers', adding for clarity's sake that the bookmaking brand did not 'endorse or support' the most oppressive and abusive regimes in the world.

Word soon got back on whether Kim Jong-un was willing to set a team of North Korean basketball players against a group of former NBA All-Stars. There was a fear that the despot would be reluctant to do so given the fact that the average height of a North Korean man is 5ft 5in and the level of basketball skills is somewhat below the NBA. However, the regime was game for the match but with its own idea of how it would play out. Kim didn't want to watch a broadcast from Zurich or Dublin – he wanted it to be in Pyongyang and he wanted it to be on his birthday, which was just five months away.

Scott was emailed a folder of pictures of Rodman, showing him on a grand tour of the hermit kingdom. In one picture the five-time NBA champion sat smiling on one of Kim Jong-un's white horses. Another showed Rodman screaming into a microphone as a string quartet looked on, less than charmed, behind him. Other pictures showed that Rodman had had unprecedented access to Kim, sipping beer and smoking cigars with him: Scott saw a photo of both men embracing, smiling widely, and one with Rodman in his branded Paddy Power cap sitting alongside the despot watching a basketball game and drinking orange juice. The pictures were watermarked with a cartoonish 'confidential' logo and shared within Paddy Power. Scott began to believe that the 'peace match' would really happen.

The international media picked up on Rodman's return trip but Paddy Power's sponsorship only got a reference in most news reports below details about the detention of Bae.

After visiting North Korea with Vice, Rodman had used the diplomatic channel of Twitter to call for Bae's release. 'I'm calling on the Supreme Leader of North Korea or as I call him "Kim" to do me a solid and cut Kenneth Bae loose,' he wrote.

When asked about it before returning to North Korea

for Paddy Power, Rodman said he would broach the issue with Kim: 'I will definitely ask for Kenneth Bae's release. I will say, "Marshal, why is this guy held hostage?" I could try and soften it up in that way. If the marshal says, "Dennis, you know, do you want me to let him loose?" and then if I actually got him loose, and I'm just saying this out the blue, I'd be the most powerful guy in the world.'

But when asked if he had done so by a throng of reporters waiting for his touchdown in Beijing airport following the trip, the man touting basketball diplomacy was markedly undiplomatic. 'Guess what? That's not my job to ask about Kenneth Bae. Ask Obama about that. Ask Hillary Clinton. Ask those assholes,' he said in comments reported around the world by Associated Press.

While Rodman was fielding questions in Beijing airport, Scott was hastily arranging a press conference in the Soho Grand Hotel on West Broadway in New York City to announce the 'Paddy Power Dennis Rodman Invitational'. Aware of Rodman's erratic time-keeping from the Rome trip, Scott, Power and Robertson arranged for him to get a late flight the night before the conference and put him up in the luxury Gramercy Park Hotel so that the temptation of the New York nightlife wouldn't be so alluring ahead of the nine o'clock briefing to the world's media the next morning.

With Rodman safely ensconced in his room, the three PR men went for a few drinks of their own and the surreality of what they were planning began to dawn on them. But there was no time to dwell on it as they had to be ready in the conference room at 8 a.m. As the clock ticked towards nine, Power, Robertson and Scott became increasingly nervous that Rodman would be a no-show or, worse, show up in an unfit state. At five to nine, the doors to the conference room swung open and in walked Rodman clutching a bottle of vodka and staggering from the night before, which had clearly blended straight into the morning now. Power, in his typically cheery fashion, wished Rodman a good morning. 'Fuck you!' Rodman shot back in a tone that was hard to discern through the slurring.

They noticed that the bottle in his hand was Original Bad Ass Premium Vodka, Rodman's own brand of alcohol. The basketball player began threatening that he wouldn't take part in the press event unless his alcoholic beverage (RRP $29.99) was on display. He went to place it on the table beside the sign bearing his name and the Paddy Power logo, when Scott snatched it away. 'Absolutely no fucking way! We're a gambling brand, we can't have any association with alcohol!'

With the world's media waiting outside for the announcement of what was billed as diplomatic and sports history in the making, Scott had instinctively reacted to British and Irish advertising standards that prohibit betting and booze being linked in commercials.

Due to some sort of divine intervention, the press conference went off without a hitch. With a bronze bust of Rodman in front of him, Paddy Power read out the decree from the DPRK Ministry of Physical Culture and Sport outlining that it had sanctioned the match: 'The ministry of sports DPR Korea invites Mr Rodman and his colleagues to return to DPR Korea to organize a basketball tournament including the best players from DPRK and a team of twelve former NBA players to be held in January 2014.'

Rodman said that Kim had offered the use of the main sports arena in Pyongyang and would ensure that its 95,000 seats were filled. Dr Pinkston handled the tricky questions and ensured the diplomatic weight of the event was covered, while Power gave his spiel.

'It all began when the Pope resigned – the first time in 900 years. That took us to Rome where we met Dennis Rodman and he told us about his incredible idea for a basketball tournament involving the North Korean team,' he said, selling the event and giving newspapers a detail too good to leave out. *The New York Times* actually used the line as the introduction to their news story about Rodman's return to North Korea ahead of the match.

PUNTERS

All that was left after the press conference was for the members of the mischief team to go out and get thrashed drunk (without Rodman) and worry about the logistics of organizing a basketball match under the most oppressive regime in the world. In five months' time.

16

Nobel Prize, or an Oscar?

'We might win the Nobel Prize here, boys,' Scott told his mischief department colleagues, with his tongue only partially in his cheek. That or a Marketing Society award, anyway.

Since getting the nod from the DPRK officials and Paddy Power's top brass that the match would go ahead, Scott had become increasingly invested in the idea that the event might have a more powerful impact than just generating the sort of controversy that might cause a few thousand people to sign up to PaddyPower.com. There was no shortage of self-belief in the company's marketing department generally but the North Korea episode supercharged everything. This was taking the PC brigade-inflaming, newsjacking agenda to a whole new level. But the mischief team believed it might also lead to something even more important: a diplomatic breakthrough.

Dr Pinkston's argument that Rodman and Paddy Power could succeed where Obama and the Western status quo had failed was persuasive. Rodman wanted the match on Kim Jong-un's birthday to be a US versus DPRK exhibition for the first half but for the players to mix together for the second half. Pinkston said this would be an important message for people in North Korea that they could trust and cooperate with outsiders. With this in mind, the Paddy Power delegation landed into a snow-covered Pyongyang in the middle of December 2013 on a recce mission ahead of the historic basketball match.

Along for the ride with Scott was Colin Offland, a documentary filmmaker who had done some ad work for Paddy Power in the past. Also on board, rather curiously, was Professor Joseph Terwilliger. A statistical geneticist associated with Columbia University in New York and the University of Helsinki, Terwilliger had a lifelong interest in North Korea since listening to short-wave radio broadcasts from Pyongyang and signing up to a propaganda mailing list.

Fortuitously he had the winning bid in an online auction to play a game of 'horse' with Rodman in 2013, the summer after he returned from the Vice trip. The unlikely pair of the tuba-playing geneticist and cross-dressing NBA icon struck it off by talking about their mutual interest in North Korea. (Terwilliger's presence on the trip and his in-depth knowledge of North Korea led to some suspicion among the Paddy Power contingent arranging the excursion that he might be a spy, but that was shaken off as too much absurdity even for this strange episode.)

Terwilliger had actually introduced Rodman's agent to Michael Spavor, who was Paddy Power's man on the ground dealing with the bureaucracy of gaining entry into the DPRK for foreigners while also attempting to secure permission to film the trip for a branded documentary and liaise with the sports department about the match itself.

Spavor runs the Paektu Cultural Exchange in China, which promotes tourism in North Korea and is the type of business that requires a good level of trust from a regime that still runs gulags. Spavor had contacts throughout the North Korean administration going back to his first visit in 2001. He is a friend of Kenji Fujimoto, Kim Jong-il's former sushi chef, who has provided some of the very few leaks from inside North Korea. Spavor had then developed close ties to Kim Jong-un's regime after he succeeded his father in 2011. Unfortunately Spavor could not be interviewed for this book because at the time of writing in 2021 he was in a Chinese prison; he has been since 2018 in apparent retaliation for the arrest in Canada of Meng Wanzhou, a prominent Chinese technology executive, at the request of American prosecutors.

Before the trip in December 2013 Spavor said he was concerned about the presence of Offland. The BBC had just shot an undercover investigation in the country and the Vice Media footage had also been badly received by the DPRK. Kim Jong-un's officials were on high alert about being embarrassed by the Western media again but Paddy Power's view was that the trip was worthless unless they could document it. Spavor's reticence about having a film crew on the trip caused a bit of consternation between Power Tower and the DPRK Ministry of Information, and when the prospect was raised by the bookmaker of the whole match being pulled if it could not be filmed, the visas were issued. Not a bad bit of diplomatic brinkmanship for the mischief department.

In line with protocol, Spavor said that Scott would need to bring gifts for the Supreme Leader as part of the journey, so Robertson arranged a bottle of Jameson and a Waterford Crystal decanter-and-glass set. Scott dispatched his mother in Rome to buy a dress for the Kims' newborn daughter Kim Ju-ae and also picked up a Mulberry handbag in the airport for Kim's wife Ri Sol-ju. It appeared that all the bumps in the road had been navigated.

But while Scott's mother was shopping for a baby dress, Kim Jong-un was dealing with a more delicate family matter.

South Korea learned through its intelligence agencies that Jang Song-thaek, Kim's uncle, had been edited out of propaganda films. This is never a good sign in a communist regime. Soon after this revelation made world news, footage was broadcast in North Korea of the four-star general and president of the Presidium of the Supreme People's Assembly being arrested at a Workers' Party meeting. The new young leader of North Korea, who had taken over in April 2012 after his father's death in late 2011, was starting a purge at the same time as his officials were liaising with Paddy Power. News reports in the West circulated that Jang Song-thaek had been stripped naked along with five aides and locked in a cage with 120 starving Manchurian hunting dogs as his nephew watched. On 9 December, two weeks before the Paddy Power trip, North Korea confirmed Jang Song-thaek's execution but in an altogether more civilized fashion. 'No, no,' Hyon Hak-bong, the North Korean ambassador to Britain told Sky News with a smile on his face, 'he was shot to death.'

Paddy Power's stunt was already being questioned as being an easy tool for North Korea to use in propaganda, but it now seemed seriously ill-timed. During discussions about pulling the plug on the whole thing the point was made that this may have rather dire consequences for the people on the ground who had been organizing this not as a Paddy Power marketing exercise but as a birthday celebration for the Supreme Leader. 'What the fuck have we got ourselves into?' was the general consensus in Dublin and London. The fact that the trip had been sanctioned by North Korea's Olympic Committee was some comfort to those about to travel as this granted them a degree of diplomatic power, which the regime was unlikely to risk damaging. The decision was taken to go ahead with the December trip to Pyongyang, while in Dublin, Paddy Power's involvement in the promotion of the basketball match to be held in Kim Jung-un's honour was reviewed.

On the first night of the delegation's trip North Korea's minister of physical culture and sports, Kim Il Guk, held up a lobster claw not much smaller than the size of a human fist, took a bite and urged the Westerners to return home and tell their countrymen how lavishly citizens in the Democratic People's Republic eat.

Right, we'll be sure to do that, Scott thought to himself at the absurdity of the situation as the effects of the first of many shots of Soju (the potent Korean liquor, which ranged in strength from 15 per cent to 55 per cent depending on the host's predilection) swirled around his brain.

This was the first of many signs, both subtle and

explicit, that the North Korean regime planned to use the presence of this unlikely delegation for both domestic and external propaganda. Scott had wanted to play the match with Paddy Power-branded green basketballs but this was rejected by the DPRK sports ministry and it was just one sign that the mischief department were not in control of the proceedings.

Offland had been to North Korea as a tourist and knew the lie of the land but was still surprised at how tightly every aspect of the trip was controlled. When he asked a minder if they could shoot footage of children playing on a snowy hill, he was told that no, any such footage would have to be arranged and staged. Offland pushed back and suggested that if the minders wanted to give the world a better impression of the country then this was a genuine way of doing that. He was met with a firm no. Other documentaries have highlighted the absurdity of this level of control on footage which leaves the country but Offland had a more pragmatic approach. 'I suppose I make adverts so I do the same kind of thing – I sort of had to respect that.'

The filmmaker was actually the one to approach Paddy Power about shooting the trip because he was excited by the idea of the bookmaker's involvement as much as the basketball diplomacy idea. Scott and Christian Woolfenden were already talking to production companies about documenting the trip but Offland's enthusiasm for the project won them over – not least because he believed Paddy Power was as interesting a participant as Rodman or Kim Jong-un. Offland was intrigued particularly by Paddy Power's belief that they would be able to place hoardings around the court in a country where the only form of advertisement is state propaganda. What he calls the 'concoction' of the mad bookmaker, out-of-control basketball legend and repressive despot was what he wanted to film.

'You take Paddy Power out and it's just not as interesting,' Offland told me in 2021, having continued to work with the gambling firm since Pyongyang.

Much of what Offland was allowed to film that December was propaganda. A trip to a hospital was notable for the lack of patients in the wards, which was explained by an official who said that this was because North Koreans were healthy. It was then that Offland and Scott noticed that the plastic wrapping was still around the plug sockets and the medical staff's livery was immaculate. The hospital had never been used.

The surreal atmosphere of the week-long trip was heightened by the fact that most of the visiting party had been living it up for almost every moment of it. Shots of Soju were downed almost continuously during the ten-course banquets that they endured every evening. Rodman augmented this with his own intake throughout the day and was becoming increasingly difficult to manage.

While Scott had flown in with aspirations of a Nobel Peace prize, the logistics of his role brought him back down to earth. Rodman was refusing to wear the branded caps Scott had brought with #HoopsNotNukes embroidered on the front – the social media call to action, as it is known in PR circles. Instead, Rodman sported a cap advertising Cheetah Gentleman's Club, a strip joint in New York where the NBA star had recently held his fifty-second birthday party. Thankfully he followed protocol by removing it when he bowed down every time he passed one of the many portraits of the Supreme Leader.

Offland's finished 2015 documentary, *Dennis Rodman's Big Bang in Pyongyang*, shows a peaky-looking Scott alongside Rodman after a night of Soju at a banquet held by the North Korean sports minister. Rodman chomps on a cigar and picks a squad of North Korean players while the PR man turns to the camera and attempts to talk up the chances of a DPRK basketball team against former NBA players.

'I tell you, these NBA folk have got their work cut out. Some of them are going to be a little bit podgy and a little bit slow. These guys look very nimble and quick, it's going to be very interesting,' Scott says, bigging up the prospect of a close match, before

Terwilliger interrupts with the rather unhelpful and obvious 'but the NBA guys are taller'.

Paddy Power didn't care if the match itself was a freak show. Back in Dublin, however, the review of the event was casting an increasingly harsh light on the company being a ringmaster in a circus celebrating a brutal dictator's birthday. Paddy Power did not enter into an arrangement with the North Korean regime naively. The marketing team knew that it was using a state that kept its citizens in poverty under the threat of violence to boost the brand recognition of a gambling company, but as the match drew nearer the stakes got higher.

Diplomats mentioned to Daniel Pinkston – who was talking to them as part of his role with the International Crisis Group – that back channels of communication, which had been closed by the North Koreans since Kim Jong-un assumed power in 2012, were beginning to reopen. It was also indicated to Spavor that if the match went well, Kenneth Bae's release could be considered.

It wasn't unknown for Paddy Power to act with humanity alongside its efforts at self-promotion. Just two months before the North Korean trip, Robertson had overseen the launch of the 'rainbow laces' campaign by working alongside the gay rights charity Stonewall to send rainbow-coloured laces to every professional footballer in the UK.

With homophobic slurs still commonplace on terraces and the lack of a single professional player in the United Kingdom feeling comfortable enough to be openly gay in any of the top leagues, the campaign was well received. 'Paddy Power can't change that we're shameless in seeking publicity,' the press release accompanying the campaign said. 'But we can help change attitudes to homosexuality in football.' A report after the first week of the campaign found that over a quarter of the entire UK adult population heard about the rainbow laces. Even *The Guardian*, which was usually sniffy about Paddy Power's attention-seeking stunts, got on board.

Maybe the North Korean trip would be seen in the same light. Swedish diplomats who had been allowed to visit Bae in hospital indicated support for the match as a way of opening up communication with North Korea on some humanitarian issues. There was also an indication that Kim Jong-un might grant an interview to the documentary team about the basketball match, which would be the first time he had ever addressed any Western media.

A few days before Christmas the delegation left North Korea. It had been a job well done, they thought. Despite the bureaucracy and Rodman's erratic behaviour, it was clear that the match would go ahead – a truly historic sporting and geopolitical event, sponsored by Paddy Power. Unbeknownst to the team in North Korea, however, media pressure had become unmanageable while Scott was in Pyongyang with the documentary crew. Some board members and shareholders were beginning to worry that the reputation of the company could face lasting damage.

Locked away from the world in North Korea, Scott was oblivious to this as regime officials showed him around pristine banquet halls and spotless hospitals. Robertson and the Dublin team were too afraid to express the true level of their concerns when contacting Scott as everyone was aware that the communication channels were likely being monitored, and they did not want to risk Scott being treated as a hostile PR man by the Pyongyang regime.

On 23 December Scott was in the air between Pyongyang and Beijing oblivious to the fact that back in Dublin, Kennedy, Kenny, Robertson and the company's long-time external PR consultant Billy Murphy had been trying to temper the fall-out from association with the dictator state. It was not a good sign when Murphy was called to Power Tower at short notice and the eerie quiet in the office two days before Christmas added to the sense of foreboding as he sat across the boardroom table.

The purging of Jang Song-thaek and the continued detention of Kenneth Bae despite international humanitarian appeals had turned the world's attention towards the barbarity of the North Korean regime. And there in the middle was a Paddy Power-sponsored circus to celebrate Kim Jong-un's birthday.

The usual internal criticism from staff unhappy that they were taking personal flak for the marketing department's controversy was adding to external criticism that was swelling and reaching shareholders and board members. The heat became too much and the decision was made to pull Paddy Power's support for the event but maintain the financial commitments so that Rodman could follow through with the plan.

A statement was drawn up, which Murphy was keen to get out to the newspapers to be carried in the next day's editions. But there was one small problem: no one was sure Scott had got out. They couldn't risk releasing a statement that would upset North Korea while the head of PR was stuck in the country. It is said to be one of the only times in his career that Murphy was left speechless.

Finally Scott was reached by mobile phone when he landed in Beijing and informed that the grand plan was over. He was deflated, having been filled with excitement over the previous months of preposterous plans turning into reality and a growing belief that the match would be a historic event with geopolitical repercussions. Plus, it was a really great marketing stunt.

'Given changed circumstances, Paddy Power has decided to withdraw its association with the Dennis Rodman basketball initiative in North Korea,' the company statement said. No explanation was given to what exactly the company believed were the 'changed circumstances' – North Korea had not turned into a starvation-ridden dictatorship overnight.

Paddy Power himself sent an email to the Associated Press newswire to be distributed to every newsroom in the world. 'This isn't a financial decision. We'll be honouring all our contractual commitments to Dennis and his team. We've reviewed the project, and with the benefit of hindsight, we've recognized we've got this one wrong. Because of this, we have decided to remove our name from the event.'

Robertson and Scott informed Offland on Christmas Eve that Paddy Power would have no more involvement in the film, but the director was not going to write them out of the story.

He returned to film the match with the twelve retired NBA stars, most of whom were dead broke and paid as little as €10,000 to put their reputations on the line. One of them, Vin Baker, had burned through $100 million since retiring in 2006 after falling into a life of alcoholism, bad business decisions and gambling addiction.

These sad stories were not told in Offland's documentary (which was shown to Scott while being edited) but it did detail Paddy Power's involvement in the match and showed Rodman alcoholically spiralling out of control while the ragtag bunch of ex-professional players along for the ride struggled to save their reputations from the American media's hostility towards their trip. The stand-out moment of the film occurred in the moments before the match tipped-off, when a visibly emotional Rodman sings 'Happy Birthday' to the despot in a style similar to Marilyn Monroe's serenade of John F. Kennedy. Matt Cooper, the Irish journalist and broadcaster, was also on the trip – having met Paddy Power chief executive Patrick Kennedy at a football match where their children were playing and asking if he could tag along to gather material for a book. The book was never written, but Cooper did get to dine out on it for years – he became an unlikely star of the documentary, barked at by an apoplectic Rodman in front of DPRK officials at one of the trip's interminable banquets.

The match itself finished in a draw between the US and North Korea before the teams mixed for the second half in a sign of cooperation between the two countries, and Paddy Power enjoyed a mixed result too. (It is worth noting that Offland and Cooper both attest to the draw being the true result of the match rather than any effort in propaganda to save face for the North Koreans. It is equally worth noting that the American players were playing under the watch of a murderous dictator and facing a hostile press at home. Some were also quite hung-over.)

On the one hand Paddy Power's North Korean sojourn could have been deemed a total failure as the bookmaker had been forced into an embarrassing climb-down from a project that most right-minded people would have said was a non-runner from the start. But really, they got away with it. Paddy Power's mischief department rode their luck, and once the thorny issue of the United Nations sanctions had been dealt with, the company came out relatively unscathed.

Those involved in the project still talk about it with giddy enthusiasm and the mischief department didn't let the short spell on the naughty step deter them from causing trouble again.

Less than three months after the company admitted it had got it wrong with the North Korea stunt, it faced international opprobrium once again.

On Sunday, 2 March 2014 readers of *The Sun* opened their papers to be greeted with an image of Oscar Pistorius mocked up to look like an Academy Award statue. The awards ceremony was to be held that night and the para-Olympian's trial for the murder of his girlfriend Reeva Steenkamp was to begin the following day.

'It's Oscar time,' the odd advert screamed in bold white letters on a bright green background. 'Money back if he walks. We will refund all losing bets on the Oscar Pistorius trial if he is found guilty.'

This was pure Stewart Kenny, pure Ken Robertson and pure Paddy Power – both the bookmaker and its eponymous spokesman.

Everybody had an opinion on the trial where the man known to the tabloids as the 'Blade Runner' was accused of shooting to death his glamorous girlfriend on Valentine's Day 2013. More than a hundred journalists had flocked to the High Court of South Africa in Pretoria and outlets from *Vanity Fair* to *Time* magazine had published stories ahead of the trial. Television cameras were going to broadcast every moment of the trial to rolling news channels. Paddy Power needed to be part of this conversation.

Former tabloid hacks who crossed over to the company's PR department noted that it had a similar set-up to a newsroom. Every morning the papers were pored over for any stories that could be covered and upcoming events were discussed for any potential that they could be conduits for Paddy Power's brand.

The Pistorius trial was prime fodder for this. There were already a number of crude jokes and memes circulating in email chains about the trial, one of which compared the Paralympian to Manchester City's poor form in the Champions League because 'they both lost both legs and had four shots on target'. Robertson wanted Paddy Power to be part of this news cycle and capture the gallows humour.

The fact that the company had opened a book on the trial the previous week, pegging the odds of a not guilty verdict at 2/5 and a guilty verdict at 7/4, had generated some controversy. The crude wording of the advert took that controversy and turned it into outrage.

The press release announcing the betting was emphatic: the company wanted in on the publicity around the trial. 'Global media attention, bar-stool conversation and pillow talk will shift from the Oscars on Sunday night to Oscar on Monday when the Blade Runner straps on his prosthetic limbs for the long walk to the high court,' a blogpost on the website said.

'As an international media circus descends on South Africa, Paddy Power's marketing department has entered the fray.'

The mischief department was prepared for some pushback but the severity and speed of the reaction caught them by surprise. Michael Moynihan, Fianna Fáil's communications spokesman, said: 'Bookmakers don't seem to care about what they do to make a profit. I think it's very inappropriate.' British politicians were widespread in their criticism as the controversy led to media coverage, including Tom Watson, a Labour MP, who called the company 'dirty' and 'money-grabbing'. (Watson later joined the board of Paddy Power's parent company Flutter Entertainment for a five-figure salary.)

The criticism that stuck, however, was from domestic abuse survivors who accused the company of trivializing violence against women and contributing to the victim-blaming culture around domestic abuse.

Holly Dustin, director of End Violence Against Women, said: 'They are making a game out of the murder and the brutal killing of a young woman, which is unacceptable. It is totally unacceptable. They should withdraw the ad.' Jean Hatchet, a domestic abuse survivor, described the bet as 'an incredibly awful, callous thing'.

Hatchet wrote an open letter to Patrick Kennedy stating that, 'The brutal death of a woman at the hands of her partner is not "sport" or "entertainment" and promoting the opportunity to make money from it is a vile and offensive act, which anyone with a sense of human dignity and respect for human life must reject.'

Within four days the petition attached to Hatchet's letter had 125,000 signatures and more than 5,000 complaints had been sent to the British Advertising Standards Authority.

Power was unrepentant. The spokesman defended the bet in phone calls with news reporters, drafted a response to be sent by email and appeared on the BBC

World Service – the exact same tactics that the company always used to maximize publicity from controversy. When *The Daily Mail* contacted the marketing department for comment and noted that the Pistorius ad had surpassed a 2005 KFC campaign that featured call centre workers speaking with their mouths full of chicken and chips, prompting concerns that it would encourage bad manners among children at dinner tables, as the most complained about of all time, Robertson responded: 'In your face, KFC!'

It was still a big laugh in Power Tower, and deemed a huge success in terms of exposure. But something was different this time around. Executives in the company could gauge the fallout on their social media feeds and as the controversy raged on, the mood changed. The blog post was updated to include an apology: 'Some people felt that by offering betting we were in some way condoning domestic violence or trivializing murder. That was absolutely not the case; we categorically do not condone domestic violence or murder. To those offended we would like to say sorry.'

It was the beginning of the end for the golden days of the mischief team. The following year Paddy Power would merge with Betfair and internal disruption would knock back the branding of the company. A more typically corporate and serious management structure would leave the company more risk averse to reputational damage. By the end of 2017 Kennedy, Kenny, Scott, Robertson and Woolfenden had left the company. References to the North Korean sojourn were purged from Paddy Power history – it did not make a 2016 list on the company blog trumpeting 'nine of Paddy Power's most controversial stunts.' Even the 'stallions or mares' advert was delisted from the company's YouTube channel.

In future there would be worried meetings about the reaction to marketing stunts on the back of angry newspaper columns, not geopolitical crises. The consensus was clear: Paddy Power was losing its bottle.

17

Betty Power

Mícheál Nagle, head of social media at Paddy Power, was used to getting in trouble for the tweets he allowed his team to put out. His crew had pissed off the former Liverpool striker Michael Owen to the point that the footballer had got a contact of his in the company to email a board member asking them to lay off calling him boring. One of the company's Premier League partners, Manchester City, gave them a rap on the knuckles when they took the piss out of the club's owner, Sheikh Mansour. There had even been an unfortunate incident when a junior staffer made an extremely ill-judged joke about the Duchess of Cambridge's pregnancy that was deleted just in time, averting serious reputational damage to the brand.

On 24 July 2015 the @paddypower Twitter account posted a half-arsed pun that caused sweaty palms in some senior management. 'Hot on the heels of the Ladbrokes/Coral merger, we can exclusively reveal that we have merged with Betfair. Our new name is Betty Power.'

The £2.3 billion merger between Ladbrokes and Coral created Britain's biggest bookmaker and was a further sign that consolidation was the only guarantee of survival in what was becoming an increasingly competitive marketplace. GVC Holdings, the London-listed gambling group that had burst into the online gambling scene in 2004, was also putting the final touches to a deal that would lead to it paying over £1 billion to buy Bwin, an Austrian online operator that had made a number of small acquisitions in European countries. It seemed that every operator was looking for a way to boost their customer base and breadth of product as a new wave of gamblers poured their money online.

Revenue in the UK gambling industry had climbed from £5.6 billion in 2010 to £7.1 billion in 2014 with most of the growth coming from the new wave of online gamblers, many of whom had never walked into a high-street outlet, picked up a tiny biro and scribbled out their bets on a slip to hand over the counter. They were betting through their phones, on buses, in pubs and while at work.

The Betty Power tweet was not getting into any of

that, though, it was just a silly pun. The first response was a follower posting a picture of a tumbleweed but the second response was a bit more insightful. 'You're both listed companies, your compliance people have just had a collective heart attack!'

Andy McCue had been – somewhat surprisingly – appointed chief executive designate in September 2014 after Patrick Kennedy's sudden announcement that he was leaving the top job. Kennedy was a maverick, perfectly balancing the mettle needed for rapid decisions to secure online expansion with the looseness necessary to lead a company that prided itself on politically incorrect campaigns. He was regularly voted chief executive of the year by *The Sunday Independent* and his standing in the Irish business community was such that he was approached to chair the Irish state's NTMA in 2013, when the recession-racked country was attempting to return to the international bond markets.

To his colleagues in Paddy Power, however, Patrick Kennedy was also good fun. Within a few months of his appointment to the job in 2006, he travelled to Ischgl, the Austrian ski resort village known as Ibiza on ice for its nightlife. Stewart Kenny had invited Kennedy, Ken Robertson, the Irish marketing chief and others along for a holiday. The presence of the new boss on the trip gave rise to concern that it might dampen the atmosphere, but Kennedy was quick to make sure there was nothing on the agenda other than a good time. He maintained that warmth with his staff throughout his tenure and when he left in 2013 the occasion was a last chance to have some fun at his expense.

On his final day in Power Tower he was greeted with a faux-marble sculpture of his face on the body of Michelangelo's *David*. The sculpture had been organized by Robertson and at its base was a note, 'Lowkey as requested', referring to Kennedy's stated desires that no fuss be made about his going-away bash.

Féilim Mac An Iomaire, a Galwegian *gaeilgeoir* who was a rising star in the marketing department – he had been hired following a billboard campaign he used his dole money to pay for asking anyone to hire him so he could avoid emigration – arranged for Karl Spain, a ruthless Irish comedian, to rip into Kennedy, Kenny and McCue in front of their families. His heart skipped a beat when he saw the three chief executives, past, present and future, making a beeline for him. Luckily for Mac An Ionmaire, they were still laughing and only wanted to make sure he had got a recording of the set.

McCue, an affable Scotsman who had worked for the OC&C consultancy often used by Paddy Power, was well-liked within the company. His bolstering of the retail division in the face of online growth had been a feat but there was widespread surprise about his elevation to top-dog position.

Cormac Barry was seen as the chief executive in waiting and was favoured by most of the board. He had supercharged the business with the Australian operation and had a strong connection to the core of the brand, having worked under Kenny, Kennedy and John O'Reilly. But Barry was enjoying life in Australia and rebuffed efforts from Kenny to take on the top job, leaving McCue to lead the company during a transformational period.

Paddy Power's near two decades of non-stop growth was plateauing by 2014 and Kennedy began a project in his final months as chief executive to look at ways to keep the upward trend going by doing a deal with a competitor. With the success in Australia, increases in the business arm and small acquisitions powering new technological developments, it was clear that the growth of Paddy Power would no longer be what is known in business as 'organic'. It would have to get into bed with another company. SkyBet and Bet365 were eating into Paddy Power's customer base by offering better versions of the same thing, and the feeling was spreading that the company was losing ground.

Rivals with strong retail networks such as William Hill and Ladbrokes were initially considered as potential partners but the obstacles to merging such legacy brands with their complex corporate structures and anchors on high streets would have made any deal a massive task. Many smaller online operations were experiencing the same problems as Paddy Power as the saturation of millions of pounds being spent to secure new customers had drenched the market – with one exception.

Breon Corcoran's establishment of the Betfair sportsbook (a traditional bookmaking product where the company offered odds on events and took on the risk itself) had completely reinvigorated the start-up, which had become bogged down in international efforts that limited its ability to compete against its rivals in Britain and Ireland. Betfair was by now camped on Paddy Power's doorstep, employed around a hundred people in a new Dublin office and had located its servers in Ireland.

Betfair was very much on the up while Paddy Power was struggling under McCue's early tenure to keep the pace with increasingly well-funded and aggressive rivals. Within months of taking the top seat at Power Tower, McCue was fretting that he would wake up one morning to news that William Hill had merged with Betfair, which would leave Paddy Power alone on the dancefloor while all the attractive potential partners were coupling up. There was almost a paranoia developing in Paddy Power that its options would be cut off before it could make a move.

The landscape was changing fast. Only a few months earlier in March 2015 one of McCue's first acts as chief executive officer had been to return €400 million to shareholders as the project to find suitable acquisitions had turned up no suitable matches. But there was still enough cash in the bank to be flexible if that opportunity arose.

The Scotsman soon took the view that in a time of consolidation Paddy Power needed to be on the front foot. Informal conversations had been held with Corcoran and the other Betfair heads, many of whom had followed Corcoran to the Hammersmith company. His 2012 departure had been a blow to Paddy Power, and many of the maths-driven staff who had helped build the online operations rankled at the direction the company was now taking. This cohort wanted Paddy Power to compete based on its products and innovations, not acquisitions and forays into what they believed were gimmicks doomed to fail.

In July 2013 Paddy Power became the first company to partner with Facebook on the idea of a social betting app within the social network's desktop website. It was seen as a coup by some as it validated their view that Paddy Power was in league with the new Silicon Valley giants.

A note to the stock market about the plan to launch

a beta version of Paddy Power's In-Play! Facebook partnership to UK customers said the 'pioneering work' would 'add social engagement to online betting, enabling customers to bet on a wide variety of sporting events through Facebook, while also giving them visibility of, and the opportunity to engage with, other users'.

This was the sort of technobabble that had permeated every industry in 2013 as they clamoured to catch a wave on the social media tsunami and it was shelved soon after. Corcoran had never believed Paddy Power's technology offering was as powerful as those of competitors such as Betfair and when he was tasked by the board in the mid-2000s with looking into the exchange, his belief was confirmed.

Andrew Black and Edward Wray's Betfair firm had moved past its growing pains, which had caused the site to sputter when the volume of new customers rushed online for big events. The exchange was powered by IT systems similar to those which ran the New York stock exchange but they just couldn't cope with the demand of tens of thousands of gamblers looking to match up their bets every day.

The potential was there for sure, but in the fast-moving world of digital start-ups it was not unknown for better innovations to lose out to inferior ones that were easy and more reliable to use.

By the end of 2005 Black and Wray were under

pressure from early investors to seek a flotation on the stock market. Under Stephen Hill's two years as chief executive Betfair's revenues had grown from £32 million in 2003 to £107.1 million in 2005. Many shareholders wanted a valuation that touched £1 billion when it eventually did float and it was believed that this could be achieved if it held out until after the 2006 World Cup, which would serve as a profit-boosting proof of concept. Some analysts were less starry-eyed and reported expected valuations as low as £30 million.

Before France's talisman Zinedine Zidane thrust his head into the chest of Italy's Marco Materazzi in the 2006 World Cup Final, Betfair had already exceeded unicorn status, as technology start-ups which reached valuations of more than one billion would come to be known. Masayoshi Son, the big-thinking chief executive of the gargantuan Japanese SoftBank investment fund, bought 23 per cent of Betfair, valuing it at £1.5 billion. Since the 1990s Son and SoftBank's money fuelled innovative Internet companies such as a fledgling Chinese e-commerce platform called Alibaba, and most notably pumping billions into Uber and WeWork – those disrupters of the old models of transport and office space. The backing of Betfair in April 2006 was a sign that the then five-year-old company was the future of gambling.

By the time Corcoran joined in 2012 Betfair had

floated on the stock market, breaking the £1 billion valuation mark, and was a force in a number of areas where Paddy Power was lagging. It had four million customers and was still growing with products that no one had thought of before. As well as in-play betting, which had by then been copied wholesale by the rest of the industry including Paddy Power, Betfair launched a cash-out option, which allowed nervous punters to settle their bets before the end of an event for a lower sum than they would pay out if the result was finalized. The feeling in Dublin was that this was an idea Paddy Power should have thought of first, but in any case they were ripped off as soon as possible.

Betfair was attracting more price-savvy customers and higher rollers to its exchange so when it launched a sportsbook in 2012, the concern in Power Tower was that the newcomer would start to take a chunk of the small-staking market too.

The rumours of Corcoran's shock switch to Betfair had swirled around Power Tower throughout 2011 as the second-in-command at the Irish bookmaker hummed and hawed about the move. It was known that he was considering it but up until the summer, there was still a belief among some who worked closely with him that he might stay.

Betfair was performing well in Britain and Ireland but had struggled under the weight of its share price and it was clear that if it did not make significant changes it could dissolve into the ether like other great white hopes of betting disruption such as Blue Square, Betmart and Matchbook. But Corcoran was game for the fight and acted boldly on his arrival in Hammersmith, sacrificing a quarter of Betfair's revenues by withdrawing from markets where regulation was unstable and cutting £20 million in costs. He sold off a stake in social gaming product to Time Warner for £18 million and ended the tech company's operations in Germany, Canada, France, Greece and other locations in order to 'press reset'.

Since the flotation the share price had halved and there were concerns that the great revolution sparked by Betfair might proceed without its instigator playing a significant part. Under Corcoran, the focus was now to remain on the core of the company: product, marketing and customer acquisition in established and regulated markets. Corcoran's strategy produced almost immediate results and the share price began to recover but Betfair's blood was in the water and the sharks were circling.

A consortium led by Richard Koch, the British heavyweight consultant, and CVC Capital put together an almost £1 billion bid for Betfair together with a ballsy new strategy. The group wanted Betfair to ditch Corcoran's efforts to secure more customers and instead focus on the 200,000 largest betting-exchange customers. The pitch was that high rollers could sustain the business in a way that small fry would not, and without a management team lined up it was proposed that Corcoran – a man who had just graduated from the Paddy Power school of fun, friendly and fair mass-market bookmaking – should lead the company through into this new stage.

In essence, Koch's pitch had been that small customers joining up for tenner free bets and pushing small sums back and forth on piddling bets were not worth the £100 million spent in marketing every year, and a more focused customer strategy would take advantage of the big dogs making up the bulk of the money on Betfair.

The bid pitted the exchange evangelists in Betfair who believed wholeheartedly in the company as an innovator against the side headed by Corcoran who theorized that the more tried and tested sportsbook arm they had launched was crucial to a better long-term strategy. The bidders put Corcoran under pressure but he held firm and the balls of the board in rejecting the billion-pound bid showed that they backed his vision too. But the CVC consortium had set a marker: Corcoran had to get the value of the stock to exceed the £955 million offered.

Betfair needed to simplify its offering, in Corcoran's view, and that was shared by analysis in Paddy Power where, while sometimes existentially envious of the power of the exchange, the ethos was that most gamblers wanted the entertainment from placing a bet. And the easier it was to do that, the better.

About three-quarters of Betfair's accounts were inactive and industry analysts believed that the novelty of the exchange was tempered by the fact that it was fiddly compared to most sportsbook websites. Corcoran had taken a crew of Paddy Power division heads with him to Betfair and they tried to poach more experience from within Power Tower over 2013. Some traders couldn't believe the salaries being offered and jumped ship while others got their own contracts fattened up in order to stay.

When at Paddy Power, Corcoran followed the mode of Google's early years where the thought leaders in the company were directly involved in hiring. Between Corcoran, Barry and O'Donovan, two of them interviewed every person who was considered for a role; they talked of the 'secret sauce' they wanted to add to every position in Paddy Power. The main ingredients in this were intellectual curiosity, and a comfort with ambiguity. They also had to be what Corcoran described as 'underconfident overachievers'.

The phrase first came up at a board meeting when Corcoran, in his typically blunt but incisive way, turned to O'Donovan and said to the rest of the executives

– 'Well look at Peter, he's your classic underconfident overachiever'. It was apparently meant more as a compliment than an insult but it got to the heart of what the culture in Paddy Power was by the time it became an Internet force. People who could set aside their uncertainty to follow through for the company showed they had internal resilience that had driven success up to that point. With Kennedy departing two years after Corcoran, who took a group from Paddy Power with him, it was an uncertain time in Power Tower. The move to the plush sports-mad take on Silicon Valley offices, with its mottos about customers on the walls and Astroturf in the place of carpets in meeting rooms, and the new position of the company as an established corporate giant in Ireland had changed the mood around the office.

Simon Moore, who had moved from his role in the quants team to be head of customer analysis by the time of the Power Tower move, explained:

We had the Zen meeting rooms and the beanbags, so you started getting these CV-builders in who weren't really interested in gambling. They definitely weren't interested in spending five or seven years at Paddy's. They just wanted something cool like Google or Facebook or Paddy Power on their CVs. It sounds mad to say it but at the time in

Dublin, Paddy Power had a pull for people liked Facebook and Google – it was blue chip, it was big time and people wanted to be part of it. That's how far we had come by the time we left the shed in Tallaght but we used to reminisce about when it was really shit, when it was professional suicide to work for Paddy's because then we knew we had someone who was committed and was into what we were trying to do.

By 2012 there were forty quants in the risk team, which now numbered 140 people. It was much easier to attract talented people and get graduates in on intern projects by this stage but for many the fun of the early days of innovation in the shed had faded. A restructuring prior to the merger following McCue's appointment had placed a new layer of management between staff and senior management and the agility of the decision-making was lost.

Rob Reck, the first quant at the company, who had been a force of nature in the trading room, had a more visceral reaction to the newly corporatized identity of Paddy Power in Clonskeagh:

They were what I would call 'man-bag wearing people' walking up the driveway with their own snooker cue under their arm to play on the tables in the office. Anyone coming up to work like that at 10 o'clock in the morning needs to be dropped. It was part of the company growing up by leaving the shed, but it was all more Google-y with an open plan office and tens of thousands being spent on birthday cakes. You can imagine what we thought of that. We couldn't get space for our servers in the shed and now we were supposed to care when it was one of 3,000 people's birthday? Fuck off.

The deal to merge Paddy Power and Betfair consolidated two rivals and was a behemoth in the scope of its products and market penetration, but it was remarkably drama-free in execution. There were no late nights in smoke-filled rooms with the two chief executives, their sleeves rolled up and ties undone, leaning on the table facing off with each other to outline why they should, no must, lead the new group. The elevation of McCue to the top job in Paddy Power effectively cleared the path for Corcoran to take over when the deal was struck. The view was that Kennedy certainly would not have done a deal where he got knocked down a rung, but McCue viewed it pragmatically. He liked Corcoran and they had shared meals in the short time since he had departed, over which the consolidation in the industry was discussed with neither chief executive revealing their own hand.

After the discussions about the Ladbrokes and Coral deal became public in June 2015, McCue's concern about being left without a dance partner intensified. Happily he found himself in step with Corcoran and the talks ran smoothly. Gary McCann, the new chairman of the board, Andrew Algeo, who had been brought in by Kennedy to lead acquisitions, and Peter O'Donovan were among those in the know when the first stages of talks were a closely kept secret.

It was clear during the talks that a big part of the appeal of the deal at Betfair was the Australian operation of Sportsbet where Cormac Barry was displaying a kind of alchemy in producing continuous growth. Sportsbet would remain a shining star in the merged operation and a crucial driver in its march towards being listed in the FTSE 100 under new chairman Gary McGann, a veteran of Irish corporate life.

The Betfair deal took about six weeks to complete and the excitement among the senior management in Paddy Power was tempered by the reality that although as shareholders they would benefit greatly from the merger, as staff they were buying outbound tickets. The share price rose by 77 per cent as the £12 billion merger was completed but the bulk of £60 million in cost saving from the deal was to be made up mostly of jobs, and there was a restructuring at board level that ushered in a new management team. It was a bloodbath that created 207 millionaires among the shareholders – but it was a bloodbath none the less.

One junior employee at Power Tower, who was not one of those made a millionaire in shares, likened the change to a scene in *Entourage*, a glitzy HBO comedy-drama series about the life of a Hollywood star and his hangers-on. In the final episode of the sixth series, the main character's agent Ari Gold returns as the owner of the talent agency which had once been his rival and takes charge of his new role, entering the building with a paintball gun and firing (literally and figuratively) all the staff who he feels had done him wrong in the past.

'It was just bang, bang, bang: you're gone,' the Paddy Power employee said. 'It was a completely different atmosphere from then on. Everything required a new layer of approval and it felt like you were no longer trusted to do your job without someone signing off on it.'

Dermot Golden, who had revolutionized risk management at the company, left, along with Rob Reck and a number of senior quants. (Reck formed Banach Technology with former Paddy Power employees Mark Hughes, Hadrien Lepretre and Alex Zevenbergen in 2015 and continued to power the risk under new products for multiple companies until it sold for €36 million to Australian firm PointsBet in 2021.) Andrew Algeo and Peter O'Donovan left soon too. In marketing, Gav

Thompson, Rory Scott and Ken Robertson were gone within sixteen months of the merger. Corcoran had made it clear early on in his tenure that any future international expansion would be under the Betfair banner 'as it has the word "bet" in it'. Rod O'Callaghan, who had led the Airton Risk Management operation, was out as well, and there were changes in finance, HR and operations which clearly indicated which brand was now running the firm to be known as Paddy Power Betfair.

Traders had their bonuses, which could be worth thousands, slashed to a few hundred pounds, while the 200+ shareholders in the company became millionaires. Cuts were made everywhere – the company even stopped paying for the staff twice-weekly five-a-side matches in the grounds of University College Dublin. After a revolt it was agreed that one of the days would be covered by the multi-billion-euro company and staff could pay for a second day themselves if they wanted it. One cad did the calculations (and shared them with his football pals) that Corcoran's bonus in March 2017 of £798,000 could have paid for 2,000 years' worth of staff five-a-sides.

A clearer example for the Paddy Power old guard of the changes in direction was the first Christmas party after the merger. Paddy Power Christmas parties were notorious affairs with different divisions organizing blowouts to mark the festive period. There were stars from the sporting world in attendance who had worked as ambassadors for the firm throughout the year and bleary-eyed staff posed for selfies with them in between live music and scrambles for the bar. The first Christmas party after the merger was held in the Odeon bar on Harcourt Street and the bar tab ran out early leading to jokes that it was another victim of the €60 million in savings the new board hoped to make.

People began to walk away, to be replaced by young graduates, or their roles were outsourced to other offices. The staff who remained felt an immediate change too as the mammoth task of merging the back-end operations of the technology began as part of the efforts to lessen duplication across the brands.

The operation created by the merger of Paddy Power and Betfair was a beast. There were now 1,000 staff working on product development across the sports-book, online casino and shops, a £300 million annual marketing budget and an IT budget of £171 million. This could all be reduced if things were run more smoothly and new firmer management styles would be used to tame the beast.

As most sport is event-based, Paddy Power's website and apps would be smashed with a wave of activity on a Saturday afternoon or just before the Grand National got under way. If the website crashed during that time, it was not just profit that would be lost, trust would be too. So Paddy Power operated at around 30 per cent capacity most of the week until the servers got red hot on a typical Saturday afternoon and everyone in operations wondered if this would be it, the day the system finally crashes.

It was a fight to keep everything up and running while introducing improvements and innovations. The merger had increased the customer base and highlighted the inefficiencies of the old software, and it became quickly apparent that the new way would be the Betfair way. So in 2016 the entire technology team was instructed to be on call all the time. Prior to this developers were releasing code to meet deadlines after weeklong 'sprints' and the operations team was left to pick up the pieces if it broke down in action. Under the new set-up, the last person to work on a project that had fallen over would be called in to fix the problem, whether it was Saturday night or Sunday morning. An immediate improvement in the quality of work was noticed. Staff were trained in each other's roles and had to take on the responsibility for any issues with their work, even if it would previously have been a different team's problem.

It was painful for many but the benefits were clear. The firm was now valued at £12 billion – more than £4 billion more than the separate entities. Only Bet365, the family-owned firm that had an edge because it did not have to answer to shareholders or the market for activity in grey markets (where online gambling was not illegal but was also not regulated), or for its tactics of allowing Chinese punters access to its platform despite betting being outlawed there, was bigger globally.

The newly merged Paddy Power Betfair now led the markets in Ireland, Britain, France, America and Australia, and 87 per cent of its £330 million profits were generated online. The merged company operated from Paddy Power's headquarters but it was clear that things were going to be very different. One person who survived the initial transition from Paddy Power into the new entity described it as 'starting as a merger, turning into a take-over, and ending in annihilation'.

By the end of 2017 some of the green walls in Power Tower had even been painted white.

18

Rise of the FOBTs

Derek Webb is about as far from a problem gambler as you could find and about as unlikely an anti-gambling campaigner as you could imagine.

Everything from the designer spectacles that sit atop his sticky-out ears to the apartment at the luxury apartment complex in Las Vegas where he avoids the British winters was paid for one way or another by the gambling industry. He spent his career as a professional card player exploiting weaker players at poker tables around the world, and such is his understanding of the game that he decided to invent his own version of poker, which would make it quicker and easier to play. When it comes to gambling he has seen it all, from the inside of the Eccentric Club above Terry Rogers' shop on Dublin's northside in the 1980s recession to the luxury tables filled with high rollers in riverboat casinos on the Mississippi Delta. Since the 1990s he has divided his time between Nevada and London, but still has his deep Derbyshire drawl as he explains his theory of the tricks gambling plays on the brain:

> The ability to trade up your bet is the danger. If the fixed stake was 100 quid at a time then nobody would bother with it to start with, but it is the ability to suck people in at a low stake and then get them to engage in repetition and give them the perception that there are patterns of play. That encourages them to increase their stake and they start gambling at levels that are too unaffordable and ultimately dangerous. That is the nature of it. If you made people pay one hundred quid for every spin, no one would get addicted 'cause no one would be able to afford to get sucked in.

Webb recognizes the absurdity of this idea given that he has dedicated much of the last decade and a small part of his personal fortune to campaigning for the maximum stake on gambling machines in bookmakers to be reduced. But he believes the theory shows that gambling interrupts the rationality of people's brains and they need to be protected from the natural inclination to bet more and bet bigger.

Every gambler will be familiar with the feeling after

a winning bet that they could have won more if only they had had the balls to back their instinct and put more on. Even losses encourage gamblers to bet more on the next bet because – well, of course the roulette ball landed on black the last time so it will be red this time. Certain types of gambling corrupt the logical part of the brain (as much as it exists in many people) and appeals to the part of the grey matter that ignores risk and seeks only the buzz of a reward.

Webb knows better than most the psyche of the gambler. After a losing streak at the tables in the 1990s, the man who grew up attending political rallies in 1960s Derby decided he needed a steadier income stream. In 1994 he patented Three Card Poker, a version of the card game played against a dealer that is more fun for the player without exposing the casino to additional risk.

The game is fast, simple and fun, often returning chips to the player – the perfect combination for keeping casino customers happy and entertained enough to play until their luck runs out, and still return to do it all again.

Webb was immensely proud of his invention and took on the role of a travelling salesman, visiting casino bosses around Europe and the United States trying to convince them that Three Card Poker could be as popular and as profitable as other table games such as blackjack. In the casinos that agreed to trial the game, Webb trained the dealers himself and stood on the floor of the card room trying to convince gamblers to give this new game a go.

He sold the rights to the game outside Britain to the established game manufacturer Shufflemaster for $3 million in 1999 but the real paydays would come in later years when Webb launched a series of lawsuits against games manufacturers for robbing his idea. He even settled out of court in 2007 with Shufflemaster for around £20 million for undervaluing his game in the original deal. He made a further $23 million from selling his gaming firm Prime Table Games to Galaxy Gaming in 2011. By the time Webb was part of another successful lawsuit in 2018, which led to a $315 million payout from Scientific Games, by then the owners of Shufflemaster, his reputation had completely changed. He was now the head of one of the most vociferous and politically charged movements bookmakers had ever come up against, a movement that was considered anti-gambling and even puritanical by many in the industry, who began to mock the campaigners as 'Sunday School prohibitionists'.

Using his personal fortune, Webb set up and began funding the Campaign for Fairer Gambling group in 2012, which was waging war on bookmakers for the FOBTs springing up in shops around Britain.

The touch-screen machines, known as FOBTs (said aloud as 'fob-tees') feature electronic versions of casino games such as roulette and blackjack, and were first introduced in 2001, providing a pipeline of profits for bookmakers. Gamblers could bet up to £100 per spin on the machines which, like all casino-style games, have a built in advantage that gives the operators a risk-free return. Typically the FOBTs returned 90 per cent to 97 per cent of the money bet to the players, guaranteeing profits for bookmakers. The machines had barely any practical limits and in theory gamblers could wager up to £18,000 an hour on them. The placement of the machines in disadvantaged areas meant that was only a theory, though they were attractive to drug dealers wishing to launder money from crime as gambling winnings.

Webb hates FOBTs for many reasons, not least because they prey on the part of the brain that encourages people to trade up to dangerous levels. They are, he says, 'addictive by design'.

When he heard the story of Matt Zarb-Cousin, a bright man forty years his junior, he knew he had the perfect face of the campaign. Zarb-Cousin first bet on a FOBT when he was sixteen years old and by the age of twenty he was in debt to the tune of £20,000 and suicidal, not just because of the money he owed but because he felt he had wasted years of his life sitting in front of the psychological tricks of the flashing lights and cheery beeps from the FOBTs. With the help of his parents he cleared his debts but remains scarred by the mental health issues, which require ongoing medication. His story on Channel 4's *Dispatches* in 2012 ignited a debate in Britain about FOBTs, their positioning in run-down areas and how they robbed disadvantaged young people of their money and prospects.

Webb, bald and pale despite his time in the Nevada sun, and Zarb-Cousin, handsome and sallow despite his time under the London clouds, are unlikely allies to an almost comical degree. The younger man worked as a communications adviser to Jeremy Corbyn, the socialist bête noire of middle Britain, and here he was leading a campaign funded by Webb, a capitalist using the courts to secure his right to the money generated from the gambling games he developed. When Webb and Zarb-Cousin launched the Campaign for Fairer Gambling in 2012 they had a powerful ally inside the bookmaking industry, though they didn't know it at the time.

Stewart Kenny had made his distaste for FOBTs known to other members of the company's board soon after Paddy Power had begun its expansion into the British retail market and for the first years of the drive into the UK the machines were not part of the company's thinking. This was not out of any moral standpoint taken by the company but rather through a lack of understanding of the British bookmaker market. Paddy Power's internal self-belief had given the board the confidence to think that they would replicate their Irish success without altering their approach too much. The original entry into the UK market was envisaged as a twin attack using the dot.com for some punters and attracting shop bettors with generous offers.

It failed, and by 2006 Paddy Power had forty-five shops in Britain and was losing around £6 million. The more shops that were opened, the more money was lost, so when Patrick Kennedy became chief executive in 2006 he worked to address the problem. Kennedy assigned the job of reviewing it to Andy McCue, the man who would go on to replace him as chief executive eight years later.

McCue was initially employed to review the online operation from Dublin but Kennedy persuaded him to take on the role of deputy head of retail and deploy the strategy he had developed under Alan Kerr. He found that the retail division was overpaying on everything from betting-coupon printing to high-street rents. The turnover looked healthy but when he dug down into the figures he found this was largely because customers were recycling their bets when they were paid out on offers. Shrewder customers had also taken advantage of Paddy Power's position as being a bookmaker who wanted to take chunky bets, which the likes of William Hill and Ladbrokes were less inclined to take.

In Ireland the culture in Paddy Power was that local shop managers should be trusted to know their customers well enough to set odds and offers that would appeal to them, but in Britain this made the company seem inconsistent and area managers were unsure of what the overall strategy was. Smart punters would travel around London seeking out Paddy Power offices with overly generous books on golf tournaments, undermining the profit on the offer as they had no interest in hanging around the shop once their bets were placed, which was a marked difference from the Irish customers.

Kerr and McCue instead started pushing out consistent offers across all shops, which would stand out from those offered by rivals, particularly around football and horse-racing. They then brought in a new team to do a deep analytical review of what drove the best Paddy Power shops versus the worst ones and developed a template that would improve the existing real estate and drive the future expansion. The analysis this model was based on was forensic and allowed the decisions for new retail opportunities to be determined by data derived from the existing shops and, more cleverly, by those of their competitors.

While Paddy Power's marketing team was pushing

the idea that the brand was a slapdash operator only interested in creating a bit of craic for the English betting market, the analysts in the company were able to determine whether one postcode of fourteen households would be more profitable in a given area than another postcode. This level of detail was outside the model's ability, however, so Paddy Power hired an external company to deploy teams of people around the country to count the number of customers going into competitors' shops, and checking what was on discarded bet slips to glean an insight into the staking levels on different types of bets being taken. The rule was that if Paddy Power was to open a shop it needed to have collected data from dozens of visits to a competitor in the area in order to determine how Paddy Power could fit with local tastes.

As a late entrant into the market, Paddy Power was determined not to make the same mistakes as its rivals and to take advantage of the fact that it was not weighed down by long leases and shops in unsuitable areas. It targeted the top-performing shops of William Hill, Ladbrokes and the rest, mimicking what they had done to the Irish independents in the 1980s. By the second half of the 2000s, however, regulation was looming and the financial crash was beginning to hit the pockets of people who had previously been spending their discretionary income in bookies, but the psyche among Paddy Power management was that they would be the last man standing when their more exposed competitors had to close shops to reduce their outgoings.

Despite Kenny's scepticism about FOBTs, by 2010 Paddy Power's 124 shops in Britain were taking in more than £24 million from 492 machines, a 74 per cent increase on 2009 and a sign that the company was fully committed to maximizing the potential of the machines.

Kenny might have expressed distaste for the social ills caused by FOBTs but Paddy Power's appetite for the fast profits from them in the UK was only growing stronger.

19

Green Street

In the summer of 2013 on Green Street in the London borough of Newham, between the DK Foreign Money Exchange and Super Housewares, a team of labourers in paint-flecked overalls were putting the finishing touches to a new retail outlet that had once been a kebab shop. That June did not leave much of a mark in the sports history books – the Tour de France was the main event, followed by the FIFA U-20 World Cup and World Aquatics Championships – but Paddy Power was fighting to get the shop open fast.

Andy McCue's team didn't need to do too much data mining to work out that gambling was popular in Newham. Paddy Power already had twelve shops in the area and was planning to open three more, which would bring close to ninety bookmakers to an area with a population of 300,000. While Stewart Kenny had been orchestrating a campaign to convince the Irish government about the dangers of FOBTs for working-class people, Paddy Power was opening multiple shops in areas in order to get around the British regulations which allowed only four machines per shop.

Kenny had written to the Irish government that the machines were 'particularly enticing to younger gamblers in disadvantaged areas' as a warning not to let them into the Irish high street, but it seemed that the firm he had co-founded took the idea of a machine that was 'particularly enticing to younger gamblers in disadvantaged areas' to be a business opportunity that was just too good to pass up. Flutter declined to comment when approached prior to publication.

The industry fervour around FOBTs was not surprising as they were literally money-making machines – and money-losing machines for punters. All they required was that someone sit in front of them, filling them with cash.

Opening from nine in the morning until ten at night, the corners of betting shops were filled with the flashes and dings from the four machines where gamblers fed the FOBTs and punched in their bets while others queued behind them. From 2013 customers were offered 'loyalty bonuses' for using Paddy Power machines and in return the machine customers provided a net revenue to the bookmaker of £63.5 million that year.

On Green Street, the former Kebabish Originals joint that was being converted to a Paddy Power was a flashpoint in the fight between multinational bookmakers and local authorities watching in dismay as their main shopping streets were being swamped with betting shops.

Paddy Power had worked hard throughout the 1980s and 90s to make spending an afternoon in a bookie's an acceptable way to pass the time, but by the second decade of the 2000s the shops were again being tarnished as dens of inequity, viewed as places of violence, drugs and anti-social behaviour.

Newham Council had had enough. By 2013 when Paddy Power applied for its licence for the former kebab shop, what was expected to be a formality turned into a protracted affair that helped turn the tide against FOBTs.

Ian Corbett, a local councillor, rejected the licence and began a pushback against the proliferation of bookies in the deprived area.

Corbett described 'violence, robbery, street drinking' taking place outside bookmakers and accused the industry of 'targeting new immigrants to the area, those who have not been steeped in the *Racing Post*, who do not understand the odds, especially in the machines'.

The council began using CCTV footage and secret-shopper surveys to build a case that bookmakers and their four FOBTs in every shop were leading to increased crime in the area. One video showed a man with a two-foot-long metal bar approaching a gang of people outside a Paddy Power shop to settle a dispute. When the news media arrived to cover the issue they got vox pops from locals who described people walking out of bookies to mug people before heading into another shop to bet again.

Paddy Power successfully pushed back against Newham's refusal by getting a magistrates' court to allow the shop licences. It was a pyrrhic victory, however, as Derek Webb, Matt Zarb-Cousin and the Campaign for Fairer Gambling had managed to drag the reputation of the bookmakers through the mud in the media before the case was settled. The campaign had got other local authorities on board and they began to push Westminster for stricter regulation of the machines. They had also found support from across the spectrum of the British press.

The left-wing *Guardian* and Tory *Daily Mail* share an editorial view on the English cricket team and not much else, but the campaign against FOBTs appealed to the sensibilities of both papers. *The Guardian* decried multinational corporations taking over British streets to pilfer the pockets of the poorest in society while *The Daily Mail* moralized about a vice that was destroying proud British towns and inflicting misery in homes across the country. Webb and Zarb-Cousin had been attending Labour and Conservative party events around England to seek support for their campaign, and though Zarb-Cousin wasn't allowed to attend certain Tory events due to his close links to Jeremy Corbyn, his story resonated and he became the face of the fight against FOBTs.

It was a slick campaign, bolstered by Katherine Morgan, a former adviser at the Treasury who was working with Interel Group, a global public affairs consultancy with clients such as Coca-Cola, Nestlé and Sony. Webb also funded Dr James Noyes to be appointed as an adviser on gambling policy to Tom Watson, the Labour Party's deputy leader.

The Association of British Bookmakers (ABB) fought back through its own political network and support from the likes of the free-market think tank the Institute of Economic Affairs (IEA), which published research attempting to show the faults in the campaign against FOBTs.

Chris Snowdon, the IEA's head of lifestyle economics, accused the campaigners and media of exaggerating the epidemic of problem gambling that was supposedly linked to FOBTs. He published a briefing paper that found no evidence for many of the claims about FOBTs being made such as an increase in the level of addicts and billions lost in specific towns.

Snowdon accused the campaigners of using Trump's method of referring to a particular product as the 'crack cocaine of gambling' in order to hide the lack of empirical evidence they had to support their claims about addiction and social harm. He said that the use of FOBTs were being wilfully mischaracterized by campaigners and the media was failing to grasp the real economics of gambling, leading to headlines that misunderstood the difference between the amount staked and the amount lost. Snowdon wrote:

Gambling is unusual in being a form of entertainment for which the cost is not known until it is concluded, and it is unique among leisure activities in that expenditure is often described as 'loss'. Nobody would talk about buying a football ticket as 'losing thirty pounds' since the money is being exchanged for entertainment. By contrast, someone who has enjoyed two hours of entertainment in a casino or betting shop will be said to have 'lost thirty pounds'. This is understandable because, unlike watching a football match, you can leave a gambling establishment with more money in your pocket than you went in and a tally of profit or loss is, in part, a measure of how successful the trip has been.

This understanding of the economics of gambling had been accepted for decades but it was now subject to a 'moral panic' that politicians were manoeuvring to be seen solving.

'More than a decade after their introduction to the UK, there has been no increase in problem gambling and no proliferation of betting shops. The real story of the last ten years in the betting sector has been the rise of online gambling, much of which remains offshore and untaxed. FOBTs are one way for the incumbent betting industry to keep pace with changing tastes in a digital world,' Snowdon wrote in the conclusion of his briefing. 'Regulation cannot afford to be anachronistic in a market in which punters can place unlimited bets on their mobile phones.'

Those words, written in 2016 about the use of FOBTs by retail bookmakers to mimic the profits of online products, would prove to be salient because the campaigners would come for online betting next.

Standing up to the gambling companies as they clustered shops in the country's poorest areas and maxed out the number of FOBTs allowed was politically profitable and garnered coverage in newspapers across the Labour–Conservative divide.

Everyone from Carolyn Harris, an ally of Jeremy Corbyn in the Labour Party, to Iain Duncan Smith, David Cameron and Theresa May in the Conservatives spoke out against FOBTs. The moral indignation and calls for politicians to act escalated in 2016 when the Gambling Commission published a damning finding about how Paddy Power had treated a FOBT addict.

The Gambling Commission found that Paddy Power had failed to prevent gambling from being a source of crime or disorder; failed to ensure that gambling is conducted in a fair and open way; and failed to protect vulnerable people from being harmed or exploited by gambling. The most damning was not a failure by omission, but a pro-active attempt by a senior staff member to bleed a man with serious addiction issues for more cash.

'Customer A' is the name given to the addict in the UK Gambling Commission's report. He was pumping so much money into FOBTs in early 2014 that staff decided they needed to look into where he was getting his cash from, concerned that he might be money laundering.

Customer A's family owned a few restaurants but even if he was able to get access to cash in the amounts he was losing, the shop staff were concerned that he had a problem. They opened a file on him, which noted his family's restaurants and added their concerns about his addiction.

In May 2014 the reasons for their concern were confirmed when he told them that he was working five jobs and had no money, but added that he was comfortable with his gambling. Following Paddy Power's internal procedure, the shop staff alerted their manager to the customer's clear signs of addiction. After seven interactions with the customer, the shop manager told a more senior figure in the company that Customer A would be visiting less frequently.

The more senior Paddy Power figure told the manager that Customer A should be encouraged to keep betting in the shop, despite the manager's concerns about his addiction. The manager said that he was struggling to marry this commercial directive from his own boss with Paddy Power's supposed commitment to social responsibility. All he could do was tell his shop staff to keep monitoring the customer's gambling while providing good service in the hopes that he would keep pumping money into Paddy Power's FOBTs. The manager saw that Customer A was still spending heavily but that he looked sick and as if he had not slept for a while.

In August 2014, seven months after staff first became concerned about the customer, the issue reached a head. A staff member from the shops Customer A frequented bumped into him outside of work and learned that he had lost his five jobs, was homeless and could no longer see his children. He was finally advised to seek help for his addiction. After this, Customer A stopped coming into Paddy Power.

It was a sordid and cruel illustration of how the gambling industry's rhetoric around social responsibility clashed with the commercial allure of FOBTs. The case was proof that gambling corporations were as addicted to the machines' easy profits as problem gamblers were to the psychological tricks and triggers the machines used to keep the customers high on the FOBTs.

In Dublin, Paddy Power's PR system kicked into gear when the Gambling Commission's report was published and the team began to consider what questions would be asked by journalists. One obvious query would be what were the repercussions for the senior staff member who told the shop manager to encourage the gambler to keep betting.

The marketing team wanted to know if they should tell the media whether he had been reprimanded in some way or even sacked. What was the official reaction to the case of a customer being encouraged to keep betting until he lost it all: his money, his jobs, his home and his children? Paddy Power told the Gambling Commission that 'it was satisfied that staff had followed social-responsibility procedures'.

There was a palpable sense in the Dublin office that was handling the media queries that they were on the wrong side on this occasion, and the case of Customer A exposed Paddy Power for a cruelty they had not imagined was possible.

Fintan Drury, the chairman of Paddy Power at the time of Stewart Kenny's lobbying in 2009 against FOBTs in Ireland, wrote an article for the London *Times* a month later in March 2016, decrying the 'damage being done to some of the most defenceless in society by one aspect of what the industry is allowed to do, unchecked by any moral code'.

The case added extra power to the anti-FOBT campaigners and provided a clear example of the real misery that Paddy Power and other gambling firms were inflicting through the FOBTs. For its failing in relation to Customer A, the sanction levied against Paddy Power, which was about to join the FTSE 100 with profits of €167 million and a valuation of €10 billion, was a paltry £280,000 payment to charity – causing a further clamour for harsh action to be taken against bookmakers.

Despite the internal differences about what level of responsibility Paddy Power had to protect customers from the dangers of addiction, it was clear in the company that if they wanted to fulfil their aim of being the biggest operator in the market they needed FOBTs. The figures showed that while Paddy Power's use of data to determine the best locations for shops had resulted in their entering the FOBT free-for-all, the company also had an equal level of turnover of customers betting over the counter on sports. The analysis of this was that while FOBTs were fuel, Paddy Power was not existentially dependent on them. But its rivals almost were.

William Hill and Ladbrokes had a retail legacy of shops in areas all over Britain from past mergers and expansions, some of which were in the more deprived areas and would have been financially unviable were it not for the FOBTs.

Under Alan Kerr and McCue's data-driven expansion in the UK, Paddy Power had opened 264 shops between 2010 and 2017, of which 211 were new outlets positioned to attack their competitors' strongest locations. The rest were bought from independent bookies who had lost in their own fights against the high-street giants. In total Paddy Power now had 357 shops in the UK.

Paddy Power had an average turnover of £2 million per shop on sports betting compared to £1 million at William Hill and Ladbrokes, and the Irish brand's average earnings per shop was £103,000 – 51 per cent higher than Ladbrokes' and 27 per cent higher than William Hill's. Paddy Power was spending millions on having live Sky Sports, BT Sports, big screens and virtual racing in all its outlets, while the British brands offered them only in selected stores.

The war on FOBTs was heating up and Kenny was adamant in his belief that the regulations would tighten. This was being heeded by David Newtown, the managing director of retail, who was opening new shops with a business model projection based on the maximum stake on FOBTs being cut from £100 to £2. After the merger, Paddy Power Betfair was the largest online operator in the UK and Ireland with 14 per cent of the total online market and 24 per cent of the sports betting market. With just 5 per cent of the British retail market, and most of that in prime locations, it would be well able to weather the hit to profits from tightening FOBTs stake limits.

The Association of British Bookmakers, however, was warning of a doomsday scenario, which would 'destroy 20,000 jobs, close thousands of betting shops, and cost millions of pounds in lost taxes for the government'. The stark effect of cutting stakes to a maximum of £2 was laid out to Her Majesty's Treasury in a report by KPMG commissioned by the association and submitted to the government.

The tactic worked and in October 2018, Chancellor Phillip Hammond announced that the cut in stakes would be delayed until October 2019 given the concerns over job losses and to allow the industry time to adjust. Of course the delay meant that almost a billion more pounds would be hoovered up from the machines before the change.

In the political fervour, Hammond was accused by the Conservative chair of the Treasury committee of putting bookmakers' profits before the welfare of addicts. Startlingly, Tracey Crouch, a minister in the Department for Digital, Culture, Media and Sport, which oversaw gambling regulation, quit her position in protest over the move.

Speaking to Rob Davies of *The Guardian* after her resignation, Crouch outlined why she felt so strongly about the issue:

> You think about the stories that you've heard and they seep into your head and heart. A group of addicts came to see me and it was absolutely silent when every person was telling their story and saying they'd contemplated suicide. Other people were crying silently because their stories were the same. It sounds like an exaggeration but I felt really lucky that they were all in the room. Really, I could have been talking to ghosts.
>
> I couldn't take the responsibility of potentially not meeting people in the future because they'd taken their lives over these machines.

The politicians were unusually forthright in the condemnation of their own Chancellor's decision and dismissed the evidence for his claims.

What was not known at the time was that Tom Tuxworth, Paddy Power Betfair's Head of Public Affairs and Corporate Social Responsibility, had shared a rebuttal of the ABB's report with anti-FOBTs campaigners and their political allies.

It said the KPMG report the ABB's submission to the Treasury was based on had explicitly stated that it was not to be relied upon as evidence for any other purpose than 'to meet the specific terms of reference agreed between the ABB and KPMG and that there were particular features determined for the purposes of engagement'.

In plain English, KPMG had found the evidence to support the purposes of the association hiring them. Using independent evidence to reach conclusions that support the lobbyist's aims is a tried-and-tested industry tactic. Kenny himself has joked with campaigners that the use of such tactics is bogus and they are only used when lobbyists have run out of good reasons for a new regulation they don't like.

The document circulated by Tuxworth dismissed the wider industry's argument and noted that the findings were based on selective data from William Hill, Ladbrokes, Coral and some small independents. The Paddy Power Betfair document dismissed the figures in the KPMG report which said that only 1 per cent of FOBT customers would migrate to another form of betting if stake limits were changed. There was no rationale or data given to support this stark drop-off in gambling if stake limits were lowered, and KPMG simply stated 'these assumptions were agreed by the industry'.

Tuxworth's document sought to pull up the planks of the ABB's argument which had successfully convinced the UK government that practically unlimited stakes on FOBTs were vital to protect jobs and high streets. The ABB had massaged the figures to claim that half of customers would simply stop betting in shops if their preferred outlet was closed. Paddy Power Betfair's analysis found that up to 90 per cent of punters would simply use another outlet.

The internal analysis done by Paddy Power Betfair on its retail network concluded that it would not have to close any shops if the stake on FOBTs were cut to £2. This revelation did not mention the fact that many of Paddy Power's new shops were already being operated on a business model that factored in a £2 limit and as such the change was already absorbed.

The document also said that bookmakers were making online profits based on their high-street presence and many firms were chains accepting loss-making outlets as in reality they generated up to £50,000 a year in online profits.

The blunt details in the Paddy Power Betfair document all served to undermine the central argument of the ABB that huge numbers of shops would close and jobs would be lost if the stakes on FOBTs were cut.

Coupled with the resignation of Crouch and wailing from Conservative backbenchers, Labour in opposition, the media, campaigners and the general public who viewed FOBTs with distaste, Hammond conceded. The cut in stakes would come into effect in April 2018, six months earlier, costing the industry a projected £450 million in turnover.

By now Stewart Kenny had left Paddy Power Betfair and moved to the side of the campaigners pushing against the excesses of the gambling industry. But the firm he had co-founded was employing similar tactics to his in Ireland when the wider industry wanted FOBTs introduced and he had fought the other side of the argument, leading to accusations that this was down to self-interest, not social responsibility.

In the UK Paddy Power Betfair knew it could absorb the cuts in FOBTs better than its rivals and reap the benefits of the competition being dragged down by lower-performing retail outlets while it fuelled its growth through select shop locations and an ever-increasing stream of money from online gambling.

The Irish company had seen early on that the battle on FOBTs would be lost, but the anti-FOBT campaign was emboldened by its success and now that the industry had conceded ground on the machines, believed that it could be beaten into retreat on its Internet operations. Further revelations about the way Paddy Power Betfair sought out and milked addicts would continue to stalk the company as it sought to take advantage of new global opportunities.

20

Addiction by Design

Every month Paddy Power's high stakes unit, or HSU as it is called internally, compiles a list of the most valuable customers on the bookmaker's books. The list contains sports stars, captains of industry and high rollers, and it is the HSU's job to ensure that they are well treated so that they don't get tempted by another gambling corporation and take their business elsewhere. In August 2016 an entrant appeared on the list for the first time under the name given to him by shop staff who had yet to learn much about him other than his first name: 'New Tony'.

The shop staff who gave him the moniker may not have been aware of the old Tony, the An Post worker whose treatment had embarrassed Paddy Power so badly, when they chose the name, but the similarities were remarkable.

New Tony was in fact Tony Parente, a shaven-headed Englishman who had relocated to Dubai where he worked as a property developer using loans from wealthy local businessmen. The HSU was already well aware of who Parente was as he had been delivered to them through Tony Carroll, an agent who had worked in the VIP section of Ladbrokes luring high-staking gamblers to bet with the firm.

Carroll's gig was that he had a group of clients who bet so big and so often that Paddy Power was willing to share the profits from them with him. Carroll and a handful of other agents like him developed relationships with high-staking punters and handled them on behalf of bookmakers, taking them to sporting events, going out for meals and furnishing them with free bets, in order to keep them betting. These punters were so profitable that a percentage of their losses was shared with the handlers. There was a slight kink in Paddy Power's use of Carroll as a handler as he was already exclusively employed by Ladbrokes, so his wife Ericka was named on the contract instead. As part of this arrangement, Carroll was paid £5,000 a month and 25 per cent of the money that Parente lost when gambling with Paddy Power. In total, Ericka Carroll, a hairdresser in her day job, made £130,000 from the gamblers introduced to Paddy Power under the agreement.

The HSU wanted Parente so much that they were

willing to pay him £20,000 as a signing-on fee, matching the gambler's first deposit into his online account in October 2015. Carroll had handled Parente for Ladbrokes and knew about his gambling style when he presented him to Paddy Power's HSU. An email from Carroll to the HSU gave them all the relevant information they required: he was a 'Dubai-based property developer' who 'plays all products' and whose 'stakes range from £500 to £5,000'. It also noted that Parente was an Arsenal fan, a useful piece of information for providing tickets and hospitality to show the new customer just how valued he was by the HSU.

The value of Parente to the HSU became immediately clear, and when a report on his gambling on an online casino game showed he had staked £548,000 on 164 bets in one session, a member of the HSU forwarded the report to his colleagues with the note: 'This Tony Parente is a wild man!!'

Despite all staff by this time receiving training to spot the signs of problem gambling as part of the Vanguard Project, the obvious wildness of Parente's gambling did not set off any alarms that might require an intervention. Instead he was given the full suite of treatment reserved for the HSU's VIPs. The day after being described as a wild man for his half-a-million-pound gambling session, he was given a bonus made up of 7.5 per cent of his losses to keep betting. Over the following months he was given access to a corporate box for the North London Derby between his beloved Arsenal and hated rivals Tottenham, with a special meeting with players as part of the tickets, which cost Paddy Power £3,000, for both Parente and Carroll, the man he considered a friend. He was taken to watch Arsenal face Barcelona at the Nou Camp in the Champions League, and to the Cheltenham Gold Cup and Aintree Grand National.

Among Paddy Power's corporate responsibilities was an adherence to run anti-money-laundering checks to ensure the business wasn't being used by criminals. It is a serious and important part of running a corporate bookmaker, requiring staff who had worked in large financial institutions and state agencies.

About seven weeks into his gambling with Paddy Power, Parente triggered the anti-money-laundering procedures with losses of £152,662.

The anti-money-laundering team decided to give Parente twelve weeks to provide the source of his funds, and told Carroll to pass on the request to him. During those twelve weeks Parente lost a further £70,000 and was treated to VIP tickets at the North London Derby at White Hart Lane designed to keep him betting with Paddy Power. By the time Parente did provide wage slips to show his source of funds, he had lost £222,000

– just four months after signing up. His wage slips showed he earned a salary of £229,000.

When Amarjeet Singh Dhir, one of Parente's business associates, became aware that he had pumped the money meant for property deals into Paddy Power, Dhir opted not to sue Parente but instead launched an action against Paddy Power, claiming that it should have known the money was the proceeds of crime. The extraordinary 2021 court case did not result in Dhir getting his money back but it did lay bare the way the HSU handled its clients.

Giving evidence to the London High Court by video link from Dublin, HSU member Ciaran McDermott was asked by Dhir's lawyer why there was no effort to intervene to help a gambler who appeared to be gambling in a 'wild' manner and losing all of his salary within a few months. McDermott said that he had received training about responsible gambling in his four years as HSU manager by 2015 and that Parente's gambling did not ring any alarm bells.

'Are you seriously suggesting to me that you weren't equipped with sufficient common sense and experience to recognize this betting in the way in which was summarized on one day as "wild" and which you now describe as "out of control" as posing a responsible gambling issue that needed to be escalated?' the lawyer asked.

'In essence, yes,' McDermott, who still works in the HSU, responded.

In the end Parente closed the account of his own volition in October 2016 and told the company he did not wish to bet any longer. Paddy Power had only recently merged with Betfair and would not have known that Parente had previously closed an account with Betfair while struggling with his addiction. Had they done so, 'TonyP10', the name of his account, would have surely rung alarm bells.

Mr Justice Griffiths found in Paddy Power's favour on all grounds regarding the need to repay Dhir the money, including in his summary that it was not possible to trace the gambling losses directly back to Dhir's business. But the judge also tore into how Paddy Power had handled Parente's addiction.

He said Paddy Power knew Parente 'was gambling like a problem gambler with an unhealthy and unsustainable gambling addiction on an escalating and desperate scale', and that his losses were unsustainable based on what the company knew were his income and assets.

'They knew all this, but they continued to accept his stakes and, indeed, by providing gambling bonuses and lavish hospitality, to encourage him to gamble more. It stopped only when he stopped it himself by self-exclusion,' he said.

He said that all Paddy Power staff who gave evidence at the hearing 'tried to defend the indefensible' by stating that the treatment of Parente was business as usual. This did not wash with Mr Justice Griffiths.

'I cannot comment on industry norms but, in my judgment, Paddy Power knew that it was dealing with a compulsive gambler who could not afford what he was doing, and Paddy Power did not really care,' he said.

The fall-out from the case in 2021 forced Paddy Power to end the contracts it had with HSU agents like Carroll, and Ian Taylor, an executive, admitted in court that he was 'deeply, deeply embarrassed' by the details of the case.

Taylor also claimed that the failures in relation to Parente were old and that Paddy Power and the wider industry had cleaned up its act in the intervening years. This was similar to what the company had said when the case of old Tony had reached the courts a decade earlier.

Taylor stated after the case: 'Our business today is unrecognizable to what it was five years ago, but we know there is more we must do as an industry to ensure the most vulnerable are protected. We are committed to leading a race to the top in safer gambling and will continue to prioritize investment in this area.'

But the case was just another example of Paddy Power failing to uphold its own commitment, and legal obligation, to prioritise problem gambling over profit.

It was also another example of how Paddy Power does everything it can to keep a steady stream of high rollers logging into its online casino.

Take the case of a gambler who was twenty-four years old in 2019 when Paddy Power made him a VIP. Over the course of the first two years of his account he lost about £40,000 and triggered the company's problem-gambling alerts forty-six times for betting large sums in sessions.

But he was such a profitable customer for Paddy Power that they wanted more like him, so in April 2020 his VIP manager emailed to ask him for the names, phone numbers and email addresses of any gambling friends. Those who passed Paddy Power's internal checks would be given a ninety-day trial as a VIP, while the young gambler was to be given £100 a month for every month they continued to meet the criteria for the HSU. If they passed the ninety-day test, he would get a bonus of £2,000 and a bottle of champagne.

The young gambler himself knew that the status of being a VIP changed how people gambled with Paddy Power. He had been given bonuses that made him feel like he could not lose in the long run. He explained to me in an email in June 2021 just as I was covering the Parente case:

You don't realize at the time you are actually funding the enhanced bonuses, rather than receiving preferential treatment. I found myself betting higher stakes than I could afford just to ensure I qualified for those free bet bonuses. I just had the mindset that I could make up any losses or any shortfall knowing I would get a large bonus at times as a consequence. There are times I did win initially and then having the VIP bonuses put on top gives you a false sense of security that you have turned the tables and will continue winning, But not only do you end up losing everything you won, you end up depositing more to win back your initial stake, which is just a vicious circle as you need to then deposit a larger amount to wager to have any chance of recovering the large amount you have deposited initially to qualify for your bonuses.

Despite the forty-six alerts on Paddy Power's internal problem-gambling system, the company only sent automated emails warning the punter he was exhibiting signs of addiction while the VIP manager got in touch with new bonuses and the offer to have his friends 'treated like betting royalty'.

The only reform in the system that the young gambler noticed was that during the fall-out from the Parente case, Paddy Power changed the name of the VIP managers to the less flashy 'relationship manager'.

Peter Jackson took over from Breon Corcoran as chief executive of Paddy Power Betfair in 2018 and soon after responded to a large fine from the Gambling Commission, for a raft of failings including allowing a punter to gamble money stolen from a dogs' home. The Gambling Commission found 'significant' amounts of stolen money had been gambled with Betfair after it failed to carry out proper anti-money-laundering checks. It also found Paddy Power did not protect three customers showing signs of gambling addiction.

The commission's inquiry centred on five customers in 2016, including two who were allowed to gamble stolen money – one of whom had defrauded his employer, Birmingham Dogs Home, and the other of whom was Parente. Paddy Power was fined £2.2 million and Jackson admitted that the company has 'a responsibility to intervene when our customers show signs of problem gambling'. 'In recent years we have invested in an extensive programme of work to strengthen our resources and systems in responsible gambling and customer protection. We are encouraged that the Gambling Commission has recognized signif-icant improvement since the time of these cases in 2016.'

That was designed to sound like the company was getting on top of problem gambling, but other indicators showed that it was the reputational damage that was causing most pain.

Paddy Power Betfair had also begun paying for the silence of punters who were being failed by the company and threatened to take their cases to the regulator. It is not just massive customers who get VIP status – Paddy Power's designation as a Very Important Person is broad, to say the least.

Take Sammy, for example. Sammy, who has asked for his identity not to be shared as he continues to rebuild his life after addiction, was in his twenties when he began gambling with Paddy Power online. Sammy was, like many addicts, pumping thousands of pounds a week into Paddy Power's online casino games. Such was his value that he was assigned a VIP manager who offered him free bets, bonuses and access to special events such as 'VIP Turnover Tuesday' and 'VIP Windfall Wednesday', which required Sammy to stake almost £10,000 a day to receive free bets in the future. These events are designed to get casino gamblers betting more and spending more time on the Paddy Power website.

As Sammy was offered more freebies, his gambling increased and he punted on in-play sports markets as well as casino games as he liked the continuous nature of gambling rather than placing a single bet on a match and waiting for the result.

Addiction experts such as Matt Gaskell, the clinical lead and consultant psychologist for the NHS Northern Gambling Service, say there is growing evidence that this continuous form of gambling is more addictive by its very design, and the advent of in-play betting on sports will lead to a wider range of people getting hooked on gambling.

For Sammy, it certainly was part of his addiction. In his first eight years of gambling with Paddy Power's online casino he had staked hundreds of thousands, losing a few thousand pounds and countless hours sitting in front of his computer betting on online roulette and slots. But after being made a VIP his behaviour changed dramatically and within 15 months he staked almost £2 million, and his losses now ran to five figures.

But as the losses mounted he could no longer afford to bet as much as he had done in the past and the bonuses and VIP treatment began to dry up, as they were contingent on him betting at high stakes continuously. When Sammy emailed Paddy Power in 2014 to complain about this, a 'customer experience manager' replied that if he wanted more bonuses, he had to earn them.

The VIP manager said that the account had been

reviewed, not for problem gambling signs, but to make sure that Sammy was not due any bonuses or the VIP scheme's 'ad-hoc bonus cash-drop strategy', which awarded free bets to punters who were betting a lot.

These had become a regular reward for Sammy since his appointment to VIP status, and he had come to depend on them as part of his betting habit but, as the VIP manager outlined, there was no 'entitlement' to them. 'So, although you are unhappy with your bonus return over the last few months, the structure was in place for you to control the amount of bonus you earned from us,' the email went on to say.

This was the manager setting out that if Sammy wanted to keep getting bonuses, he would have to keep gambling large amounts. But the manager also expressed concern about Sammy's frustration at not being given bonuses, and questioned if he was in control of his gambling.

He said that what Paddy Power wanted was for customers to enjoy their time on the site and that he hoped that the lack of bonuses would not cause him to enjoy his betting any less. The function of the VIP section was to ensure high staking customers turned over large amounts on Paddy Power products, but customers who began begging for more bonuses triggered the problem gambling warnings and this had led to the concerns about Sammy's behaviour. The VIP manager was clear that the frequency with which Sammy had been raising this had recently 'caused us great concern.'

The email went on to outline in plain English why the company might take a strong view on someone showing signs of addiction. It said the company was bound by new licencing regulations which dictated how gambling companies were obliged to provide information on how to get help with gambling addiction.

But then, having set out the concerns about Sammy's addictive traits and showing him the tools that had been developed to assist him, the VIP manager offered him an out from any restrictions being placed on his bets and apologised for even raising the issue.

'We are sorry to have caused any offence to you by the manner in which we broached the area of customer protection with you, but based on the concerns I outlined above, in order to allow your continued uninterrupted usage of our site and to discuss the bonus issues, please confirm for us if you are in full control of your gambling,' the email said. The VIP manager then warned Sammy that if his 'current correspondence pattern persist' he would be forced to ask more questions and would possibly even consider closing the account, depending on the answers.

In a return email Sammy showed that he was still frustrated about the lack of bonuses being awarded to him and he threatened to leave Paddy Power. He told the customer experience manager that his VIP level had recently been increased after he staked six figures over a five-week period. This was the same 'correspondence pattern' that Sammy had been using in the previous emails. 'To make it worse, I get accused of having a gambling problem for asking the same thing as I've been asking for months. As I said previously, why continue to accept bets from me if you think I've got a gambling problem?'

Sammy then expressed more frustration at the lack of contact from the VIP manager and the way his bonuses appeared to have dried up. He said his upset and frustration was especially pronounced as he been 'suffering heavy losses during the week'. He ended the email: 'For your records, I can confirm that I am in full control of my gambling.' That was all it took.

The customer experience manager's next response showed that despite Sammy's pattern of begging for free bets, his own assessment that he was in control of his gambling was enough to push ahead with his VIP treatment. The email read: 'I am happy to look into this further for you now that you have reassured me that you are in control of your play. To be clear, we did not think you had a problem but always ask customers to ask the question of themselves when we see this kind of behaviour.' The manager reviewed

Sammy's account and found that he was not due any more bonuses than he had already received, and although Paddy Power did not want to be in a position where complaints led to bonuses, he was going to credit a small sum to Sammy's account as a gesture of goodwill.

To Sammy's annoyance, this was a bonus that needed to be gambled in full on the site before any potential winnings could be withdrawn, rather than cash, which he badly needed at the time. In frustration he asked for his account to be closed and deleted, which the manager agreed to. But a week later, when Sammy felt the urge to gamble again he was able to reopen the account, which had already been flagged by staff as that of a potential problem gambler, and start betting again.

Sammy lost a couple of grand in a single session and complained again about not receiving bonuses, but this time asked for his account to be closed under Paddy Power's responsible gambling rules so that it could not be reopened again. A bright guy from England, Sammy had gambled himself into a corner and was living in a small bedsit with barely any furniture when he shared the details of his addiction with me a few years ago.

A year after he had self-excluded, and soon after he began speaking to me, he heard the familiar ping of a text message on his phone. 'It's been too long. So here's a £5 FREE BET! Just go to a PP shop and login with your rewards card.' Two days later his phone pinged again. '20% MONEY BACK as a free bet when you play with BIG REWARDS. This WEEKEND only in PP shops!' Then another, 'Last chance to get 20% MONEY BACK on any losses with BIG rewards TODAY. Don't miss out!' Then another, 'Paddy's feeling twice as nice today! Get 2X points all day on your rewards card. More points – more free bets.' And another, 'Fancy a cheeky £5 FREE BET tomorrow? Just spin £10 with your BIG REWARDS card on ANY game TODAY & it's all yours!'

Paddy Power's promotions team was trying to get Sammy to return to FOBTs in shops where he had been betting in addition to his online betting, despite the online staff just a few months earlier advising him to seek help for his gambling issues. This was in the midst of Project Vanguard and years after the company had warned Irish politicians about the danger of FOBTs to vulnerable people.

Sammy, still in the midst of his addiction, responded angrily to the company for sending him text messages after closing his account because he was an addict – a diagnosis they had first raised.

Within weeks of his complaint, the customer experience manager rang him, then followed up with an email:

As discussed, we both wish to close off this matter as we agree it is in your best interest to discontinue all contact with Paddy Power as you seek help for your gambling issues. Further to our discussions I have agreed to make a small payment as a gesture of goodwill.

It then advised Sammy again of the organisations that assist gambling addicts and set out the legal terms he had to agree to in order to get the money they offered:

1. He had to accept the nominal sum offered as full and final settlement of all claims of any nature, both now and in the future.

2. He had to acknowledge that the payment did not constitute any admission of liability by Paddy Power.

3. He had to agree to not contact any Paddy Power staff in future.

4. Finally, he had to agree not to 'publicize, communicate or disclose to any party' any information about the agreement, and agree that he would not contact the media about the matter.

As with many addicts, the lure of gambling was too much, and soon after Sammy opened an account with Betfair, which was merged with Paddy Power, and lost several thousand pounds. He then asked a customer service agent if Betfair and Paddy Power shared data between the two different brands.

'I didn't mention having a problem or anything like that. The next day my account was closed. I asked and they said it was due to information from Paddy Power,' Sammy told me.

> I've put it to them that they obviously held this information, had no technical or legal issue sharing it – as proved by sharing and closing my account so quickly after I contacted them. So at both Paddy Power and Betfair they could share this information, ban a lot of people who they know have a gambling problem . . . but they choose not to. They choose to keep profiting from these people.

There is evidence of more cases of Paddy Power Betfair paying for the silence of punters with addiction issues and complaints about what they claim is mistreatment by the firm. Others have been paid for their silence after raising concerns about data protection.

When issues of the use of non-disclosure agreements with customers emerged, the UK Gambling Commission issued an industry warning notice: 'Some of these agreements may have had the effect of preventing those consumers from reporting regulatory concerns to us, by either excluding disclosure to any third party or, in some cases, explicitly preventing customers from contacting the Gambling Commission.'

Jackson's 2018 statement after the £2.2 million fine that the company had 'invested in an extensive programme of work to strengthen our resources and systems in responsible gambling and customer protection' was a public pitch to the regulator and politicians that Paddy Power Betfair was getting on top of the problem.

What was said behind closed doors showed they were less advanced in their efforts. The Irish government has been in the process of putting together an independent regulator for the gambling sector since 2013, with little sign of progress.

In 2019, as part of its attempts to draw up regulation of the sector, the Irish Department of Justice held a meeting with bookmakers, gambling technology companies and addiction groups to get their views. Speaking at a private event at the Department of Justice, Tanya Horgan, the chief risk officer, spoke candidly about the limitations of the current systems. A recording of her comments on a panel at the event was shared with me, much to the company's frustration.

What Horgan revealed was that Paddy Power Betfair had begun dividing the people who triggered the responsible gambling responses into test groups and control groups to run new systems:

When all of this debate started happening we did things like increasing our levels of responsible gambling interactions, in particular with people who were triggering our systems. But what we found from talking to those people afterwards, what they told us was: 'I was not in control, you rang me up, I would have told you whatever you needed to hear for you not to turn off that product.' So what do we do instead? That is the difficulty at the moment.

The comments revealed what campaigners and critics have long argued about the self-regulation of addiction interventions for the gambling corporations – it was not enough to help people, as Horgan put it, in 'the throes of addiction'.

'You have this 0.9 per cent who are problem gamblers and have addiction issues. Frankly, there, the responsibility is on operators, in so far as it is possible, to identify those individuals and literally remove them from the gambling experience and take that level of intervention. Because it doesn't matter what you tell someone in the throes of addiction, you are not going to take them out of that behaviour until something else happens.'

Paddy Power's system of intervening with problem gamblers is light-touch. When a punter begins depositing more money in their account than they have previously over the life of their account, the internal system marks them out on a 'spike report', signalling that their account should be looked at as being owned by a person who is potentially falling into addiction. The response is an email, which has been similarly worded for almost a decade, and refers customers to the same tools that were first developed as part of Project Vanguard.

'We want you to enjoy your visits to PaddyPower. com because if you don't you may not come back. That's why we like to inject all our products and services with a little bit of fun and the occasional risqué joke,' it says in the same tone the brand uses when promoting its products. 'However, part of making it an enjoyable experience lies with you. If you stay in control and only bet when you decide to you can enjoy the experience. To aid our customers in this, we offer certain tools to help them control their time and spend with us.'

The company does not place any restriction on the account which has been flagged in the spike report at this stage, but alerts the punter to the voluntary tools to limit the amount they can spend on a daily, weekly or monthly basis; block their access to the account for a period of time or block themselves from certain products such as casino games, which are believed to be more addictive.

The company does not publicize how many people

use these tools, but some figures obtained from the United Kingdom's Gambling Commission indicate that there is a significant proportion of Paddy Power Betfair's customers who believe they have a problem.

Data from the British regulator show that in 2016 and 2017, more than 10 per cent of problem gamblers with the company who asked to be blocked under a 'self-exclusion' scheme as part of their recovery were able to place bets again. The failings in the company's system were higher than the industry average. The matter was rectified in 2018, when there were 216,123 self-exclusions of which 700 were breached by the account being reopened before the exclusion ended.

That figure of 216,123 includes some duplication as many customers who self-exclude return to gambling when the period ends, only to feel the need to block their accounts for a period again. The iteration of Project Vanguard which has survived the Betfair merger is called the Customer Activity Awareness Programme (CAAP) and it tracks over 100 different behaviours and prompts varying levels of pro-active intervention with 70,000 accounts each month. The issue seems to be that because gambling addicts are like moths to flames, that even when they are tracked by CAAP and told that they are in danger they will ignore that warning.

Of course, many accounts who appear on spike reports for potential problem-gambling issues have already been assigned VIP managers to entice them to bet more money and more frequently. These accounts are the cash cows of online gambling, turning over eye-watering amounts on casino games and other products, which are designed with set returns for Paddy Power.

These VIP managers are employed to increase the turnover on the accounts in their lists and ensure the customer does not depart with their cash to a rival gambling website. But what do they do when their customers are flagged by the internal system for spotting addicts?

In 2013 a gambler who had permanently self-excluded from Betfair in 2010 was able to open a new account with the company, providing the same details for full name, date of birth, email and home address, simply by altering their account name. The person does not want to be named publicly for fear of difficulties in rebuilding their life if they are revealed to be a problem gambler, but the change in the account was just adding the number 1 to the end. So, without revealing their identity, it went from John1985 to John19851.

After losing £30,000 in three months 'John' was betting enough to be designated as a VIP with Betfair and given regular free bets of £200 and free tickets to sporting events. He even had £500 returned to his account after losing it on a casino session. As the punter's total losses reached £60,000, they triggered the responsible gambling interventions. Every time he deposited amounts above £1,000, he got an automated email saying: 'We noticed you recently deposited more than your daily average. From time to time we may get in touch to discuss your account activity and make you aware of ways in which you can manage your betting, such as deposit limits, loss limits and time outs. No need to email us back unless you'd like to chat about our Player Protection Tools.'

That is hardly the tone which reflect the seriousness of someone's slide into addiction. The cheery email was headed with a black banner with the logo 'Betfair VIP'. The customer received the same email twelve times over a six-month period, during which his deposits were more than six times his typical amounts previously, triggering the spike reports. At the same time 'John' was being granted VIP status and getting bonuses to keep him betting.

The clash between gambling corporations' profit incentives and their self-declared interest in social responsibility is never more clearly illustrated than in the use of VIP managers to implement responsible gambling measures with customers. There is, even now, tension within Flutter Entertainment, the rebranded group established by Paddy Power Betfair in 2019 to manage its growing global operations, about the need to balance the two.

Insiders in Paddy Power's risk department acknowledge that people who are given VIP status are also triggering responsible gambling alerts (Flutter declined to comment when approached prior to publication). In fact I have seen the files of a professional gambler, which show that the same behaviour can be determined by Paddy Power staff to be addiction or VIP. A professional gambler who set up accounts with Paddy Power and Betfair in his wife's name in order to evade detection by the risk team was awarded VIP status on Paddy Power. Betfair, however, flagged him as someone with a potential gambling problem and asked him to provide details on his earnings and answer questions about his control over his habits. This was despite the exact same bets being placed on both accounts and the two brands sharing risk and problem-gambling functions.

The fact that some VIP managers are asked to take on responsible gambling roles in relation to customers also poses problems as their main job as a VIP manager requires them to increase turnover on accounts and retain high-staking customers, while responsible-gambling interventions are designed to do the opposite.

While there is no quick solution, Stewart Kenny and

others such as Richard Flint, a current non-executive director with Flutter and previous chief executive officer of SkyBet – once Paddy Power's rival but now a stablemate – believe that more can be done.

Evidence is mounting that substantial proportions of bookmakers' profits come from vulnerable gamblers. A 2021 study by the Centre of Social Justice found that problem gamblers, who make up just 0.8 per cent of the UK population, contribute 25 per cent of the gambling industry's profits. That is not so far off what Paddy Power discovered in 2013 when it launched its Project Vanguard.

Kenny has told campaigners and experts that the industry's internal measures amount to them 'acting as a fire brigade putting out fires rather than changing the design and materials used in the building of the house to prevent any fires breaking out'.

He believes that they should simply make the product less addictive, particularly for young people in the 18–25 age group when the brain is not fully developed. Young gamblers should not be targeted by companies for the cross-selling of more addictive casino games and a catch-all tool should be deployed to stop so many people falling into addiction by chasing their losses, Kenny has said.

A mandatory deposit limit, which would require every customer to set an amount they are willing to lose in a specific period, would stop people spinning out of control from pumping more money into their accounts when they are in a spiral. Instead they would be required to set a limit on their betting before they started gambling and if they wished to raise that limit, it would require a time delay so it could not be done within a gambling session.

In 2021 Kenny wrote an article for *The Daily Mail*, which has been waging an editorial campaign calling gambling companies 'predators'. He accepted that he had failed to see the problem until it was too late.

'All online bookmakers have voluntary deposit limits where a customer can put a maximum amount in their betting account each day, week or month. Sadly, the very people who most need to apply these limits are the ones who choose not to. Optional limits are really no more than an industry fig leaf. The deposit limits need to be mandatory, enabling "at risk" customers to avoid self-destructing at a point where rational behaviour has been compromised,' Kenny wrote.

He also called for a £2 stake limit on online slots so that they would fall in line with the FOBTs in shops and for the protection of 18- to 25-year-olds to be increased. 'None of these suggestions would lessen the enjoyment of those who love having a bet, but they would protect the young and vulnerable. For the majority of their customers betting is an enjoyable pastime, but for hundreds of thousands it leads to despair,' Kenny wrote.

What followed was a profuse *mea culpa* from Kenny, who had previously resisted making public statements about his own role in facilitating the creation of the online gambling giant: 'As an industry veteran, I accept my responsibility for not seeing just how much the development of online gambling would damage vulnerable people and parts of society. I acknowledge that I shoulder some of the blame for the harm caused by the addictive nature of some online gambling products. I wish I'd been a lot more pro-active. The fact I did not do more leaves me with deep regret.'

From what Kenny has told politicians, psychologists and campaigners, it is clear that he does not believe the gambling industry can be reformed without radical change to the way it operates. As he explains to anti-gambling campaigners when he talks to them, the reason he walked away from Paddy Power was because it was not possible to reform from within an industry dependent on addictive products. He still face accusations of hypocrisy. Some campaigners are wary of dealing with someone with such close ties to corporate gambling, while a handful of industry figures quietly accuse him of merely seeking attention as he did during his days as the face of Paddy Power. In July 2021 he gave his first on-air interview to RTÉ's on *PrimeTime* and defended his campaigning: 'I must take responsibility for some of the developments. I was part of it, and I have deep regrets that I was not more proactive. Of course, I've faced bundles of accusations of hypocrisy,' he said, 'but I think it is better to speak up than shut up.'

Epilogue

The punters began to line up in the air-conditioned lobby of the Meadowbanks Racetrack in New Jersey. The early heatwave had turned into a sticky, humid summer in July 2018, and the crowd of men in XXL T-shirts and baggy shorts waited patiently to enter the 5,300-square-foot betting shop. Many had travelled the six short miles from New York, where it was still illegal to bet on sports unless you were in a casino.

Only days earlier Paddy Power Betfair had completed the purchase of FanDuel, an online fantasy sports app with ambitions to open a sports book, after New Jersey had legalized sports betting following a US Supreme Court decision that was the first major liberalization of the country's prohibitionist gambling laws.

This long-awaited change in the US had been war-gamed in Paddy Power's offices going back to the mid-2000s, when Breon Corcoran had instructed the staff to run trials on what they would need to do if they could operate on the other, more lucrative side of the Atlantic. But the possibility of Irish and UK-style gambling in the US had always seemed a long way off, even if Paddy Power always had it in mind. It was one of a few corporate bookmakers who had always refused to take bets from the US in case it led to licensing issues when the great Wild West eventually did open up.

But here they were, finally. Peter Jackson had restructured his executive team after taking over from Corcoran and deployed Johnny Hartnett to the role of group development officer, tasked with expanding the group into new markets.

Hartnett had worked his way up from a sports trader, joining as the Internet operation was getting off the ground in the Village Green office in Tallaght. He had followed Cormac Barry to Australia and returned to Clonskeagh as head of operations.

He had identified a number of opportunities for the company, which was about to be renamed Flutter Entertainment – a generic and techie-sounding rebranding that signalled its American ambitions. The main goal was always to land on the shores of the United States and Hartnett struck a deal with FanDuel, a fantasy sports game with seven million registered accounts.

Americans longing to give their opinions on the sports

they watched had made do with fantasy sports games and mafia-controlled illegal betting for a long time. But that was about to change.

The $158 million deal with FanDuel merged all of Paddy Power Betfair, existing American interests and a couple of horse-racing TV networks into one group.

A team from Paddy Power's retail operations were flown over to work on the opening of a network of sportsbook locations that would give a bricks-and-mortar presence at racetracks and near NFL stadiums. They couldn't believe the amounts the American gamblers were bringing to gamble. People were driving miles with tens of thousands in cash to do all their betting.

On 14 July 2018 FanDuel took its first bet at the Meadowlands. The gamblers waiting outside had entered through the doors past two mock-stone signs standing ten feet high, each spelling out the word 'VICTORY'.

While FanDuel was opening up, Jackson was about to take the company that started with the meeting of Stewart Kenny and John Corcoran on Kildare Street in 1980s Dublin onto Wall Street.

Jackson believes that once the US betting market is fully opened up it could be bigger than the Internet market has been to date. Flutter's estimation is that the market will be worth $20 billion by 2025, but the

American Gaming Association believes that it could be $150 billion if it can break through the long-established illegal gambling operations. Whatever it is, it will represent an existential change for multinational gambling corporations who will be able to tap into the most lucrative population of consumers in the world.

Before his appointment as chief executive, Jackson, who had been on the Paddy Power Betfair board for four years, met with Rafi Ashkenazi, a shaven-headed Israeli engineer who had worked in a number of online gaming companies before becoming chief executive of the Stars Group.

At the time of his meeting with Jackson, the Stars Group had an international and online footprint that included PokerStars, which had run foul of the US ban on Internet gambling during a 2011 crackdown, resulting in its sites being blocked and ominous-looking seizure notices appearing under the seals of the FBI and the US Department of Justice. This showed the perilous nature of investing in operations with a US presence before the 2018 ruling overturned the Professional and Amateur Sports Protection Act, which banned sports betting in all but four states, Oregon, Delaware, Montana and Nevada, where it had been allowed prior to 1992.

Ashkenazi declined Jackson's overture of a merger and told him he was concentrating on two deals, one big and one small. Two months later, Ashkenazi oversaw the $120 million purchase of CrownBet, Paddy Power Betfair's rival in Australia, leaving Jackson wondering if that was the big deal.

It wasn't even close. A $4.7 billion deal was announced to buy SkyBet, the company that had taken advantage of Paddy Power and Betfair's struggles after the merger to become the favourite of the casual punter in the UK. The Stars Group now owned SkyBet in the UK, CrownBet in Australia, and FOX Bet in the US, a Murdoch family-owned gambling company that was linked to the media mogul's television networks.

The spree of acquisitions put a huge strain on the Stars Group's share price and in the summer of 2019, Jackson moved again. The Yorkshire son of a car salesman who had had a career in retail banking and technology before joining Paddy Power Betfair convinced Ashkenazi that merging Flutter Entertainment and the Stars Group would give the new conglomerate a dominant global position. But Ashkenazi was a dealmaker and after Gary McCann made a formal approach for a 'merger of equals', with Flutter getting 57 per cent of the new group, GVC Holdings, the owner of Paddy Power's lifelong enemy Ladbrokes, approached with its own deal.

The wrangling between Flutter and Stars began with both knowing they had to move fast to take first-movers' advantage in the liberalized US market. McCann tabled a new deal at the start of August with Flutter's stake reduced to 55 per cent, and the Irish group got a much more favourable reception. Then the complications began to emerge around the exclusivity deals FOX Bet, FanDuel and a casino partner had around online operations.

Jackson had to cut a deal that gave FOX Bet a 18.5 per cent stake in FanDuel and the firms backing it a pay-off based on the future value of FOX Bet. The negotiations with Lachlan Murdoch, the tattooed son of Rupert, who was co-chairman of News Corp and chief executive of Fox Corporation, was a far cry from Paddy Power's deals to buy out family-owned book-makers in rural Irish towns in the early 1990s. It would lead to a $4 billion legal dispute that threatened to cut off FanDuel's access to the Murdochs' television networks showing major sports in the US, but that was all to come.

The merger between Flutter Entertainment and the Stars Group was announced in October 2019, creating the biggest sports and online gambling operation in the world. The €12 billion merger created a group that had had more than €4 billion in revenue in the previous year and the chance to multiply that every year as the United States market opened up.

This consolidation put Flutter on par with dominance

in the global gambling market that rivalled how the tech giants consolidated their powers over their markets. With more states likely to liberalize their markets in the near future, Flutter has already engaged consultants on the ground to do market research and make sure every potential opportunity is pursued.

But by the time the merger of the companies – which would operate under the Flutter Entertainment name – was completed in May 2020, the world was in the grips of the Covid-19 pandemic. Stadiums were shuttered, international events including the European Championships, Tokyo Olympics and every horse-racing meeting was cancelled. It looked like there was nothing to gamble on.

Still, Flutter's revenue rose as people, bored and stuck at home, signed up for online gambling sites. The group revenue grew by 49 per cent to £1.52 billion in the first half of 2020 despite the shutdown of sporting events due to the pandemic as punters piled cash into online casino games. By the end of 2020 it had grown 106 per cent to £4.4 billion. The number of people who opened online accounts broke the seven million figure during the social distancing restrictions that kept bookies' shops closed while televised sports resumed in empty stadiums.

Jackson saw that the trend was speeding up as everything was now being conducted online. As Amazon packages and Deliveroo pizzas landed on people's doorsteps during lockdowns, gambling was all done on laptops and smartphones. It illustrated the strength of Flutter Entertainment's business model but has also increased the concerns around addiction caused by online gambling as the types of markets offered, even on sports, are suspected of leading to the same sort of loss of control that caused the panic about FOBTs.

Matt Gaskell, who works at the coalface of addiction, believes that the technology behind online gambling is 'addictive by design' and that the social-media targeting of 18- to 25-year-olds will create a new generation of gambling addicts who are hooked on poorly regulated products such as in-play betting.

'The goal here is to make as much money as possible – that's obviously the main aim of most businesses, but gambling has to have different responsibilities. This is a harmful commodity, so that model of growth which counts each person's value in how much more time they can get out of this person gambling, and trying to maximize the amount that person will spend; you can't reconcile that model with having a public health perspective of protecting people,' Gaskell says, punching his fists together to illustrate the clash between gambling corporations' desire for growth and the protection of problem gamblers.

Gaskell believes that the new products and advertising campaigns centred on placing multiple bets while watching live football matches or other events could lead to more people falling into addiction.

Sports betting has long been viewed as the safest form of gambling, as it traditionally requires the punter to place a bet and wait until the end of the event to know the result. But the rise of in-play betting will fuel online sports betting in the United States where the sports are much more suited to it. Gaskell says that everyone he treats at his clinic is someone who has fallen into addiction through 'continuous gambling':

Continuous gambling experiences are half an hour, an hour, three hours, five hours, ten hours, where you're in it. Your adrenaline is going, your motivation is going, and you're encouraged to bet at high frequency and each bet is going to influence your next behaviour, and your next behaviour after that. It lends itself to impaired decision-making, impulsive behaviour and continuing despite the negative consequences. Emotionally you want to remain in play – it's the same for a slot machine or in-play football betting. A lot of people now sit and bet in play for ninety minutes on football matches, which compared to putting a fiver on the outcome of the match and just watching it is a completely different level of risk.

From a business point of view, it's brilliant, because you know young lads are gonna sit and watch the match for ninety minutes. So why not create a gambling product which means they're continually gambling through it? So yeah, it's genius on the one hand, but it's a recipe for disaster on the other.

There is a growing body of research that shows that, through their design, online gambling products are more dangerous because of how they use psychological triggers to keep people betting, Gaskell says:

These are very, very deliberate environments, carefully organized and constructed to keep gamblers there and to retain their loyalty. The construction of specific products is just a bag of psychological tricks to maintain desire and motivation to persist gambling, and to keep going no matter what is going on around you. The trick and the delusion is that you maintain a high level of motivation while you are losing. Normally you would never hand over £100 without thinking about it but with online gambling it is happening while you are feeling engaged and motivated, there is a level of adrenaline and there are dopamine spikes. There are lots of things going on that are neurochemical, biological and psychological.

He adds: 'It is an environment that focuses the attention and keeps the user in the zone of continual gambling and a high-frequency betting process, without allowing them to reflect, get fresh air and break from it. If you create those circumstances, you're going to deliver harm.'

This high-frequency, continual betting is how many people are now gambling on Flutter's growing range of products and the research that is being conducted into continual gambling raises the alarm that corporations are nudging people into this more harmful form of betting. Already in-play betting and 'flash markets', which encourage people to gamble on what will happen in the next minute of a live event, are used by 20 per cent of Flutter sports-betting customers, and account for more than 10 per cent of sports betting revenues.

A 2019 study by scientists at the Centre for Gambling Education and Research at Southern Cross University in Australia made a stark finding.

They surveyed 1,812 Australians who placed in-play bets on micro-events such as the next ball in cricket, or the next point in tennis, or anything where the outcome is determined almost immediately after the bet. 'This enables rapid, impulsive and continuous betting and may heighten the risk of problem gambling,' the paper published in the *Journal of Gambling Studies* said.

It found that micro-event bettors are likely to be 'younger, well-educated and single; engaged in a wider variety of gambling activities; and to have high trait impulsivity'. The researchers concluded that 'Micro event betting appears to appeal almost exclusively to bettors with gambling problems, so a ban would represent a highly targeted intervention to reduce gambling-related harm.'

The structural change in how people bet on sports when betting online is part of a reckoning facing the gambling industry in regulated markets such as the UK and Australia. The same conversations are likely to be had in the United States as well, where the media is increasingly sceptical of technology and data-powered companies since the reporting of the Cambridge Analytica scandal and use of data targeting in the campaign to elect Donald Trump. Already there have been efforts to attach strict data protection laws into gambling legislation.

Ravi Naik, a lawyer who has launched a legal case against Cambridge Analytica, believes the Flutter brand is using webs of data to target gamblers to increase their betting activity. And he is not alone.

The focus on data harvesting by gambling corporations could lead to uncomfortable questions for the original wave of innovators including Paddy Power and Betfair, which use hosts of tracking software and analytics to determine how to treat punters and are already facing scrutiny over how much data they have harvested from their customers. It ranges from personal data relating to age and location to much deeper financial information pulled from credit-check sites.

As part of the Campaign for Fairer Gambling's anti-FOBT campaign, Derek Webb paid for Dr James Noyes to work with Tom Watson, the former deputy Labour Party leader who was a prominent figure in the fight.

Watson has been appointed to Flutter's board as a non-executive director to review its responsible gambling initiative, a high-profile move that Jackson and the new executive believe show the corporation is serious about its social responsibility.

Stewart Kenny thinks otherwise, branding Watson's appointment as a PR exercise. He likens it to Nick Clegg, the former deputy prime minister's appointment to Facebook as part of the social media giant's efforts to fend off harsher legislation following Cambridge Analytica and myriad other issues facing it.

'The bookies already know what they need to do to deal with gambling addiction. All they have to do is engage with British politicians who are already investigating the area, but the fact is that the only thing that will make them take gambling addiction seriously is legislation,' Kenny told me after Watson's appointment in 2020.

While Watson is working within the industry, his old adviser Noyes is continuing to fight for change from outside. The Social Market Foundation think tank where Noyes now works has challenged the idea promoted by other groups that gambling is a free market activity that does not require extra levels of state intervention. Noyes believes the use of data to power companies like Flutter has reduced their customers' agency to the point where extra checks are needed.

He has pushed the idea, along with Matt Zarb-Cousin and politicians from Labour and the Conservatives, of requiring gambling companies to check that every customer can afford their level of betting once they reach a loss threshold of £100 a month. It was a radical idea that gained a significant foothold in the UK and resulted in Entain, the renamed Ladbrokes owner, introducing its own version ahead of any regulation.

In a research paper submitted to the UK government in February 2021, Noyes outlined why he believes that online gambling companies are fundamentally different from the high-street bookmakers they have grown from:

At the heart of the question over consumer affordability is the question of consumer data: data as the mechanism by which operators control – and restrict – both consumer identity and economic agency through interaction. In this context, libertarian accusations of intrusion do not hold water. Intrusion has already happened from the beginning of the customer journey. And operators, through internal systems of consumer profiling and the sharing of these profiles with third parties through mechanisms such as cookie syncing, already capture from their customers a framework of affordability, which they can choose to apply either for the purpose of harm prevention or for commercial gain. When it comes to the ecosystem of surveillance capitalism, remote gambling operators are at the top of the food chain.

Harvard professor Shoshana Zuboff popularized the theory in her 2019 book *The Age of Surveillance Capitalism*, a 700-page tome about the social impacts of the digital era and the undermining of the free agency of individuals by the business model of technology giants.

Noyes believes that the sharing of data by gambling corporations with third-party companies, which can profile punters in more refined ways than even the internal models of firms like Flutter can, places too much power in the hands of operators. To redress it, Noyes believes, the companies should be required to show they are not looking to push people into losing more than they can afford.

The slow dawning upon politicians, regulators and theorists about how data is integral to gambling corporations will soon lead to a reckoning for betting corporations. The past use of VIP schemes and targeting losers with the Future Expected Margins model reveals the hunger in the industry for fast profits that governments are sure to temper with extra scrutiny and increased regulation.

Whatever measures are introduced to combat the perceived problems, Flutter will be well placed to withstand any hit to profits. The firm that was once a chain of forty Irish shops is now a diverse brand of sports betting, online casinos, poker operators and broadcast networks with websites, smartphone apps, cookie-tracking systems and other digital tubes to filter all the data to reduce the risk to profits.

From John Corcoran, Stewart Kenny, David Power and John O'Reilly's attempts to battle against the British firms through to Breon Corcoran, Cormac Barry and Patrick Kennedy's stewardship during the transition to an online giant, to Peter Jackson's current positioning of Flutter as a global behemoth, the company is likely to dominate the global gambling sector for decades to come.

It has market-leading positions that may soon be near monopolies in Ireland, the United Kingdom and Australia. The big bet is on the United States, and if it lands in Flutter's favour the future growth will be multiples of what has been built in the last thirty years. The Covid-19 pandemic will likely lead to the speeding up of liberalization in the United States as state governments seek to cash in on the easy money from taxes generated by punters.

Jackson has already upgraded the goal for Flutter from being among the biggest operators in the United States to leading the whole sector. On a call with investors in March 2021 announcing the £4.4 billion in turnover achieved during 2020 despite a global pandemic that shut down sports and the energy-sapping efforts to push through a multinational merger while working from home, Jackson declared victory for Flutter Entertainment. 'Let's be really clear. We are number one in America.'

Back in Dublin, the company that began as a deal by three bookies to compete against British rivals is now the largest company on the Irish stock market, with a valuation of €30 billion. It is also the biggest gambling company in the world.

Acknowledgements

This book is the culmination of more than five years' reporting on Paddy Power that began at *The Times* Ireland edition and has continued at the *Business Post*. I owe thanks to all the company's employees, rivals, customers and higher-ups who have spoken to me in that time, and particularly the dozens who agreed to speak again or for the first time for this book. Many did so at some personal risk, and a few did at great length to explain to me the intricacies of what powered Paddy Power's growth over that last three decades.

I am also indebted to the gambling addicts and frustrated winners who have shared their stories and the data from their accounts with me. That offered invaluable insight into how online gambling firms operate, and it informed my interviews with people who worked at Paddy Power over the years.

I would also like to thank the professional gambler who assisted me in a botched experiment to see how my own Paddy Power account would be treated if run like a high-stakes customer. It provided some insight, but nothing like that of those who have shared their true experiences with me.

While I have been reporting on Paddy Power for five years, this book was written in just over a year and would not have been possible without the work of the many other reporters who have covered the company and wider gambling industry.

Particulary, I would like to praise the work of John Martin, who died in 2014, for detailing the changes on the Irish gambling scene in the 1980s and 1990s. I've drawn from his work and other public interviews with Paddy Power staff in the times before my reporting to assist me in recreating the events that came up in my own interviews with insiders.

Elsewhere, my editors at the *Business Post*, Richie Oakley, Mark Brennan, Aiden Corkery and Gillian Nelis, have my thanks for giving me leave to write this all up at a time when the world was adjusting to life under a pandemic.

I am also grateful to my colleagues Peter O'Dwyer, Daniel Murray, Killian Woods, Rosanna Cooney, Rachel Lavin, Roisin Burke, Michael Brennan and the rest of the newsroom crew for covering for me if I ever got

ACKNOWLEDGEMENTS

distracted from my day job by this book. Particularly, I want to thank Barry J. Whyte, who offered a kind ear and well-timed rant on a number of occasions that served me to push on. I also owe thanks to John Walsh for some steadying advice very early on in the project.

Conor Nagle, Nora Mahony, and Catherine Gough at HarperCollins Ireland have all been great in helping me navigate the process of writing a book, and Djinn von Noorden's copy-editing saved me from a few embarrassing blunders – any that are left are my doing.

Outside of work, friends, including Seán Mac Fhearraigh, Conor Donoghue, Ronan Kenny, Rob Mannering, and the Shamrock Rovers lads Denis, Dermo, Donal, Mark, Barry, Conor and Bill, have offered much-needed distraction.

A special thanks too to Adrian Mannering RIP for the use of his desk and the view of his back garden while writing. The cat, Cosmo, deserves a word also for putting up with me using his armchair to work late into the night.

My parents, Catherine and Paddy, and my in-laws, Alice and Gerry Canny, have also shown remarkable interest and patience in this project.

Most of all I want to thank my wife, Aisling, who has had to listen to over a year's worth of dinner-long monologues about breakthroughs and set-backs in my reporting, and never once wavered in her support. That support and the darling distraction of our daughter, Rose, bunny-hopping into my office has kept me sane in moments when finishing the book seemed to be undoable. Finally, I can follow Rose's instruction to 'stop writing that book, Daddy, and come and play'.